Alan Bennett
Plays Two

Alan Bennett first appeared on the stage in 1960 as one of the authors and performers of the revue Beyond the Fringe. His stage plays include *Forty Years On*, *Getting On*, *Habeas Corpus*, *The Old Country* and *Enjoy*, and he has written many television plays, notably *A Day Out*, *Sunset Across the Bay*, *A Woman of No Importance* and the series of monologues *Talking Heads*. An adaptation of his television play, *An Englishman Abroad* was paired with *A Question of Attribution* in the double bill *Single Spies*, first produced at the National Theatre in 1988. This was followed in 1990 by his adaption of *The Wind in the Willows* and in 1991 by *The Madness of George III*, both produced at the National Theatre.

ALAN BENNETT

Plays Two

Kafka's Dick

The Insurance Man

The Old Country

An Englishman Abroad

A Question of Attribution

Introduced by
the author

faber and faber

This collection first published in 1998
by Faber and Faber Limited
3 Queen Square London WC1N 3AU

Photoset by Parker Typesetting Service, Leicester
Printed in England by Mackays of Chatham PLC, Chatham, Kent

Contents

Introduction

1 On *Kafka's Dick* and *The Insurance Man*

I have written two plays around if not altogether about Kafka and in the process have accumulated a good deal of material about and around the Prague insurance man. Some of this is fanciful; sketches and speculations that never had a hope of being included in either piece; some of it is the kind of stuff that's always left over after writing a play, the speeches one has not managed to get in or the jokes that have had to be cut out and which are invariably the jokes and the speeches of which the playwright is most fond. Indeed he often thinks them the heart of the play, whereas the director (who never had to sweat over them) can see they're diversions, distractions or ornament. Not wanted on voyage. There is a word for this kind of thing which I have just come across (and having come across it can't think how I've managed so long without it); it is *paralipomena* – the things omitted but which appertain and are put in later as afterthoughts. It describes half my life as well as the notes that follow.

Besides these notes I have also included, as an introduction to *The Insurance Man*, a diary that I kept during the shooting of the film, which was first shown on BBC2 in February 1986. *Kafka's Dick* was produced at the Royal Court Theatre six months later. The play was not as well received by the critics as was the film and, though I could not imagine it better done and it played to packed houses, it did not transfer for a longer run. Shortly after it opened, I was working in Yugoslavia and drove into Italy for the day. Depressed about the reception the play had had I came by chance on the village of Aquileia, went to look at the church and found there a huge mosaic

vii

floor laid down in the fourth century. I say 'by chance' but
to read Kafka is to become aware of coincidence. This is to
put it at its mildest. His work prefigures the future, often
in ways that are both specific and dreadful and this is part
of his popular reputation. Sometimes though, his
premonitions are less haunted, lighthearted even: he has a
notion of the answering machine, for instance, and a
dream of Berlin divided by a wall that seems more strange
than tragic. In *Kafka's Dick*, Kafka is metamorphosed
from a tortoise and is also sensitive about the size of his
cock. So to find inside the west door of this church at
Aquileia, a mosaic of a cock fighting a tortoise seemed not
quite an accident. In the play cock and tortoise are not
symbols; in Aquileia, so said the guide book, they
represent a battle between the forces of light and darkness.
I bought a postcard of the mosaic and the postcard-seller
told me of a better example in the crypt. This took some
finding, as the tortoise wasn't so much in the crypt as in a
crypt beyond the crypt, and even there hidden behind the
furthest pillar, just where Kafka (were he a tortoise) would
have chosen to be. This seemed if not quite a nod then at
least a wink and I drove on in better spirits.

I would like to thank Richard Eyre, who directed the
plays and the film (and who was always in good spirits)
and for her unstinting help and encouragement, the best of
editors, Mary-Kay Wilmers.

A.B., 1987

2 On *An Englishman Abroad* and *A Question of Attribution*

Some years ago a stage play of mine, *The Old Country*,
was running in the West End. The central character,
Hilary, played by Alec Guinness, was a Foreign Office
defector living in Russia. Hilary was generally identified as

Philby, though that had not been my intention, the character having much more in common with a different sort of exile, W. H. Auden. However during the run of *The Old Country* friends and well-wishers would come round after the performance, often with reminiscences of Philby and his predecessors, Burgess and Maclean. One of these was Coral Browne who told me of her visit to Russia with the Shakespeare Memorial Theatre in 1958 and the particular incidents that make up *An Englishman Abroad*.

The picture of the elegant actress and the seedy exile sitting in a dingy Moscow flat through a long afternoon listening again and again to Jack Buchanan singing 'Who stole my heart away?' seemed to me funny and sad but it was a few years before I got round to writing it up. It was only when I sent Coral Browne the first draft of the television film that I found she had kept not merely Burgess's letters, thanking her for running his errands, but also her original notes of his measurements and even his cheque (uncashed and for £6) to treat her and one of her fellow actors to lunch at the Caprice. The original script of the television film was quite close to the version now presented on the stage. It had no exterior shots because I knew no BBC budget would run to filming in Moscow or some foreign substitute. I introduced the exteriors only when a suitable (and a suitably economic) substitute for Moscow was found in Dundee.

I have put some of my own sentiments into Burgess's mouth. 'I can say I love London. I can say I love England. I can't say I love my country, because I don't know what that means', is a fair statement of my own, and I imagine many people's position. The Falklands War helped me to understand how a fastidious stepping-aside from patriotism could be an element in characters as different as Blunt and Burgess. Certainly in the spy fever that followed the unmasking of Professor Blunt I felt more sympathy with the hunted than the hunters.

I never met Blunt, but though he seems to have been an altogether less likeable character than Burgess he is a more familiar type, at any rate in academic circles. Championed by his pupils, he was less favourably regarded by some of his colleagues, who found him arrogant and opinionated. There are plenty of dons like this, in whom shyness, self-assurance and deep conviction combine to give an uncongenial impression. Housman and Wittgenstein are perhaps the most distinguished examples. In death such characters are invariably filed under the obituarist's catch-all 'Did not suffer fools gladly'.

In the first play it is suggested that Burgess was a spy because he wanted a place where he was alone, and that having a secret supplies this. I believe this to be psychologically true, but there is a sense too that an ironic attitude towards one's country and a scepticism about one's heritage is a part of that heritage. And so, by extension, is the decision to betray it. It is irony activated.

I find it hard to drum up any patriotic indignation over either Burgess or Blunt, or even Philby. No one has ever shown that Burgess did much harm, except to make fools of people in high places. Because he made jokes, scenes and, most of all, passes, the general consensus is that he was rather silly. Blunt was not silly and there have been attempts to show that his activities had more far-reaching consequences, but again he seems to be condemned as much out of pique and because he fooled the Establishment as for anything that he did. It is Philby who is always thought to be the most congenial figure. Clubbable, able to hold his liquor, a good man in a tight corner, he commends himself to his fellow journalists, who have given him a good press. But of all the Cambridge spies he is the only one of whom it can be proved without doubt that he handed over agents to torture and death.

It suits governments to make treachery the crime of crimes, but the world is smaller than it was and to conceal information can be as culpable as to betray it. As I write evidence is emerging of a nuclear accident at Windscale in 1957, the full extent of which was hidden from the public. Were the politicians and civil servants responsible for this less culpable than our Cambridge villains? Because for the spies it can at least be said that they were risking their own skins whereas the politicians were risking someone else's.

Of course Blunt and Burgess and co. had the advantage of us in that they still had illusions. They had somewhere to turn. The trouble with treachery nowadays is that if one does want to betray one's country there is no one satisfactory to betray it to. If there were, more people would be doing it.

A.B., 1989

KAFKA'S DICK

Introduction

There are many perils in writing about Kafka. His work has been garrisoned by armies of critics with some 15,000 books about him at the last count. As there is a Fortress Freud so is there a Fortress Kafka, Kafka his own castle. For admission a certain high seriousness must be deemed essential and I am not sure I have it. One is nervous about presuming even to write his name, wanting to beg pardon for doing so, if only because Kafka was so reluctant to write his name himself. Like the Hebrew name of God it is a name that should not be spoken, particularly by an Englishman. In his dreams Kafka once met an Englishman. He was in a good grey flannel suit, the flannel also covering his face. Short of indicating a prudent change of tailor the incident (if dreams have incidents) serves to point up the temptation to English Kafka and joke him down to size. The Channel is a slipper bath of irony through which we pass these serious continentals in order not to be infected by their gloom. This propensity I am sure I have not escaped or tried to; but then there is something that *is* English about Kafka, and it is not only his self-deprecation. A vegetarian and fond of the sun, he seems a familiar crank; if he'd been living in England at the turn of the century and not in Prague one can imagine him going out hiking and spending evenings with like-minded friends in Letchworth. He is the young man in a Shaw play who strolls past the garden fence in too large shorts to be accosted by some brisk Shavian young woman who, perceiving his charm, takes him in hand, puts paid to his morbid thoughts and makes him pull his socks up.

Charm he certainly had, but not at home. Chewing every mouthful umpteen times so that at meals his father cowered behind the newspaper, Kafka saved his charm for work and for his friends. Home is not the place for charm anyway. We do not look for it around the fireside so it's not so surprising Kafka had no charm for his father. His father, it seems, had none for anybody. There is something called Home Charm though. In the forties it was a kind of distemper and nowadays it's a chain of DIY shops. In that department certainly Kafka did not excel. He was not someone you would ask to help put up a shelf for instance, though one component of his charm was an exaggerated appreciation of people who could, and of commonplace accomplishments generally. Far from being clumsy himself (he had something of the dancer about him) he would marvel (or profess to marvel) at the ease with which other people managed to negotiate the world. This kind of professed incompetence ('Silly me!') often leads to offers of help and carried to extremes it encourages the formation of unofficial protection societies. Thus Kafka was much cosseted by the ladies in his office and in the same way the pupils of another candidate for secular sainthood, the French philosopher Simone Weil, saw to it that their adored teacher did not suffer the consequences of a practical unwisdom even more hopeless than Kafka's.

One cannot say that Kafka's marvelling at mundane accomplishments was not genuine, was a ploy. The snag is that when the person doing the marvelling goes on to do great things this can leave those with the commonplace accomplishments feeling a little flat. Say such a person goes on to win the Nobel Prize it is scant consolation to know that one can change a three-pin plug.

Gorky said that in Chekhov's presence everyone felt a desire to be simpler, more truthful and more oneself. Kafka too had this effect. 'On his entrance into a room', wrote a contemporary, 'it seemed as though some unseen attendant had whispered to the lecturer, "Be careful about everything

you say from now on. Franz Kafka has just arrived."' To
have this effect on people is a not unmixed blessing. When
we are on our best behaviour we are not always at our best.

This is not to say that Kafka did not make jokes in life and
in art. *The Trial*, for instance, is a funnier book than it has
got credit for and Kafka's jokes about himself are better
for the desperate circumstances in which they were often
made. He never did win the Nobel Prize of course, but
contemplated the possibility once in fun and in pain, and
in a fairly restricted category (though one he could have
shared with several contemporaries, Proust, Katherine
Mansfield and D. H. Lawrence among them). When he
was dying of TB of the larynx he was fetching up a good
deal of phlegm. 'I think,' he said (and the joke is more
poignant for being so physically painful to make), 'I think
I deserve the Nobel Prize for sputum.' Nothing if not sick,
it is a joke that could have been made yesterday.

Dead sixty-odd years Kafka is still modern and there is
much in the present day world to interest him. These days
Kafka would be intrigued by the battery farm and
specifically, with an interest both morbid and lively, in the
device that de-beaks the still-living chickens; in waste-
disposal trucks that chew the rubbish before swallowing it
and those dubious restaurants that install for your dining
pleasure a tank of doomed trout. As the *maître d'* assists
the discerning diner in the ceremony of choice, be aware of
the waiter who wields the net: both mourner and
executioner, he is Kafka. He notes old people in Zimmer
frames stood in their portable dock on perambulatory trial
for their lives. He is interested in the feelings of the squash
ball and the champagne bottle that launches the ship. In a
football match his sympathy is not with either of the teams
but with the ball, or, in a match ending nil–nil, with the
hunger of the goalmouth. He would be unable to endorse

the words of the song by Simon and Garfunkel 'I'd rather be a hammer than a nail', feeling himself (as he confessed to one of his girlfriends) simultaneously both. And in a different context he would be concerned with the current debate on the disposal of nuclear waste. To be placed in a lead canister which is then encased in concrete and sunk fathoms deep to the floor of the ocean was the degree of circulation he thought appropriate for most of his writing. Or not, of course.

Kafka was fond of the cinema and there are short stories, like *Tales of a Red Indian* that have a feeling of the early movies. He died before the talkies came in and so before the Marx Brothers but there is an exchange in *Horse Feathers* that sums up Kafka's relations with his father:

Beppo Dad, I'm proud to be your son.

Groucho Son, you took the words out of my mouth. I'm ashamed to be your father.

The Kafka household could have been the setting for many Jewish jokes:

Father Son, you hate me.

Son Father, I love you.

Mother Don't contradict your father.

Had Kafka the father emigrated to America as so many of his contemporaries did, things might have turned out differently for Kafka the son. He was always stage-struck. Happily lugubrious, he might have turned out a stand-up Jewish comic. Kafka at Las Vegas.

Why didn't Kafka stutter? The bullying father, the nervous son – life in the Kafka household seems a blueprint for a speech impediment. In a sense, of course, he did stutter.

Jerky, extruded with great force and the product of tremendous effort, everything Kafka wrote is a kind of stutter. Stutterers devise elaborate routines to avoid or to ambush and take by surprise troublesome consonants of which K is one of the most difficult. It's a good job Kafka didn't stutter. With two Ks he might have got started on his name and never seen the end of it. As it is he docks it, curtails it, leaves its end behind much as lizards do when something gets hold of their tail.

In thus de-nominating himself Kafka was to make his name and his letter memorable. Diminishing it he augmented it and not merely for posterity. K was a significant letter in his own time. There were Ks on every banner, palace and official form. Kafka had two Ks and so in the *Kaiserlich* and *Königlich* of the Habsburg Emperors, did the Austro-Hungarian Empire. The Emperor at the time was Franz Joseph and that comes into it too, for here is Franz K writing about Joseph K in the time of Franz Joseph K.

There was another emperor nearer at hand, the emperor in the armchair, Kafka's phrase for his father. Hermann Kafka has had such a consistently bad press that it's hard not to feel a sneaking sympathy for him as for all the Parents of Art. They never get it right. They bring up a child badly and he turns out a writer, posterity never forgives them – though without that unfortunate upbringing the writer might never have written a word. They bring up a child well and he never *does* write a word. Do it right and posterity never hears about the parents; do it wrong and posterity never hears about anything else.
 'They fuck you up your Mum and Dad' and if you're planning on writing that's probably a good thing. But if you are planning on writing and they haven't fucked you up, well, you've got nothing to go on, so then they've fucked you up good and proper.

Many parents, one imagines, would echo the words of Madame Weil, the mother of Simone Weil, a child every bit as trying as Kafka must have been. Questioned about her pride in the posthumous fame of her ascetic daughter Madame Weil said, 'Oh! How much I would have preferred her to have been happy.' Like Kafka Simone Weil is often nominated for secular sainthood. I'm not sure. Talk of a saint in the family and there's generally one around if not quite where one's looking. One thinks of Mrs Muggeridge and in the Weil family it is not Simone so much as her mother who consistently behaves well and elicits sympathy. In the Kafka household the halo goes to Kafka's sister Ottla, who has to mediate between father and son, a role in weaker planetary systems than that revolving round Hermann Kafka which is more often played by the mother.

Kafka may have been frightened that he was more like his father than he cared to admit. In a letter to Felice Bauer, Kafka indulges in the fantasy of being a large piece of wood, pressed against the body of a cook 'who is holding the knife along the side of this stiff log (somewhere in the region of my hip) slicing off shavings to light the fire.' Many conclusions could be drawn from this image, some glibber than others. One of them is that Kafka would have liked to have been a chip off the old block.

Daily at his office in the Workers Accident Insurance Institute Kafka was confronted by those unfortunates who had been maimed and injured at work. Kafka was not crippled at work but at home. It's hardly surprising. If a family is a factory for turning out children then it is lacking in the most elementary safety precautions. There are no guard rails round that dangerous engine, the father. There are no safeguards against being scalded by the burning affection of the mother. No mask is proof against the suffocating atmosphere. One should not be surprised that so many lose their balance and are mangled in the machinery of love. Take the Wittgensteins. With three of their five children committing suicide they make the Kafkas seem like a model family. One in Prague, the other in Vienna, Kafka and Wittgenstein often get mentioned in the same breath. Socially they were poles apart but both figure in and are ingredients of the intellectual ferment of the last years of the Austro-Hungarian Empire. Not at all similar in character, Kafka and Wittgenstein sometimes sound alike, as in Wittgenstein's Preface to his *Philosophical Investigations*: 'I make [these remarks] public with doubtful feelings. It is not impossible that it should fall to the lot of this work, in its poverty and in the darkness of this time, to bring light into one brain or another – but, of course, it is not likely. I should not like my writing to spare other people the trouble of thinking. But, if possible, to stimulate someone to thoughts of his own. I should have liked to produce a good book. This has not come about, but the time is past in which I could improve it.'

Though Nabokov was sure he had travelled regularly on the same train as Kafka when they were both in Berlin in 1922, Kafka and Wittgenstein could meet, I suppose, only in the pages of a novel like *Ragtime* or in one of those imaginary encounters (Freud and Kafka is an obvious one) that used to be devised by Maurice Cranston in the days of the BBC Third Programme. But if Wittgenstein had never heard of Kafka, Kafka would certainly have heard of Wittgenstein. It was a noted name in Bohemia where the family owned many steelworks. A steelworks is a dangerous place and the Wittgenstein companies must have contributed their quota to those unfortunates crowding up the steps of the Workers Accident Insurance Institute in Poric Street. So when Kafka did come across the name Wittgenstein it just meant more paperwork. It must have been a strange place, the Workers Accident Insurance Institute, a kingdom of the absurd where it did not pay to be well and loss determined gain; limbs became commodities and to be given a clean bill of health was to be sent away empty-handed. There every man carried a price on his head, or on his arm or his leg, like the tariffs of ancient law. It was a world where to be deprived was to be endowed, to be disfigured was to be marked out for reward and to trip was to jump every hurdle. In Kafka's place of work only the whole man had something to hide, the real handicap to have no handicap at all, whereas a genuine limp genuinely acquired cleared every obstacle and a helping hand was one that had first been severed from the body. The world as hospital, it is Nietzsche's nightmare.

Kafka's career in insurance coincides with the period when compensation for injury at work is beginning to be accepted as a necessary condition of employment. Workers' compensation was and is a pretty unmixed blessing but it did spawn a new disease – or at any rate a new neurosis. Did one want a neurosis, the turn of the century in Austro-Hungary was the time and place to have it, except that this condition was a product of the factory not the drawing room, not so richly upholstered or so literate or capable of literature as those articulate fantasies teased out at No. 19 Berggasse. Compensation neurosis is a condition that affected and affects those (they tend to be women more than men) who have suffered a slight accident at work, and in particular an accident to the head: a slight bump, say, a mild concussion, nothing significant. Before the introduction of compensation such a minor mishap was likely to be ignored or forgotten. With no chance of compensation there was no incidence of neurosis, grin and bear it the order of the day. But once

there is the possibility of compensation (and if the –
scarcely – injured party does not know this there will be
well-wishers who will tell him or her) then the idea is
planted that he or she might be owed something. One does
not need to be a conscious malingerer to feel that some
recompense is perhaps called for, and from this feeling is
bred dissatisfaction, headaches, wakefulness, the whole
cabinet of neurotic symptoms.

With Lily in *The Insurance Man* I have assumed that
such a case did occasionally get as far as the Workers
Accident Insurance Institute. If so then here was one more
hopeless quest going on round the corridors of that
unhappy building. This kind of quest, where what is
wanted is the name of the illness as well as compensation
for it, has something in common with Joseph K's quest in
The Trial. He wants his offence identified but no one will
give it a name; this is his complaint. Until his offence is
named he cannot find a tribunal to acquit him of it.

Kafka and Proust both begin on the frontiers of dreams. It
is in the gap between sleeping and waking where Marcel is
trying to place his surroundings that Gregor Samsa finds
himself transformed into a beetle and Joseph K finds
himself under arrest. *Metamorphosis* and *The Trial* are the
two works of Kafka that are best known, are, if you like,
classics. Classics – and in particular modern classics – are
the books one thinks one ought to read, thinks one has
read. In this category particularly for readers who were
young in the fifties come Proust, Sartre, Orwell, Camus
and Kafka. It isn't simply a matter of pretension. As a
young man I genuinely felt I ought to read Proust and
Eliot (though it did no harm to be seen reading them).
However, a few pages convinced me that I had got the gist
and so they went on to the still uncluttered bookshelf
beside Kafka, Camus, Orwell and the rest.

The theory these days (or one of them) is that the reader

brings as much to the book as the author. So how much more do readers bring who have never managed to get through the book at all? It follows that the books one remembers best are the books one has never read. To be remembered but not read has been the fate of *The Trial* despite it being the most readable of Kafka's books. Kafka on the whole is not very readable. But then to be readable does not help a classic. Great books are taken as read, or taken as having been read. If they are read, or read too often and too easily by too many, the likelihood is they are not great books or won't remain so for long. Read too much they crumble away as nowadays popular mountains are prone to do.

The readers or non-readers of *The Trial* remember it wrong. Its reputation is as a tale about man and bureaucracy, a fable appropriate to the office block. One recalls the office in Orson Welles's film – a vast hangar in which hundreds of clerks toil at identical desks to an identical routine. In fact *The Trial* is set in small rooms in dark houses in surroundings that are picturesque, romantic and downright quaint. For the setting of *The Trial* there is no blaming the planners. It is all on an impeccably human scale.

The topography that oppressed Kafka does not oppress us. Kafka's fearful universe is constructed out of burrows and garrets and cubby-holes on back staircases. It is nearer to Dickens and *Alice* and even to the cosiness of *The Wind in the Willows* than it is to our own particular emptiness. Our shorthand for desolation is quite different: the assembly line, the fence festooned with polythene rags, the dead land between the legs of the motorway. But it is ours. It isn't Kafka's. Or, to put it another way, the trouble with Kafka is that he didn't know the word Kafkaesque. However, those who see *The Trial* as a trailer for totalitarian bureaucracy might be confirmed in this view on finding that the premises in Dzherzhinsky Square in Moscow now occupied by the Lubianka Prison formerly housed another institution, the Rossiya Insurance Company.

Joseph K's first examination takes place one Sunday morning in Juliusstrasse, a shabby street of poor tenements. The address he had been given was of a gaunt apartment building with a vast entrance that led directly into a courtyard formed by many storeys of tenement flats.

Futile to go looking for that courtyard in Prague today. It exists after all only in the mind of a dead author whom you may not even have read. But say you did go looking for it, as a Proust reader might go looking for Combray, or Brontë fans for Wuthering Heights and say even that you found the address, it still would not be as Kafka or as Joseph K describes it. These days the stone would have been scrubbed, the brick pointed, the mouldings given back their old (which is to say their new) sharpness in what the hoarding on the site advertises as a government-assisted programme of restoration and refurbishment. Go where you like in the old quarters of Europe it is the same. Decay has been arrested, the cracks filled; in Padua, Perpignan and Prague urban dentistry has triumphed.

The setting for Joseph K's first examination is a small room with a low ceiling, a kind of upstairs basement, a rooftop cellar. It is a location he finds only with difficulty since it can be reached only through the kitchen of one of the apartments. It is this block of apartments, let us imagine, that has now been restored, the architect of which, grey hair, young face, bright tie and liberal up to a point (architects, like dentists, being the same the world over) here shows off his latest piece of conservation:

What we had here originally was a pretty rundown apartment building. The tenants, many of whom had lived here literally for generations, were mainly in the lower-income bracket – joiners, cleaners, factory workers and so on, plus some single ladies who were probably no better than they should be. I believe the whole district was rather famous for that actually. My problem was how to do justice to the building, improve the accommodation while (single ladies apart) hanging on to some sort of social mix.

Stage 1 involved getting possession of the building itself, which, since it's situated in the heart of the conservation area, we were able to do by means of a government grant. Stage 2 was to empty the apartments. Happily many of the tenants were elderly so we could leave this largely to a process of natural wastage. When the overall population of the building had come down to a manageable number, Stage 3 involved locating this remnant in local-authority housing on the outskirts. Which brings us to Stage 4, the restoration and refurbishment of the building itself.

Initially what we did was to divide it up into a number of two- and three-bedroom units, targeted, I suppose, on lawyers, architects, communications people, the kind of tenant who still finds the demands of urban living quite stimulating. We've got one or two studios on the top floor for artists of one kind and another, photographers and so on, and a similar number of old people on the ground floor. Actually we were obliged to include those under the terms of the government grant but though they do take up some very desirable space, I actually welcome them. A building of this kind is after all a community, old, young – variety is of the essence.

The particular unit associated with the gentleman in the novel is on the fifth floor. Trudge, trudge, trudge. I'm afraid the lifts are still unconnected. Bureaucracy, the workings of.

And so they go upstairs to the fifth floor as Joseph K went up that Sunday morning in the novel, looking for the room where his examination was set to take place.

'Actually I remember this particular apartment,' says the architect, 'because it was a bit of an odd one out. Whereas most of the other flats amalgamated quite nicely into two- and three-bedrooms units, this particular one wouldn't fit into any of our categories. Here we are. You come into a small room, you see which has obviously served as a kitchen . . .'

'Yes,' says the visitor. 'That's described in the book.'

'Never read it alas,' says the architect. 'Work, pressure of. Come in, have supper, slump in front of the old telly box and that's it for the night. However, this kitchen rather unexpectedly opens into this much larger room. Two windows, rather nicely proportioned and I think once upon a time there must have been a platform at the far end.'

'Yes,' says the visitor. 'That's in the book too.'

'And does he mention this?' asks the architect. 'This rather attractive feature, the gallery running round under the ceiling?'

'Yes,' says the visitor. 'People sat up there during his examination. They were rather cramped. In fact they were so cramped they had to bend double with cushions between their backs and the ceiling.'

'Is that in the book?' asks the architect.

'Yes. It's all in the book,' says the visitor.

'Really,' says the architect. 'It sounds jollier than I thought. I thought it was some frightful political thing. Anyway we had a site conference and all of us – architects, rental agents and prospective tenants – agreed it would be a great pity to lose the gallery. Someone suggested converting the place into a studio with the gallery as a kind of sleeping area but that smacked a little bit of alternative life-styles which we were quite anxious to avoid, so in the end we've given it a lick of paint and just left it, the upshot being that the management are probably going to donate the room to the tenants. If it has some connection with this fellow in the novel perhaps we could call it after him.'

'The Joseph K room,' says the visitor. 'But what would you use it for?'

'Well, what will we use it for?' says the architect. 'I don't want to use the dread words "community centre" with all the overtones of Bingo and Saturday night hop. But it could be used for all sorts. As soon as you say the word "crèche", for instance, you've got the ladies on your side. Encounter groups and suchlike, keep-fit classes, and then, of course, we have the Residents' Association. What we are hoping you see is that the residents will *join in*. After all this is a co-operative. Everybody needs to pull their weight and to that end all the tenants have been carefully – I was going to say screened, but let's say we've made a few preliminary enquiries in terms of background, outlook and so on, nothing so vulgar as vetting, you understand, but if we are all going to be neighbours it makes for less trouble in the long run.

'And supposing anybody does step out of line, stereo going full blast in the wee small hours, ladies coming up and down a little too often (or indeed gentlemen in this day and age), kiddies making a mess on the stairs, then in that event I think this room would be the ideal place for the culprit to be interviewed by the Residents' Association, asked to be a little more considerate and even see the error of their ways. After all I think a line has to be drawn somewhere. And the Joseph K Memorial Room would be just the place to do it.'

In our cosy little island, novel readers must seldom be accused of crimes they did not commit, or crimes of any sort for that matter: PROUST READER ON BURGLARY RAP is not a headline that carries conviction. Few of us are likely to be arrested without charge or expect to wake up and find the police in the room, and our experience of bureaucracy comes not from the Gestapo so much as from the Gas Board. So *The Trial* does not at first sight seem like a book to be read with dawning recognition, the kind of book one looks up from and says, 'But it's my story!'

Nor is it a book for the sick room and seldom to be found on those trolleys of literary jumble trundled round the wards of local hospitals every Wednesday afternoon by Miss Venables, the voluntary worker. The book trolley and the food trolley are not dissimilar, hospital reading and hospital food both lacking taste and substance and neither having much in the way of roughage. The guardian and conductress of the book trolley, Miss Venables, seldom reads herself and would have been happier taking round the tea, for which the patients are more grateful and less choosy than they are over the books. But in the absence of a Mr Venables and because she has no figure to speak of, Miss Venables is generally taken to be rather refined and thus has got landed with literature. The real life sentences come from judgements on our personal appearance and good behaviour, far from remitting the sentence, simply confirms it and makes it lifelong. Kafka was always delicate and his father therefore assumed he was a bookworm, an assumption his son felt was unwarranted and which he vigorously denied.

Miss Venables is not a bookworm either, seldom venturing inside the books she purveys, which she judges solely by their titles. Most patients, she thinks, want to be taken out of themselves, particularly so in Surgical. In Surgical novels are a form of homeopathy: having had something taken out of themselves the patients now want something else to take them out of themselves. So coming out of Surgical Miss Venables finds her stock of novels running pretty low as she pauses now in Admissions at the bedside of a patient who has come in, as he has been told, 'just for observation'. Presumptuous to call him Mr Kay, let us call him Mr Jay.

'Fiction or non-fiction?' asks Miss Venables.

'Fiction,' says Mr Jay, and hopes he is going to do better than last week. Last week he had wanted a copy of *Jake's Thing*, but could not remember the title and had finished up with *Howards End*.

'Fiction,' says Miss Venables (who would have come in handy in the Trinitarian controversy), 'fiction is divided into Fiction, Mystery and Romance. Which would you like?'

Truthfully Mr Jay wants a tale of sun and lust but daunted by Miss Venables's unprepossessing appearance he lamely opts for Mystery. She gives him a copy of *The Trial*.

How *The Trial* comes to be classified under Mystery is less of a mystery than how it comes to be on the trolley at all. In fact it had originally formed part of the contents of the locker of a deceased lecturer in Modern Languages and had been donated to the hospital library by his grateful widow, along with his copy of Thomas Mann's *Magic Mountain*. This Miss Venables has classified under Children and Fairy Stories. So leaving Mr Jay leafing listlessly through Kafka she passes on with her trolley to other wards and other disappointments.

It does not take Mr Jay long to realize that he has picked another dud, and one even harder to read than *Howards End*. What is to be made of such sentences as 'The verdict doesn't come all at once; the proceedings gradually merge into the verdict.'? Mr Jay has a headache. He puts *The Trial* on his locker beside the bottle of Lucozade and the Get Well cards and tries to sleep, but can't. Instead he settles back and thinks about his body. These days he thinks about little else. The surgeon Mr McIver has told him he is a mystery. Matron says he has

baffled the doctors. So Mr Jay feels like somebody special.
Now they come for him and he is carefully manoeuvred
under vast machines by aproned figures, who then
discreetly retire. Later, returned to his bed, he tries again to
read but feels so sick he cannot read his book even if he
really wanted to. And that is a pity. Because Mr Jay might
now begin to perceive that *The Trial* is not a mystery story
and that it is not particularly about the law or bureaucracy
or any of the things the editor's note says it is about. It is
about something nearer home, and had he come once
again upon the sentence 'The verdict doesn't come all at
once; the proceedings gradually merge into the verdict' Mr
Jay might have realized that Kafka is talking to him. It *is*
his story.

In the short story *Metamorphosis* Gregor Samsa wakes up
as a beetle. Nabokov, who knew about beetles, poured
scorn on those who translated or depicted the insectified
hero as a cockroach. Kafka did not want the beetle
depicted at all but for the error of classification he is
largely to blame. It was Kafka who first brought up the
subject of cockroaches though in a different story,
Wedding Preparations in the Country. 'I have, as I lie in
bed,' he writes, 'the form of a large beetle, a stag beetle or
a cockchafer, I believe.' Cockroach or not, Gregor Samsa
has become so famous waking up as a beetle I am
surprised he has not been taken up and metamorphosed
again, this time by the advertising industry. Since he wakes
up as a beetle why should he not wake up as a
Volkswagen? Only this time he's not miserable but happy.
And so of course is his family. Why not? They've got
themselves a nice little car. The only problem is how to get
it out of the bedroom.

The first biography of Kafka was written by his friend and
editor Max Brod. It was Brod who rescued Kafka's works

from oblivion, preserved them and, despite Kafka's instructions to the contrary, published them after his death. Brod, who was a year younger than Kafka (though one somehow thinks of him as older), lived on until 1968. The author of innumerable essays and articles, Brod published some eighty-three books, one for every year of his life. Described in *The Times* obituary as 'himself an author of uncommonly versatile stamp' he turned out novels at regular intervals until the end of his life, the last one being set during the Arab–Israeli war. These novels fared poorly with the critics and were one able to collect the reviews of his books one would find few, I imagine, that do not somewhere invoke the name of Kafka, with the comparison inevitably to Brod's disadvantage. This cannot have been easy to take. He who had not only erected Kafka's monument but created his reputation never managed to struggle out of its shadow. He could be forgiven if he came to be as dubious of Kafka's name as Kafka was himself.

Never quite Kafka's wife, after Kafka's death Brod's role was that of the devoted widow, standing guard over the reputation, authorizing the editions, editing the diaries and driving trespassers from the grave. However, living in Tel Aviv, he was spared the fate of equivalent figures in English culture, an endless round of arts programmes where those who have known the famous are publicly debriefed of their memories, knowing as their own dusk falls that they will be remembered only for remembering someone else.

Kafka was a minor executive in an insurance company in Prague. In *Kafka's Dick* this fact is picked up by another minor executive in another insurance firm, but in Leeds seventy-odd years later. Sydney, as the insurance man, decides to do a piece on Kafka for an insurance periodical (I imagine there are such, though I've never verified the fact). As he works on his piece Sydney comes to resent his subject, as biographers must often do. Biographers are only fans after all, and fans have been known to shoot their idols.

'Why biography?' asks his wife.

Sydney's answer is less of a speech than an aria, which is probably why it was cut from the play:

I want to hear about the shortcomings of great men, their fears and their failings. I've had enough of their vision, how they altered the landscape (we stand on their shoulders to survey our lives). So. Let's talk about the vanity. Read how this one, the century's seer, increases his stature by lifts in his shoes. That one, the connoisseur of emptiness, is tipped for the Nobel Prize yet still needs to win at Monopoly. This playwright's skin is so thin he can feel pain on the other side of the world. So why is he deaf to the suffering next door; signs letters to the newspapers but holds his own wife a prisoner of conscience? The slipshod poet keeps immaculate time and expects it of everyone else, but never wears underwear and frequently smells. That's not important, of course, but what is? The gentle novelist's frightful temper, the Christian poet's mad, unvisited wife, the hush in their households where the dog goes on tiptoe, meals on the dot at their ironclad whim? Note with these great men the flight and not infrequent suicide of their children, their brisk remarriage on the deaths of irreplaceable wives. Proud of his modesty one gives frequent, rare interviews in which he aggregates praise and denudes others of credit. Indifferent to the lives about him he considers his day ruined on finding a slighting reference to himself in a periodical published three years ago in New Zealand. And demands sympathy from his family on that account. And gets it. Our father the novelist, my husband the poet. He belongs to the ages, just don't catch him at breakfast. Artists, celebrated for their humanity, they turn out to be scarcely human at all.

Death took no chances with Kafka and laid three traps for his life. Parched and voiceless from TB of the larynx, he was forty, the victim, as he himself said, of a conspiracy by his own body. But had his lungs not ganged up on him there was a second trap, twenty years down the line when the agents of death would have shunted him, as they did his three sisters, into the gas chambers. That fate, though it was not to be his, is evident in his last photograph. It is a face that prefigures the concentration camp.

But say that in 1924 he cheats death and a spell in the sanatorium restores him to health. In 1938 he sees what is coming – Kafka after all was more canny than he is given credit for, not least by Kafka himself – and so he slips away from Prague in time. J. P. Stern imagines him fighting with the partisans; Philip Roth finds him a poor teacher of Hebrew in Newark, New Jersey. Whatever his future when he leaves Prague he becomes what he has always been, a refugee. Maybe (for there is no harm in dreams) he even lives long enough to find himself the great man he never knew he was. Maybe (the most impossible dream of all) he actually succeeds in putting on weight. So where is death now? Waiting for Kafka in some Park Avenue consulting room where he goes with what he takes to be a recurrence of his old chest complaint.

'Quite curable now, of course. TB. No problem. However, regarding your chest you say you managed a factory once?'

'Yes. For my brother-in-law. For three or four years.'

'When was that?'

'A long time ago. It closed in 1917. In Prague.'

'What kind of factory was it?'

'Building materials. Asbestos.'

This is just a dream of Kafka's death. He is famous, the owner of the best-known initial in literature and we know he did not die like this. Others probably did. In Prague the consulting rooms are bleaker but the disease is the same and the treatment as futile. These patients have no names, though Kafka would have known them, those girls (old ladies now) whom he describes brushing the thick asbestos dust from their overalls, the casualties of his brother-in-law's ill-starred business in which Hermann, his father, had invested. A good job his father isn't alive, the past master of 'I told you so'.

In the last weeks of his life Kafka was taken to a sanatorium in the Wienerwald and here, where the secret of dreams had been revealed to Freud, Kafka's dreams ended.

On the window sill the night before he died Dora Dymant found an owl waiting. The owl has a complex imagery in art. Just as in Freudian psychology an emotion can stand for itself and its opposite, so is the owl a symbol of both darkness and light. As a creature of the night the owl was seen as a symbol of the Jews who, turning away from the light of Christ, were guilty of wilful blindness. On the other hand the owl was, as it remains, a symbol of wisdom. It is fitting that this bird of ambiguity should come to witness the departure of a man who by belief was neither Christian nor Jew, and who had never wholeheartedly felt himself a member of the human race. He had written of himself as a bug and a mouse, both the natural prey of the bird now waiting outside the window.

Alan Bennett
1987

Characters

Kafka
Brod
Linda
Father
Sydney
Hermann K

Kafka's Dick was first performed in an earlier version at the Royal Court Theatre, London, on 23rd September, 1986. The cast was as follows:

Kafka, Roger Lloyd Pack
Brod, Andrew Sachs
Linda, Alison Steadman
Father, Charles Lamb
Sydney, Geoffrey Palmer
Hermann K, Jim Broadbent
Julie, Vivian Pickles

Director, Richard Eyre
Designer, William Dudley
Lighting Designer, Mark Henderson
Sound, Christopher Shutt
Music, Effects and Arrangements, George Fenton
Dances, David Toguri

Act One

The date is immaterial, though it is around 1919.
Kafka, a tall, good-looking man is sitting in a chair,
dying. Max Brod, his friend, is smaller, slightly hump-
backed, and very much alive.

Kafka Max.

Brod I hoped you were sleeping.

Kafka Max.

Pause.

Brod What?

Kafka I think I shall die soon.

Brod says nothing.

Did you hear me, Max?

Brod Let's cross that bridge when you come to it. You've
said you were dying before.

Kafka I know. But I won't let you down this time, I promise.

Brod Kafka, I want you to *live*.

Kafka Forgive me. If I die . . .

Brod What's this if? He says he's dying then suddenly it's
'if'. Don't you mean 'when'?

Kafka When I die I want you to do me a favour.

Brod Come to the funeral, you mean? Look, this is Max,
your best friend. I'll be up there in the front row.

27

Kafka No. The funeral can take care of itself.

Brod Pardon me for saying so, but that's typical of your whole attitude to life. A funeral does not take care of itself.

Kafka (*overlapping*) I know, Max. I know.

Brod Take the eats for a start. You're dealing with grief-stricken people. They want to be able to weep secure in the knowledge that once you're in the grave the least they'll be offered will be a choice of sandwiches.

Kafka But after the funeral . . . this is very important . . . I want you to promise me something, Max. You must burn everything I've ever written.

Brod No.

Kafka Stories, novels, letters. Everything.

Brod What about the royalties?

Kafka I've published one novel and a few short stories. Does it matter?

Brod But where would they go in a bereavement situation?

Kafka My father, where else? Which is another reason to burn them. I've got stuff in technical periodicals to do with my work at the insurance company. Don't worry about that . . .

Brod But the rest I burn, right?

Kafka Yes.

Brod That is your honest decision?

Kafka Cross my heart and hope to die.

Brod That's not saying much; you are going to die.

Kafka Max, I *mean* it. All my works burned. Understand?

28

Brod All your works burned.

Kafka Everything. When I go, they go. Finish.

Brod You've got it. Message received and understood.

Pause. Brod starts to go.

Kafka Where are you going?

Brod To buy paraffin.

Kafka Max. Stay a minute. After all, my writings are worthless. They wouldn't survive anyway. They don't deserve to survive.

Pause.

Don't you think so?

Brod You're the one who's dying. I'm Max, your faithful friend. You say burn them, I burn them. (*Going again*) Maybe I'll get petrol instead.

Kafka Max! (*Pause.*) If you want to read them first, feel free . . . just to remind you.

Brod (*going again*) No. I read them when you wrote them. If I'm going to burn them I may as well press on and burn them. Only . . .

Kafka (*brightening*) What?

Brod Well, I ask myself, are we missing an opportunity here? Why not juice up the occasion? . . . Ask one or two people over, split a bottle of vino, barbecue the odd steak then as a climax to the proceedings flambé the Collected Works? Anyway, old friend, don't worry. All will be taken care of.

Kafka Good. Still, if in fact you can't get hold of all my stuff, no matter. Some of it has been published. It could be anywhere.

Brod You're kidding. I mean, what are we saying here? This is your faithful friend, Max. Kafka wants his stuff burned, Max will find it and burn it. It won't be difficult. You'd be surprised how helpful people are when it's a dying wish.

Kafka But I'm in libraries, Max. You can't burn them. *Metamorphosis*, my story about a man who wakes up as a beetle. That's in libraries. Ah well. I shall just have to live with that.

Brod Don't be so negative. Here's the plan. I go to the library, borrow your books, go back and say they've been stolen. Then it's burn, baby, burn.

Kafka Some are in America. London. Paris.

Brod So? I've always wanted an excuse to travel. I can't wait. Max Brod. Search and destroy! (*Pause.*) Hey, you look really depressed.

Kafka Wouldn't you be depressed? I'm dying.

Pause.

Brod Look. Vis-à-vis your books. I've just had a thought.

Kafka (*clutching at a straw*) Yes?

Brod Maybe I won't burn everything. Not every single copy. Could you live with that?

Kafka Well . . . I . . . I'm not sure. I really wanted them burnt . . .

Brod Can I just let you in on my thinking? We're in 1920 now, right? You're going to die soon . . . give a year, take a year, say 1924 at the outside. Well, less than ten years later we get the Nazis, right? And, as prefigured in some of your as yet unrecognized masterpieces (which I'm going to burn, I know, I know), the Nazis seize power and put into operation the full apparatus of totalitarian bureaucracy.

Kafka Max, I saw it coming.

Brod You did.

Kafka Would that history had proved me wrong, Max.

Brod Would that it had. Only, tragically it didn't. Because in 1933 the Nazis are scheduled to stage their infamous Burning of the Books . . .

Kafka Burn books? Who in his right mind would want to burn books? They must be sick.

Brod The Nazis ransack libraries for what they term decadent literature. Film shows Brownshirts bringing out books by the armful and casting them into the flames.

Kafka In civilized Europe! I can't bear it. It's tragic. It's insane. (*Pause.*) Max. Which books in particular?

Brod Freud. Proust. Rilke. Brecht.

Kafka Er . . . anybody else?

Brod Hemingway. Thomas Mann. Gide. Joyce . . .

Kafka Max . . . Don't I figure?

Brod Well, this is the point . . . I'll have burnt your stuff already.

Kafka But nobody will know that.

Brod Exactly. People will look at the credits and say: They burnt Proust. They burnt Brecht. They burnt Joyce. Where is Kafka? Not worth burning, maybe.

Kafka God. I was depressed before. Now I'm suicidal.

Brod Maybe I can fix it.

Kafka You think?

Brod I can see it now: a shot of flames licking round a book jacket, the name Kafka prominently placed.

Kafka Dreadful.

Brod Sure, but burn one and you sell ten thousand. Believe me, if the Nazis hadn't thought of it the publishers would.

Kafka Max, I'm still not sure. Do I want to survive?

Brod Of course you do. I'm a successful novelist, so I'm headed that way myself. I know you've got talent. You haven't made it big yet, in fact you haven't made it at all, but once you're dead I've a hunch your fame is going to snowball. Who knows, you could end up as famous as me. Whereas, you burn everything, you've squandered your life.

Kafka You're right.

Brod Believe me, in ten years' time, your stuff is going to be classic. That one you mentioned, *Metamorphosis*, where he wakes up one morning and finds he's a cockroach. Brilliant.

Kafka (*leaping from his chair*) That's it. That is *it*. I've changed my mind. As you were. Burn them. Burn everything!

Brod What did I say?

Kafka What did you *say*? What did you say? He didn't wake up as a cockroach. I never said he woke up as a cockroach. He woke up as a beetle.

Brod Cockroach, beetle, they're both bugs, who cares?

Kafka Me! Don't you see? That's the trouble with words. You write one thing, the reader makes it into another. You try to be honest, only words fail you. They always do in the end. They're the worst method of communicating with anybody.

Brod Look . . .

Kafka No, I was right first time. Burn them.

Brod If you say so.

Kafka And Max. No biography.

Brod Who'll want to write your biography? You won't have written anything.

Kafka Promise.

Brod I promise.

Kafka Forgive me. I'm a terrible human being.

Brod Don't worry about it. (*He yawns.*)

Kafka I'm just a dog pretending to be a person, an ape.

Brod Yeah, yeah. We've been through all that. Now try and sleep a little. Come to bed.

The Lights begin to fade, with music possibly.

Kafka I would sleep, only I dream.

Brod Everybody dreams.

Kafka Not like me. I dream the future.

Kafka and Brod exit.
    Lights up immediately on:

SCENE 2

The present day. A room in a middle-class house, possibly a kitchen cum living-room. I am not sure how

33

representational the room should be. Since some of the happenings that take place in it are downright unreal perhaps the room should look unreal also, but the reverse could be more convincingly argued. An over-scrupulous naturalism would be out of place, though the reality of the bookcase is crucial. There are doors or exits to other parts of the house, and an entrance, say, french windows on to the garden.

Sydney, a mild, middle-aged man, is reading. Linda, his wife, stares out into the garden. Sydney's Father, an old man with a Zimmer frame, is consulting the bookcase.

Linda That fool of a tortoise is out again. Galloping across the lawn.

Father When are they coming?

Linda (*ignoring him but without rancour*) They are not coming.

Father (*taking an orange Penguin from the bookcase and carrying it over to Linda*) Is that a detective?

Linda (*still ignoring him*) There are no detectives. Nobody is coming.

Father What have I done?

Sydney (*kindly*) Nothing, Father. You have done nothing. (*Pause.*) There can be few people who realize that Hitler went to the same school as Wittgenstein.

Linda The way he went on to behave I'm surprised he went to school at all.

Sydney Another five years they might have been sharing the same desk.

Linda You are clever, Sydney.

Father (*now poised to leave*) When are they coming?

Linda They are not coming.

Father exits.

When are they coming?

Sydney They didn't say. (*He looks unhappy.*)

Linda Now it's making a beeline for the road. It must want to die.

Sydney I wonder if there was a school magazine. Old Boys' Notes. Wittgenstein, L. (Class of 1904) has just published his *Tractatus Logico-Philosophicus* and been elected a Fellow of Trinity College, Cambridge. Contemporaries will recall the model sewing machine he made out of matchsticks. Hitler, A. (Class of 1899) has recently been elected Chancellor of Germany. He will be remembered as an enthusiastic secretary of the Art Group.

Linda Does Mr Cunliffe read?

Sydney I don't know. As Deputy Supervisor Vehicle Insurance North Western Area I doubt if he gets much chance.

Linda says nothing.

I didn't want the job. And remember this: Mr Cunliffe has never had an article in the *Journal of Insurance Studies*.

Linda No, but Mrs Cunliffe's got a new bedroom suite and they pop over to Jersey quite regularly. (*Pause.*) Why do you never read novels?

Sydney I'm an insurance man, I prefer facts. Biography. I'd rather read about writers than read what they write.

Linda Yes, I know why. More dirt.

Sydney (*at the bookcase*) Not necessarily. *The Life of E. M. Forster.* Hardly dirt.

Linda Really? I thought he lived with a policeman.

Sydney He was a friend. Forster had friends in many walks of life.

Linda Not merely walks. You said one was an Egyptian tram-driver. And there were umpteen darkies.

Sydney Linda. (*Pause.*) We complain about my father: Kafka's father used to rummage in his ears with a toothpick then use it to pick his teeth.

She hangs over his shoulder, looking at his books. She would probably like to be in bed.

Linda No pictures?

Sydney No. I sometimes wish biographies carried nude photographs.

Linda Sydney.

Sydney It would settle this argument anyway. (*He holds up a book.*) This is by two psychologists at the University of North Carolina, who having analysed everything Kafka ever wrote, deduce that one of his problems, of which there were many, was a small penis.

Linda I never liked the word penis. I don't mind the pee . . . after all that's what it's for. It's the -nis I somehow don't like. Anyway, he's not unique in that department.

Sydney Linda.

Linda I was thinking of Scott Fitzgerald.

Sydney How do you know Scott Fitzgerald had a small . . . thing?

Linda The same way I know W. H. Auden never wore underpants, that Kafka's grandfather could pick up a sack of potatoes in his teeth and that Kafka's father used to rummage in his ears with a toothpick. Because that kind of conversation is all I ever get. If it weren't for looking after your father I could still be a nurse.

Sydney I like odd facts.

Linda When are you going to tell me the bits in between? I'd thought of taking a course. So I can help you in your work.

Sydney An insurance course?

Linda This work.

Sydney If there are courses in Kafka, which I doubt, they would be the first casualty of cutbacks.

Linda Literature in general.

Sydney Ah. Literature in general.

Linda I should have stayed a nurse. What do I do now? Hang about. I'm nothing.

Sydney I know it's a wicked thing to say nowadays but you are not nothing. You are my wife.

Linda It's not enough.

Sydney It's enough for Mrs Cunliffe.

Linda Couldn't I do research? File your papers?

She makes a move to do so. He stops her.

Sydney Linda.

Linda Let me at least read it.

Sydney (*taking back his manuscript*) You wouldn't understand it.

Linda I might. After all he's got a nice face. Would I have liked him?

Sydney He was never short of symptoms. You could at least have nursed him. You wouldn't like his stories. Not what you'd call 'true to life'. A man turns into a cockroach. An ape lectures. Mice talk. He'd like me. We've got so much in common. He was in insurance. I'm in insurance. He had TB. I had TB. He didn't like his name. I don't like my name. I'm sure the only reason I drifted into insurance was because I was called Sydney.

Linda Sydney's a nice name. I like Sydney.

Sydney Now this is interesting. Kafka had read *Crime and Punishment*, which is a novel by Dostoevsky. In *Crime and Punishment* the student Raskolnikov commits a murder for which another man is wrongly arrested; the man is a house painter. In Kafka's *The Trial*, Joseph K is wrongly arrested. Who has actually committed the crime? A house painter. And someone in whose name millions of people were wrongly arrested was Adolf Hitler. Who is himself wrongly accused of being . . . a house painter.

Pause.

Linda And?

Sydney Linda, it's interesting.

Linda It is, it is.

Sydney One of the functions of literary criticism is to point up unexpected connections.

Linda With you being in accident insurance I thought your only interest in unexpected connections was when they occurred between motor cars. Sydney.

She draws him out of the chair.

Sydney Linda. It's two-thirty in the afternoon.

Linda It'll be another unexpected connection.

The doorbell goes. They stop.

Sydney Is his case packed?

Linda nods.

Linda (*meaning 'Be brave'*) Sydney.

Linda answers the door, but the visitor has already come round to the french windows. It is Brod, who is just as we have seen him previously, except that he is minus his hump. He carries in his hand a large Homburg hat which conceals a tortoise.

Brod I ring your doorbell with reluctance. I have met with an accident. I am a visitor to these shores. Suddenly a temperamental prostate and a total absence of toilet facilities necessitates my emptying my bladder outside your front door.

Linda returns.

Linda Sydney, it's all over the step.

Brod Worse is to follow. Picture my distress as I am rebuttoning my trousers when I discover I have urinated not only over your doorstep but also over your tortoise. (*He removes the Homburg to reveal the tortoise.*)

Linda Our tortoise? (*She puts out her hand for the tortoise then thinks better of it.*) He's wet through!

Brod puts the tortoise down on the floor. It begins to move off – Brod, without looking, puts his Homburg hat over it.

Sydney It was an accident, I'm sure.

Brod Blame the disappearance of your public conveniences. Time was when they were the envy of the civilized world. To be incontinent here is some problem, I can tell you.

The doorbell has alerted Father and he has come in.

Father It's not true. Someone's been telling lies about me. I am not incontinent. Furthermore I can tell you the name of the Prime Minister. Are you them?

Sydney No, he is not them. There is no them. This gentleman has just urinated over the tortoise.

Father I know what that means. You want my room.

Brod Why does urinating over the tortoise mean they want your room?

Sydney My father imagines things.

Father I don't imagine things. You say I imagine things. I never imagine things.

At which point Brod's hat begins to move slowly across the room towards Father, who retreats before it in shocked silence, then (Zimmer frame permitting) bolts.
    Linda picks up the hat and hands it to Brod. Ignoring the cue to go he sits down and opens a book.

Sydney Should we offer him a cup of tea?

Linda And put another innocent tortoise at risk? No.

Brod How singular! I open a book and what do I find? Kafka. (*Opening others*) Kafka, Kafka.

Sydney You know his work?

Brod Only by heart. 'As Gregor Samsa awoke one morning from uneasy dreams he found himself transformed into a gigantic cockroach.' 'Ah, ha,' says the browser at the airport bookstall. 'The very thing to while away my flight to Sri Lanka.' And ring a ding ding. It's another sale for our Czech Chekhov.

Linda I was a nurse. Waking up people was half my job. I never came across anyone waking up as an insect.

Brod You probably never came across metaphor either. She says no one wakes up as a cockroach. Next to her I'd wake up a wild beast. So what is it about our Prague Proust that interests you?

Sydney It's not generally known but Kafka worked all his life in an insurance office . . .

Brod It is known to some people.

Sydney And as I'm in that line myself, I'm writing a piece about him for *Small Print*, the *Journal of Insurance Studies*.

Brod For a moment I thought you were yet another of those academic blow flies who make a living buzzing round the faeces of the famous. You've read his biography?

Sydney I've read several.

Brod Excuse me. There is only one. Mine.

Sydney You've written a biography of Kafka?

Brod I wrote the biography. I edited the diaries. I published the novels. You want to know about Kafka, start here. Max Brod.

They shake hands.

Sydney Max Brod! You are Max Brod? You're pulling my leg. No. (*He laughs nervously.*) How could you be?

Brod Why?

Sydney You're Kafka's closest friend.

Brod Correction. Not his closest friend. His only friend. His only real friend.

Sydney You're a great man. A legend. What could you be doing here? Max Brod! (*He shakes hands again.*)

Brod What about Nurse Cavell? Doesn't she want to shake hands with a legend?

Linda Brod? You spell it B-R-O-D? (*She goes to look it up.*)

Sydney No need to look him up. I know all about him.

Brod (*to the audience*) She's about to discover I'm dead. But then I'm also famous. These are the dead ones. Nobody's ever heard of them. That's death. You read my book?

Sydney Every word.

Linda (*beckoning him with the book*) Sydney.

Sydney I've read half a dozen biographies but I always come back to yours.

Brod Of course you do. I knew Kafka. They didn't.

Linda Sydney, can I have a word?

Sydney In a minute, Linda. Tell me, was Kafka as saintly as you make him out?

Brod's interest throughout this conversation is in Linda, not Kafka and still less Sydney.

Brod I should lie? Kind, modest and with that clod of a father . . . what type of a nurse was this, crisp, white uniform, thin black stockings . . . that type?

Linda Yes. Strict. And I was a past master of the enema. Sydney.

Sydney (*eluding Linda's attempts to draw him aside*) To me Kafka is the last, authentic, modern saint. It's interesting that one by one the moral giants of the twentieth century have all been toppled. I say that in my article. 'It is interesting that one by one the moral giants of the twentieth century have all been toppled.' But not Kafka.

Brod That's fascinating. Nurses have a reputation for unbridled promiscuity. How does that accord with your experience?

Linda Sydney.

Sydney Take Wittgenstein. People said he was a saint, but not any more.

Linda (*feigning interest*) No?

Sydney Biography reveals that his less philosophical moments were spent picking up youths.

Brod What for, when there's so much else on offer?

Sydney And who nowadays admires Freud?

Linda Oh? Where did he slip up?

Sydney Dishonest. Freud was quite small . . .

Brod Minute. He would only have come up to here (*on Linda*).

Sydney And yet in a photograph of Freud with his colleagues he's head and shoulders above everybody else. Why? Biography reveals he's stood on a box.

Linda Oh. Like Alan Ladd.

Sydney Alan Ladd?

Linda Alan Ladd wasn't tall. He often had to stand on a box. Either that or his leading lady stood in a trench. Maybe Freud wasn't on a box. Maybe the others were in a trench.

Sydney Linda. Nursing, though an admirable profession, doesn't exactly hone the mind.

Brod Don't worry about it.

Linda But Sydney. You said literary criticism was about unexpected connections. You can't get more unexpected than Freud and Alan Ladd.

Brod That's the danger with big tits. The mind goes on holiday.

Linda Sydney. I want to tell you something.

Sydney Linda, I'm talking. You wouldn't catch Kafka standing on a box. Wanting to make himself bigger. Not your friend Kafka, eh?

Brod No.

Sydney In fact, I'd have said the reverse. I'd have said he wanted to make himself smaller. Would you agree?

Brod Larger, smaller, one or the other. You don't still have your uniform?

Linda Where's the tortoise gone?

She gets down on her hands and knees to look, further fascinating Brod.

Sydney We only have to look at his work. Who does Kafka identify with? An ape, a mouse, a cockroach. Smaller and smaller.

Brod Can I help?

Sydney I tell you, give him a few more years and he'd have needed a microscope to see what he was writing about. I actually say that in my article: 'Give him a few more years and he'd have needed a microscope to see what he was writing about.'

Brod How interesting. Will it ever stop? If I never hear the name Kafka again it will be too soon. (*He sits down again.*)

Linda Sydney. You don't think he is this man?

Sydney I'm not sure. Max Brod was a hunchback.

Linda Sydney. He's also dead. I looked him up for you. (*She shows him the book.*) Died in 1968.

Sydney In Tel Aviv, yes.

Linda You know?

Sydney Of course.

Linda So who is he?

Sydney He could be to do with father. A health visitor perhaps.

Linda Masquerading as a friend of Kafka?

Sydney The social services are notorious for their imagination.

Linda So why not ask him?

Sydney Linda. Don't *worry*. We are having a conversation. Ideas are being exchanged, hypotheses put forward. For me this is a treat. A picnic of the mind. How often do I find someone who's even heard of Kafka let alone someone who can't wait to discuss him?

Linda Yes, Sydney.

Sydney All in good time.

Linda Yes, Sydney.

Sydney (*finding the tortoise*) Here he is. Why don't you put him under the tap?

Linda I'll go put him under the tap.

Brod Can I help?

Linda No. You stay and have a picnic with my husband.

She exits.

Sydney There's one question I must ask you.

Brod I won't answer it.

Sydney You don't know the question.

Brod I don't know the question? I don't know the question? There is only one question. Always there has been just one question. 'Why did you not burn the papers?' Nobody, *nobody* is grateful. But for me there would have been no Kafka. He would not have existed. He would have been a no-name. A big zero. I made Kafka. Me! Max Brod. So is it 'Thank you, Max', 'Much obliged, Max', 'Good thinking, Max'? No. Always it's 'Why did you not burn the papers?' Well, there is one person who would thank me. The man himself. If Kafka were around today he'd be the first person to shake my hand.

There is a shrill scream from Linda, off.
Kafka appears on the stage beside Brod.

Linda (*off*) Sydney! Sydney!

Brod You!

Kafka takes his hand as Linda enters.

Linda It's that tortoise. I'd swilled it under the tap and put it on the draining board. Just then it popped its little head out . . . I don't know what made me do it . . . I gave it a kiss.

Brod Kafka.

Sydney Kafka? Linda. I believe this is Kafka. It is. It is. Linda. This is Kafka.

Linda Sydney.

Kafka How are you?

Brod Good. Terrific. You?

Kafka Terrible.

They laugh.

Brod You haven't changed.

Kafka (*embracing him*) Max, Max. Old friend.

Sydney (*shyly*) How do you do.

Kafka (*taking Linda's hand*) How do you do.

Linda (*panicking*) Sydney.

Sydney Have I the pleasure of addressing Mr Kafka?

Kafka nods graciously and diffidently shakes hands.

I just don't believe it. Kafka!

Kafka Max. Who is this man?

Sydney Linda. It's him. It's Kafka.

Linda Sydney. Kafka's dead. They're both dead.

Sydney I know. But it's Kafka.

Linda Sydney.

Kafka Max. Kindly ask him not to keep saying my name. You remember I never liked my name. The persistent repetition of it is still deeply offensive.

Brod Sure, I remember. Listen, boys and girls. Kafka doesn't like his name. Point taken. No more Kafka. (*To Kafka*) The husband's very dull but the wife has possibilities.

Sydney I love you. You're my hero.

Kafka Hero? Max, what is this?

47

Linda Excuse me. I hope I'm not out of order but two minutes ago you were a tortoise. Suddenly you're a leading light in European literature.

Brod My dear Miss Marple. This is someone who wrote a story about a man waking up as a cockroach. So? Now it's a two-way traffic.

Linda That was fiction. Wasn't it, Sydney? This is non-fiction.

Kafka (*to the audience*) What is this about a leading figure in European literature?

Sydney Kafka at 27 Batcliffe Drive!

Kafka Max. Is this man deaf? He is still saying my name.

Brod Please. Please. This is the second time of asking. Drop Kafka's name.

Sydney and Linda draw aside.

Kafka What is all this 'leading figure in European literature' stuff?

Brod Well?

Kafka I'm nobody. I brought out a few short stories and an unsuccessful novel – that was seventy years ago in Czechoslovakia. How am I a leading figure?

Brod Did I say modest? Move over E. M. Forster. A saint.

Kafka And Max. A beetle.

Brod Say again.

Kafka Not a cockroach. You said cockroach. It was a beetle.

Brod Will you listen to this man. I make him world famous and he quibbles over entomology.

Brod and Kafka draw aside.

Linda Call the police.

Sydney What for? Nobody's committed a crime.

Linda Sydney. It's a Tuesday afternoon. We're expecting someone from the Health Authority and meanwhile you're kicking around some thoughts about Kafka. A knock on the door and it's a stranger with a dripping wet tortoise in his hand, who, lo and behold, turns out to be the world's leading authority on Kafka. Notwithstanding this person seems to have died several years ago you engage him in conversation while I go and swill the tortoise. The next minute it's gone, we've got Kafka in the lounge and these two are falling into one another's arms.

Sydney Well?

Linda It just seems a bit too plausible to me.

Sydney So who are they?

Linda Burglars.

Sydney Don't be absurd. How many burglars have heard of Franz Kafka?

Linda Sydney, they read all sorts in prison. They no sooner get them inside nowadays than they're pestering them to read Proust. That's all some of them go to prison for, the chance of a good read.

Sydney It would have to be a subtle burglar who got in disguised as a tortoise. It's not logical.

Linda Criminals have no logic. A woman last week answers the door, the caller shoves a dishcloth in her mouth and steals the television set. You say he couldn't be a tortoise, she's now a vegetable, so don't talk to me about logic. Call the police. Let them decide if he's Kafka.

Sydney What with? Sniffer dogs trained in Modern Studies?

Linda Sydney, he's dead. They're both dead.

Sydney They're alive to me. Franz Kafka is more present, more real to me than . . . than . . .

Linda I know. Than I am.

Sydney When do we ever talk, Linda?

Linda Sydney, we're always talking.

Sydney Not about ideas, Linda. About candlewick bedspreads. The electricity bill. Your mother's eczema. That's what you talk about.

Linda I do not. Mother's eczema cleared up last week. I told you, she got some new ointment. And I know I don't talk about candlewick bedspreads because they went out years ago. That's why we should get rid of ours. We want a continental quilt. (*Pause.*) We could afford one. The electric bill's quite reasonable. All right. I'm not clever. Why do you think I want to learn? Only you won't teach me. So I'm boring.

Sydney Linda . . .

Linda But if it's a choice between boredom and burglary I'm calling the police.

She goes off with Sydney in hot pursuit.

Kafka I just think it's odd her calling me a leading figure in European literature.

Brod It is odd. (*Aside.*) Wait till I tell him he's world famous, the author of several major masterpieces.

Kafka He seemed to think I was somebody too.

Brod This is England. It doesn't take much to be a celebrity here. (*Aside.*) He is going to be over the *moon*.

Kafka I published so little and you destroyed the rest.

Brod (*aside*) God job I didn't.

Kafka You did, didn't you?

Brod Of course. It was your last wish.

Kafka Dear, faithful Max.

Brod Though say I hadn't burned it all. And say . . . it's ridiculous of course . . . but say you turned out to be quite famous. You wouldn't mind?

Kafka Mind? No. I wouldn't mind. It's just that I'd never forgive you.

Brod But I'm your best friend.

Kafka So, it's worse. You'd have betrayed me. No. That would be it between us. Over. Finish. Still, what are we talking about? You burned them. I'm not famous. Everybody's happy.

Brod Happy? I'm ruined.

Linda returns with Sydney in hot pursuit, Linda bent on confronting Kafka.

Sydney You know nothing about this.

Linda I just want to find out exactly who they are.

Sydney Linda.

Linda Can I ask you some questions?

Kafka Of course.

Sydney She means about your work.

Linda I mean about you.

Brod His work. She mustn't ask him about his work. Oh, my God.

Kafka Feel free. Ask any questions you like.

Brod I'm sorry. Sorry. I don't want any questions. Kafka does not want questions.

Kafka What about my work?

Brod What about his work? There is no work. I burnt all the work.

Kafka I don't mind talking about my work.

Brod Exactly. Who are these people anyway? . . . You don't?

Kafka Why should I? I worked in an insurance office.

Brod What am I talking about? Of course you did. Kafka worked in an insurance office. Tell us about it. It sounds fascinating.

Linda Sydney works in insurance too.

Brod Really? How boring.

Sydney I didn't mean that work I meant your real work.

Brod What is this, some kind of interrogation? (*Recovering himself.*) I have to tell you, this is a shy man.

Kafka Max, I'm not. He always thought I was shy. I wasn't. I even went to a nudist colony.

Linda That is brave.

Brod Not if you don't take your trunks off.

Sydney Excuse my asking, but why didn't you take your trunks off? Had you something to hide?

Kafka Yes. *No.*

Sydney I have this theory that biographies would benefit from a photograph of the subject naked.

Kafka Naked? What a terrible idea.

Brod Shocking. And who, pray, is talking about biography. *No one.* No one at all. In the meantime, old friend, let's recall why you went to that nudist camp in the first place. You were delicate. You had a bad chest, remember. So why don't you just step out into the garden and fill what's left of your lungs with some fresh air.

Kafka Max. It is raining.

Brod Here is an umbrella.

Kafka Max!

But he goes, bundled out into the garden by Brod.

Linda I'm calling the police now, while he's in the garden.

She exits.

Sydney (*ready to go after her*) Why? They can't arrest him. He's committed no crime.

Brod Calm down. He wrote the script for that one. (*He sits down.*) Cigar?

Sydney I don't smoke.

Brod Neither do I. Look . . .

Sydney Sydney.

Brod Syd. There's been a small misunderstanding. Nothing of importance. You recall how at one point in his life Kafka intimated I might consider burning his writings?

Sydney On his deathbed, yes.

Brod (*furious again*) It was not his deathbed. It was prior to his deathbed. He was around for years after that. (*To the audience.*) Blood and sand, why does everybody round here think they're an authority on Kafka? He thinks he knows about Kafka. *Kafka* thinks he knows about Kafka. I'm the only one who really knows.

Sydney What is he doing in the garden?

Brod God knows. Giving the kiss of life to an ant, probably. Why wasn't I a friend of Ernest Hemingway? Where are you going?

Sydney I've some questions I want to ask him . . .

Brod No, look . . .

Sydney Sydney.

Brod OK, Syd. I didn't burn the papers . . .

Sydney (*trying to go out into the garden again*) That's one of my questions. Does he mind?

Brod *Syd.* No! Of course he doesn't mind. Why should he mind? Still if it's all the same to you I'd rather you . . . deferred the question a while.

Sydney Why?

Brod Why? Yes, why? Because . . . because he doesn't know.

Sydney He doesn't know what?

Brod He doesn't know I didn't burn the papers.

Sydney He doesn't know you didn't burn the papers!

Brod So what? He is not going to mind.

Sydney No?

Brod No. Why should he?

Sydney Why should he? That's right. As you say in your book, this is a saint.

Brod Sure, sure.

Sydney He'll forgive you.

Brod Nothing to forgive.

Sydney In fact he'll be pleased.

Brod Pleased? He'll be ecstatic.

Sydney I would be. Can I be the one to tell him? I'd like that.

Brod No. Not yet.

Sydney When?

Brod When? Well, I think we've got to be very careful about this. Choose the moment. And while we're on the subject, less of this 'leading figure in European literature' stuff.

Sydney Why?

Brod Because, dummy, if I had burnt his papers he wouldn't be, would he?

Sydney No, I suppose he wouldn't. What you're saying is he doesn't know he's Kafka.

Brod He knows he's Kafka. He doesn't know he's *Kafka*.

Sydney Mmm. It's a tricky one.

Brod Why don't we play a game? He thinks he has no reputation at all. Let's pretend he *has* no reputation at all. Then come the right moment Max here will spill the beans and we can all have a big laugh.

Sydney Yes. A big laugh, yes. Ha ha.

Brod Where is the bathroom?

Sydney Follow me. Wouldn't that be a lie?

Brod Listen, Syd. I am Max Brod. I was short-listed for the Nobel Prize. Don't tell me about lies. Here he comes.

ALAN BENNETT

Sydney Wait. Let me get this right. The game is: I don't know him, I've never heard of him.

Brod Right.

Sydney Though when you do get round to telling him, I'd like him to autograph his books.

Brod Weidenfeld and Nicolson! His books! We've got to get rid of his books.

Brod rushes to the bookcase and starts removing books as Kafka comes in.

Kafka Books?

Brod Yes. Well, no. You could call them books. They're dirty books. Pornography. Smut.

Sydney looks hurt, and opens his mouth to protest but thinks better of it.

Kafka How despicable. His poor wife. I remember I once said 'A book should be like an axe to break up the frozen seas within us.'

Brod joins in to finish the quotation.

Brod Well, these are some of the ones that failed the test.

Sydney is helping to shift the books outside also. Sydney often has to retrieve books right from under Kafka's nose.

Kafka Excuse me. I – I thought I saw my name.

Sydney Your name? Sorry . . . (*Winking at Brod.*) What was your name again?

Kafka Kafka. Franz Kafka.

Sydney No, no. This is the Hollywood movie director. Frank Capra.

Kafka (*wistfully, looking at the bookshelves*) It's like looking for one's headstone in a cemetery.

Brod is carrying another pile of books out when Sydney bumps into him and the books go all over the floor.

What's that?

Sydney What?

Kafka That one. It says *Kafka's Novels*.

Sydney This? *Kafka's Novels*? No. *Tarzan's Navel*.

Brod (*quickly taking it*) Anthropology.

Kafka And that one. *The Loneliness of Kafka*.

Sydney *The Loneliness of Kafka*? No. *The Loneliness of Raffia*. As an adjunct to her nursing course my wife did occupational therapy. Hence this one: *Raffia: The Debate Continues*. *The Agony of Raffia*, the endless plaiting, the needle going in and out, suddenly the needle slips, ah! Few people realize the single-minded devotion that goes into the humble table mat.

By this time Sydney thinks he has gathered up all the fallen books. However, one has eluded him. Sydney and Brod are transfixed with horror as Kafka picks it up.

Kafka Proust.

They sigh with relief.

Sydney Great man. A genius.

Kafka You think?

Brod Listen. A bit more get up and go and you'd have run rings round him.

Kafka I was ill. I had a bad chest.

Sydney Proust had a worse chest than you.

Kafka How does he know about my chest?

Brod He doesn't (Fool!) Anyway, what is this, the TB Olympics?

Kafka (*reading Proust*) 'For a long time I used to go to bed early.' For a long time I scarcely went to bed at all.

Sydney Yes, only Proust wrote a major novel. What did you do? Sorry, what *is* your name again?

Brod (*aside*) Don't overdo it.

Sydney Then *hurry*.

Kafka (*to Max*) Who is this Proust?

Sydney Who is this Proust? *Who is this Proust?* Beg pardon. Only the greatest writer of the twentieth century.

Kafka (*meaning 'protect me against this terrible information'*) Max.

Sydney (*playing for time while Brod clears the books*) Proust is a lifelong invalid and sufferer from asthma. Lesser men this would stop. *Oui*. Does it stop Proust? *Non*. He lives on a noisy street, the noisiest street in Paris. So, does he sit back and say 'It's too noisy. I can't write here' *'Il y a beaucoup de bruit. Je ne peux pas écrire ici'*? Not at all.

Brod *Pas du tout.*

Sydney *Eh bien*, what does he do?

Brod *Qu'est-ce qu'il fait?*

Sydney *Le voilà.* He builds himself a cork-lined room . . . *une chambre* (*looking to Brod for the translation*) . . .

Brod (*lamely*) Cork-lined.

Sydney And in this room . . . (*showing signs of weariness by now*) *dans cette chambre . . . il . . .*

Kafka Oh shut up. Max. My room was noisy. It was next door to my parents. When I was trying to write I had to listen to them having sexual intercourse. I'm the one who needed the cork-lined room. And he's the greatest writer of the twentieth century. Oh God.

Brod Listen. More than Proust ever wrote you burned. Or I burned . . .

Brod thinks he has cleared the books when Linda returns with a pile.

Linda Sydney. These don't belong in the hall.

Brod Oh my God!

Linda What's the matter with the bookcase?

Sydney Full. Chock-a-block.

Linda There's tons of room.

Kafka (*helping*) Allow me.

Linda Thank you.

Sydney No. (*Seizing the books.*) I'm – I'm throwing them out.

Linda What for?

Sydney (*nonplussed*) What for?

Brod He's – he's selling them to me.

Linda (*seizing the books back*) The penny drops. I've heard about people like you. Insinuating yourself into people's homes. Sydney. This is how mother lost her gate-legged table.

A book falls. Kafka stoops for it, but Brod is there first.

Brod Give me that.

Linda Look. He can't wait to get his hands on them.

Sydney Linda, (*seizing the books again*) I just want them outside.

Linda Why?

Sydney (*desperately to Brod*) Why?

Brod I need to go to the toilet. Now.

Sydney Well, for God's sake don't do it over the goldfish or else we'll be entertaining the Brontë sisters.

He rushes out after Brod carrying the books, leaving Kafka and Linda alone for the first time.

Kafka You think I'm a criminal?

Linda I think your friend is.

Kafka Perhaps you should think of me as a dream.

Linda I've rung the police.

Kafka The police also have dreams.

Linda They didn't think you were from the Health Authority.

Kafka That's not surprising. I never had much to do with either Health or Authority. The only authority I had came from sickness. TB.

Linda Sydney had TB. That's how we met. They can cure it now.

Kafka I'm sure people find other things to die of.

Linda If they take that attitude they probably do.

Kafka You sound like a girl I used to know.

Linda sits down and crosses her legs.

I say, that's good.

Linda What?

Kafka The way you took one of your legs and just flung it over the other. You've done it again. Perfect.

Linda Don't be silly. Everybody can do that.

Kafka No.

Linda I just don't think about it.

Kafka But in order not to think about it one has to give it a good deal of thought.

Linda tries again and muffs it.

Linda It's a simple thing. Like walking.

Kafka Is walking simple? Stand up.

Linda stands up.

You are going to cross the room. For a start you must decide which leg you're going to move first. Have you come to a decision? Wait. Remember when you're moving whichever leg it is you've decided to move first you should meanwhile be thinking about the one you're going to move after that. Slowly. Oh, you've chosen that leg. I see. Now the other leg. Now the first leg. Now the same leg as you used the time before last. And now this one again, which is the one you used the time before that.

Linda starts to laugh and stagger and, pealing with laughter, falls into Kafka's arms.
At which point Brod and Sydney enter.

Sydney Linda.

Linda He was just teaching me how to walk.

Sydney Oh. I thought you'd just about got that licked.

Brod Can I help?

Linda Don't touch me.

Brod It's always the same. As soon as they meet him it's good-night Max.

Linda How slim you are.

Kafka I know. Forgive me.

Sydney Odd when one remembers what a big man your father was.

Kafka A giant . . . how did you know that?

Sydney Er, he told me. Didn't you?

Brod Did I? Of course I did. 'What a big man his father was', I remember saying. This isn't a game.

Sydney I thought you said it was.

Brod What about her? She won't give us away.

Sydney No. She's not an intellectual. This is just an ex-nurse. Say Heidegger to her and she thinks it's a lager.

Linda Sydney has a father too.

Kafka It's not uncommon.

Linda Only he doesn't pick his ears with a toothpick.

Kafka My father used to do that.

Linda I know.

Kafka How?

Sydney I told her.

Brod And I told him.

Kafka You say this Proust is well thought of?

Brod Not by me. It's a sick mind.

Linda He liked boys.

Kafka (*shocked*) Boys?

Linda I know. Some men do. Wittgenstein did. Whoever he was.

Brod Not an intellectual? This is Susan Sontag! What does it matter? Nobody blames them. They're dead. Death does that for writers. 'Death is to the individual like Saturday evening is to the chimneysweep: it washes the dirt from his body.'

Kafka That's not bad, Max. I'd like to have said that.

Brod You did, Kafka, you did. It was one of the things I burnt.

Kafka I was better than I thought.

Brod You were.

Kafka What a pity.

Sydney (*nudging Brod*) Go on. Now.

Brod There's something I have to tell you.

Sydney I can't wait for this.

Linda What?

Brod It's about burning your books.

Sydney Here it comes.

Kafka No need to tell me, old friend. I know.

Brod You know?

Kafka I know.

Brod (*to Sydney*) He knows.

Sydney (*to Linda*) He knows.

Linda Knows what?

Brod And . . . you don't blame me?

Kafka Why should I blame you? How could I?

Brod Will you listen to this man. Did I say a saint? Shake hands with a saint. He knows.

Linda What do you know?

Kafka Once upon a time I asked my friend here to destroy all my writings. I know that he feels bad because he obeyed me.

Brod He doesn't know.

Kafka Don't *worry*. I sometimes feel the same. But what's done is done.

Brod I'm going to have to try a different tack.

Sydney You are.

Linda Sydney . . .

Sydney Be quiet.

Brod Old friend, from that distinguished bundle which I so dutifully thrust into the incinerator I'd like to recall a particularly choice example of what perished that day: 'Somebody must have been telling lies about Joseph K –'

Brod and Kafka (*together*) '– because one fine morning he woke up and found himself under arrest.'

Kafka I remember. Two mysterious men arrive to arrest Joseph K who doesn't know what offence he has committed. Then he has to appear before a tribunal somewhere.

Brod And to get to the courtroom he has to go through somebody's kitchen –

Linda Really? (*She glances round her kitchen.*)

Kafka – where people just seemed to take him for granted. He never does find out what he's done.

Brod And in the end he's executed.

Kafka Did I ever give that one a title?

Brod A great title: *The Trial* by Franz Kafka.

Kafka That doesn't make it sound like a detective story?

Sydney The public like detective stories.

Brod Only what have we got instead? A short story about a guy who wakes up as a cockroach.

Kafka A beetle, Max. A beetle. Why can you never get it right?

Brod Listen, for all the good you would have done for yourself he could have woken up a fucking centipede.

Kafka Max!

Linda One more off-colour remark and he'll have to leave, won't he, Sydney? Won't he?

Father has entered in his overcoat with a little attaché case. He is carrying the orange Penguin book he took in the beginning. He catches Linda's last phrase and assumes it was meant for him.

Father Leave? Well, I'm ready. Somebody's been telling lies about me. They've come to take me away and I don't know what I've done.

Sydney Sit down, Father.

Linda I'll get him a tablet. Father thinks we're going to put him in a home.

Kafka And are you?

Linda We didn't want to. But he's driven us so mad asking when, we decided in the end we'd better.

Kafka I sympathize. I hated my father. I once wrote him a letter telling him so. Why one can't just get rid of parents I don't understand. One puts the cat out when it's a nuisance. Why not them?

Sydney Your father was different.

Kafka How do you know?

Brod How many more times? Because I told him.

Brod exits to the garden. Linda exits for a tablet.

Sydney Listen, Father. They won't take you away if you can answer some simple questions. The day of the week.

Father Yes. I've got that off by heart.

Sydney The name of the Prime Minister.

Father Yes.

Sydney And some simple sums. Hang on to those and you'll be all right.

Kafka In youth we take examinations to get into institutions. In old age to keep out of them.

Father (*putting the Penguin down*) You said this was a detective. It's not a detective at all.

Linda returns with the tablet.

Linda There are no detectives.

Sydney assists Linda as she takes Father out.

You have a beautiful Portuguese rug in your room. I can't think why you want to keep coming down here.

Kafka is alone on the stage. He picks up the Penguin and looks at it idly. Then less idly.

Kafka (*reading aloud the first sentence*) 'Somebody must have been telling lies about Joseph K because one fine morning he was arrested . . .' (*He turns the book over to look at the title. There is a moment of shocked silence, then shouting*) MAX!

Nobody comes.
    Kafka rushes off and comes back with some of the books taken off the bookshelf.

(*looking at them and throwing them down as he comes*) Kafka! Kafka! Kafka! Novels, stories, letters.

Brod creeps on.

Brod (*faintly*) Sorry.

Kafka Sorry? SORRY? Max. You publish everything I ever wrote and you're *sorry*! I trusted you.

Brod You exaggerated. You always did.

Kafka So, I say burn them, what do you think I mean, *warm* them?

Brod I thought it was just false modesty.

Kafka All modesty is false, otherwise it's not modesty. There must be every word here that I've ever written.

Linda comes in.

Linda What did he do?

Kafka It's not what he did. (*Indicating the books*) It's what he didn't do. *This* is what he did.

Sydney comes in with a further pile of books.

Did I write these too? Oh my God!

Sydney No. These are some of the books about you. Only a few. I believe the Library of Congress catalogue lists some fifteen thousand.

Kafka Max. What have you done to me?

Brod Ask not what I've done to you, but what you've done for humanity. You, who never knew you were a great man, now rank with Flaubert, Tolstoy and Dostoevsky, called fellow by the greatest names in literature. As Shakespeare spoke for mankind on the threshold of the modern world you speak mankind's farewell in the authentic voice of the twentieth century.

Kafka (*in a small, awe-stricken voice*) Shit.

Sydney He's taking it very badly.

Brod Don't worry. He'll be all over me in a minute. But who else would treat fame like this, eh? Chekhov? He'd be round to the estate agents, looking at a little place in the country with paddock and mature fruit trees attached. Zola would be installing a jacuzzi. Even T. S. Eliot'd have people round for drinks. But what does Kafka do?

Sydney Finds the whole thing a trial.

Brod Exactly. The humility of the man. I tell you, if I were Jesus Christ I'd be looking over my shoulder.

Kafka Judas!

Sydney He's made you one of the biggest names in twentieth-century literature.

Linda Even I've heard of you.

Kafka (*with exaggerated patience*) I didn't want a big

name. I wanted a small name. I shrank my name. I pared it down to nothing. I'd have been happy with no name at all.

Sydney But that's the secret of your success. You've got a name for anonymity. *The Trial*: a nameless man's search for justice in a faceless bureaucracy. When Eastern Europe went communist this was the book that told you about it before it happened. In so many words . . .

Kafka That's it. That's it. So many words. I've added so many words to the world I've made it heavier.

Brod Some day you'll thank me.

Kafka Max, this is some day.

Brod is going to speak.

I don't want to speak to you. If you want to talk to somebody talk to Kafka.

Sydney But you are Kafka.

Kafka No, I'm not. Kafka is a vast building; a ramshackle institution in every room and department of which, in every corridor, attic and cellar, students and scholars pore over my text and worry over my work. That isn't me. That is Kafka. Communicate with that. Preferably in triplicate.

Sydney This piece I'm writing about you for the *Journal of Insurance Studies* . . .

Kafka Don't talk to me about it. He's the expert.

Sydney No, but . . .

Kafka Please.

An awkward silence in which Brod and Sydney are at one side of the stage, Kafka and Linda at the other.

Linda When did you first get the writing bug then?

Kafka I'd rather not talk about it.

Linda I have to confess, I've never read a word you've written.

Kafka Good.

Sydney Wouldn't understand it if she did.

Linda I might. How would you know? You never talk to me. I know tons of things about literature.

Sydney Such as?

Linda I know about Scott Fitzgerald for a start.

Kafka What about Scott Fitzgerald?

Linda He had a small p . . . Nothing.

She smiles. Kafka smiles back. She crosses her legs.

Who's a clever girl then? (*Peal of laughter.*)

Sydney He seems to like her.

Brod You mean she seems to like him. They always did. He has that kind of social ineptitude women mistake for sincerity.

Another peal of laughter.

Sydney Linda. You're making a fool of yourself.

Linda No, I'm not. He's nice. You said he was nice. He is nice.

Brod Listen, you can do better than her. That's what fame means. Walk down the street and you'll be mobbed by autograph hunters, girls ready to do anything, anything just for your signature.

Kafka But what do I sign? My name. I hate my name. Fame is my name everywhere.

Brod That's right. Even on T-shirts. Worn by girls. Girls with no morals and degrees in European Literature. Girls who can mix Jane Austen with the latest developments in foreplay.

Linda How does he know?

Brod Because, *sister*, I'm famous too.

Kafka You? What for? Not your novels? They were terrible.

Sydney (*indicates the books*) For these. As you're famous so is he. His name is synonymous with yours.

Kafka How? I'm not even synonymous with my own name.

Brod The ingratitude!

Linda I understand.

Sydney She doesn't.

Linda I wish I could make you happy.

Kafka There's only one thing that could make me happy. It's the look on my father's face.

Linda Pride?

Kafka Disgust. 'Look at this lot, Dad, I showed you.'

Brod You want to be careful. He might turn up.

Kafka is instantly alarmed.

Kafka How could he?

Linda You turned up.

Kafka I'm famous. I exist.

Sydney Your father's famous.

Kafka My *father*? My father ran a fancy goods store.

Sydney You were a minor civil servant.

Kafka My father was a bully. He made my life a misery. I blame him for everything.

Brod So. Why do you think he's famous?

Kafka No. Tell me it's not true. He's buried and forgotten.

There is a ring at the bell.

No. Max, what do I do? Hide me. Help me.

Linda answers the door.

Linda (*off*) I'd forgotten I'd called you.

Linda enters.

Don't be silly. It's not your father at all. It's a policeman.

The Policeman, a burly figure in a raincoat, is also Kafka's father, Hermann K. He enters and surveys the company without comment, then circles the room to stand behind Kafka.

Policeman/Hermann K Hello, my son.

Kafka confronts his father as –
  – the Curtain falls.

Act Two

Kafka is alone on the stage, his novels and all the books about him in a pile in front of him. Very nervously, and with many precautions lest he be seen doing so he takes up one of the books. Before he can open it –
    Linda enters, carrying two plates of food.
    Kafka hurriedly puts the book back.

Linda (*showing Kafka one of the plates*) I've done you a hamburger.

    Sydney enters R.

Sydney He won't want that.

Linda Why?

Sydney He doesn't like meat.

Linda How do you know?

Sydney It's a matter of historical record.

    Sydney exits L.

Linda (*to Kafka, showing him another plate, on which is a piece of quiche*) Try this instead.

Kafka What's that?

Linda It's something unexpected I do with avocadoes. Tuck in.

    Linda exits R.
    Sydney enters L.

Sydney I imagine avocados must have been pretty thin on the ground in turn of the century Prague.

Kafka What do they taste like?

Sydney Soap.

Sydney exits R.

Kafka looks at the plate with intense suspicion and puts it down. He starts to sneak another look at one of his books but is again interrupted, this time by Father.

Father enters.

Father This is him. He's got authority written all over him.

Kafka I want to ask you a question.

Father Here it comes.

Kafka Have you ever heard of someone called Kafka?

Father (*who has been about to answer, finds himself baffled*) Er . . .

Kafka It's supposed to be a household name.

Father You don't want the Prime Minister?

Kafka He was a Czech novelist. He died in 1924.

Father Six fours are twenty-four.

Kafka shakes his head.

I know the Prime Minister. I know the date and I can manage on the toilet with the bare minimum of assistance but if you're supposed to know the name of Czech novelists everybody's going to end up in a home. I had fifteen men under me.

Father exits.

Kafka examines the quiche suspiciously. Smells it. Holds it up to the light. Looks for somewhere to hide it. Behind a cushion? In a vase? Finally, hearing someone coming, he makes a dash for the bookcase and slips it in there.

Linda enters with a glass of milk, a napkin and a box of Black Magic chocolates. She spots the empty plate.

Linda I knew you'd enjoy that.

Kafka A novel experience. (*He checks the shelf*) I put it somewhere between Dostoevsky and Henry James.

Linda You know how to flatter a girl. Something else? A chocolate perhaps? I have a box of Black Magic I keep for emergencies.

Kafka shakes his head.

Linda Your father ate the hamburger.

Kafka He would.

Linda I was hoping he'd do that trick of rummaging in his ears with a toothpick then using it to pick his teeth.

Kafka And did he?

Linda No. He has dentures now anyway.

Kafka That's an improvement.

Linda He thinks so. He passed them round for inspection.

Kafka groans.

Kafka And he used to lecture me about *my* eating!

Linda The cheek. You're twice the man he is. Your constipation is in text books. (*Pause.*) You've never had a stab at marriage then?

Kafka How could I? I was on such bad terms with my own body there was no room for a third party. You should see me in a bathing costume.

Linda It could be arranged.

Kafka It wasn't that I didn't like women. In fact I

75

frequently got engaged to them. My fiancées tended to regard me as a species of invertebrate. Marriage was going to give me backbone.

Linda Clever, were they?

Kafka By and large. The last one, Dora, was very like you.

Linda I'm not clever.

Kafka But you are. You are a highly accomplished person.

Linda Me? What at?

Kafka How you enter a room, for instance, as a few moments ago you entered this room, bringing me a glass of milk. In the left hand you carry the milk. In the other hand a napkin and a box of chocolates. With an object in one hand and two objects in the other you have no hand to close the door, but no sooner does this dilemma present itself than you solve it, the right hand bringing the napkin and the box of chocolates over to the left side and tucking it between the upper part of the left arm and the rest of your body, which together co-operate to keep it clasped there, the linen and the chocolates sandwiched between the material of your dress and the arm, which is partly covered in the same material and partly . . . not. The right hand is now free so you place it on the doorknob and the fingers on that hand clasp the knob and pull it to. Free at last of the door, you take three steps into the room one leg effortlessly passing the other (your dress seems to consist of some light, woven fabric) until both legs come to a tentative halt at a point which (even with all these things on your mind, the milk, the chocolates, the moving legs) you have yet managed to find time to select as appropriate. Standing gently at rather than on this spot you lift the glass of milk towards me, managing as you do so to combine it with fetching the right hand over to the left side to take the napkin and the chocolates, now released by an agreement between your arm and your body. The two hands, one with milk, the other with the napkin and the chocolates, are now brought gently up towards me. I take the napkin and the milk but not the chocolates. To console the chocolates for this rebuff your left hand steals comfortingly into the box, selects one and carries it to your mouth. Finally, and still holding the chocolates, you sit down.

Linda I'm not surprised. I must have been exhausted. You forgot something.

Kafka Yes?

Linda When I was handing you the glass one of my fingers touched one of yours.

Kafka I hadn't forgotten. It was this finger. (*He holds up a finger.*)

Linda And this.

> *She holds up her finger. It almost looks as if they might kiss, but they don't as Linda breaks away.*
> *Brod and Sydney have entered.*

Sydney Was it always like this?

Brod No. I have to tell you. His girlfriends were women of great poise and intelligence or nubile young creatures of seventeen. In either category your wife hardly hits the bull's-eye.

Sydney This is intolerable. Linda.

Linda Excuse me. Sydney?

Sydney He should talk to his father.

Linda I don't believe he wants to, do you?

Kafka No.

Linda No.

Sydney Don't listen to her. She doesn't understand you. I've read your books. I admire you. I am a *fan*.

Kafka (*to Sydney*) You say you know me. I don't want to be known. (*To Linda.*) He says he understands me: if he did understand me he'd understand that I don't want to be understood.

Linda Of course. I understand that. (*She doesn't.*)

Sydney I read his books and this is the thanks I get.

Brod It's more thanks than I get and I practically wrote them.

Sydney I've had enough. I'm going to break this up.

Sydney exits.

(*Calling as he goes.*) Mr Kafka.

Kafka is instantly alarmed.

Kafka Help me.

Linda I'm going to make a silly suggestion. Why don't you and your father just shake hands?

Kafka I can't.

Linda Why?

Kafka My hand is shaking.

Linda You're a grown man.

Kafka Not with my father around I'm not.

Hermann K enters, followed by Sydney.

Hermann K Funny. They said I had a son here. They get

into the dumbest places, sons. Some even get to the top of the tree. Only a good father tracks them down and brings them back to earth. I'm waiting.

Linda What for?

Hermann K I'm waiting for this son to fling his arms around me in heartfelt welcome, sink to his knees in abject remorse. I'm waiting for the brittle body and the hot consumptive breath. I'm braced for a kiss.

Kafka doesn't move, frozen in terror.

Still as thin as a tram ticket. Did he eat?

Many of Hermann K's remarks are addressed to the audience. It's important that he should be on good terms with the audience, have a relationship with them, or he will just seem a bore and a bully. Perhaps it is that only the dead people can talk to the audience and are conscious of them, though Father talks to the audience too.

Linda Every scrap.

Hermann K He didn't put it down the toilet?

Linda No.

Hermann K That was his usual trick. Shepherd's pie floating in the toilet: show me a quicker way to break a mother's heart. So where? (*He looks round the room. Behind cushions, under the sofa, etc.*) My son had a problem with food. He didn't like it.

Kafka I ate nuts, raisins. Salad.

Linda Very healthy.

Hermann K For squirrels. I'm told he's done pretty well.

Sydney An understatement.

Brod No thanks to his father.

Hermann K I could debate that with you, Professor. My son is a near-delinquent. A spent condom.

Linda You've no business talking like that. This is a sensitive man.

Hermann K Lady. I'm the sensitive man. My son is about as sensitive as a gannet.

Sydney You're proud of him. You must be.

Hermann K Why? What's he done? Written a book or two. My father could lift a –

Hermann K and Brod (*together*) – sack of potatoes in his teeth.

Brod He won't have read a word he's written.

Hermann K I tried to read one once. Flat as piss on a plate. When he makes *Reader's Digest* then I'll read him.

Brod *Reader's Digest*! Last week I had a telegram from the *Oxford English Dictionary*. Your son is so famous that they named a word after him.

Hermann K What kind of word?

Brod An adjective. Kafka-esque.

Hermann K I never heard it. Has it caught on?

Brod Caught *on*? Your son now has adjectival status in Japanese.

Kafka Is this true?

Sydney Don't ask her, ask *me*. Of course it's true.

Brod They don't only write about you. They have to use you to write. Now you're a tool of the trade.

Kafka Thanks for nothing, Max.

Sydney Of course you're not the only one.

Kafka Proust?

Sydney Afraid so. Proustian.

Brod Kafka-esque is better.

Linda Look on the bright side. Most people have never heard of either of you.

Hermann K How's this word doing?

Sydney Famously. It crops up all the time. (*He picks up a newspaper.*) Here we are. It's an article about Yves St Laurent.

Kafka Who's he?

Linda A dress designer.

Kafka A dress designer?

Sydney 'He is adept at coping with the Kafka-esque intrigues of high fashion'.

Kafka High fashion? What's this high fashion? I never had anything to do with high fashion. What has Kafka to do with high fashion?

Brod Words don't always get used correctly. What matters is that they get used.

Hermann K Do we get a percentage?

Brod Words are free.

Hermann K If you make people a present of them, sure they are. My son has rights here. I told you this was a no-good friend. Your name exploited all over the world and what does he get you? Can you believe it? Nothing. Well, you'd better get out and stop them.

Brod How?

Hermann K The law. The authorities. Don't the police have some control over words?

Brod Yes. In Eastern Europe.

Kafka I don't understand it. 'Kafka-esque intrigues of high fashion.' I work in an insurance office. I have maybe three or four suits the whole of my life. I die a failure at the age of forty-one. I get into the dictionary and suddenly I'm . . .

Sydney Yves St Laurent.

Hermann K So, you should have listened to your father. Incidentally, does my son get to meet any of the models?

Brod turns away in despair.

Some friend. He gives his name to a word and he can't even get a fuck out of it.

Linda (*to Kafka*) We didn't hear that, did we?

Sydney I'm sure your new friend has heard it before. He may even know what it means.

Hermann K I wouldn't bank on it. What would I have done with your chances. (*At the bookcase.*) Edith Sitwell. You could have her. Evelyn Waugh. *Vile Bodies*. She sounds as if she knows how to please a man. I'm still waiting for this kiss.

Brod His name's an adjective in Japanese. Why should he kiss you?

Hermann K I was a simple man. I came from nothing. What was so wrong with my footsteps he didn't want to follow in them?

Kafka He sold *buttons*.

Hermann K Buttons, would you tell my son with the sick

mind, that put him through college. I can see through him. You don't have to go to university to see through your own son . . . So, he wound up a writer. Did I stand in his way? Go, I said. Go. Walk in the high places of the earth. Be rich. Be famous. Only one day come home and lay a single flower on your father's grave.

Kafka I died before he did.

Hermann K He did. On purpose.

Brod I was at the funeral. You weren't upset. He wasn't upset at all.

Kafka That's right.

Hermann K How does he know? He was dead. He was where he always wanted to be, safely tucked up in his grave. He makes me sick standing there.

Linda And you make me sick, turning up and laying down the law. You . . . you great bladder of Czechoslovakian lard.

Sydney Linda.

Linda Why don't you and I go next door?

Kafka Yes.

Linda Then I can fix you something more to eat.

Kafka Maybe not.

Brod Old friend. Come with me into the garden.

Kafka Yes.

Brod Then I can tell you how big you are in New Zealand.

Kafka I don't want that either.

Hermann K Why don't you just talk to your father?

Kafka I want that least of all. Oh God!

Cornered, he finally makes a bolt for it into the kitchen.

Linda (*smiling happily, and about to follow Kafka off*) Incidentally, what was the woman's role in this household? What was his mother doing?

Brod Backing up his father.

Hermann K Naturally. We were a normal family.

Linda exits L.
Brod exits into the garden.
Sydney and Hermann K are alone.

Hermann K So. You're a big fan of my son?

Sydney I'm writing an article about him if that's what you mean. I'm a fool. I thought he'd be interested.

Hermann K I'm not interested either. These books, articles . . . they're all the same. For him whitewash, for me excrement.

Sydney Mine would have been different.

Hermann K Yes?

Sydney Having met your son I begin to think the books may have got him wrong.

Hermann K That's interesting. In what way?

Sydney He's not quite the person I imagined him to be. I thought he was a saint.

Hermann K You mean you don't any more?

Sydney No. I think posterity's got him wrong. He has faults like everybody else.

Hermann K Ladies and gentlemen I have lain in my grave and dreamed of this moment! Look . . .

Sydney Sydney.

Hermann K Syd. I'm not an intellectual, I sold knicker elastic, so you'll forgive me if I spell it out.

Sydney Do. I'm still trying to spell it out myself.

Hermann K Misjudge him, they misjudge me. If my son wasn't so good as all the books make him out to be, and I wasn't so bad . . . if we were, say, more just a routine father and son then I wouldn't be the villain any more and . . .

Sydney And all the books would have to be re-written.

Hermann K And then people would see I was just an ordinary fellow and you'd be famous.

Sydney I'd be famous? How?

Hermann K A new view of Kafka, of course you would.

Sydney I hadn't thought of that. I could take time off from insurance.

Hermann K Time off? Time off? Fifty years of Kafka studies turned on their heads, you could travel the world, lecturing, giving talks . . .

Sydney People would know my name, students. I'd be famous! (*Pause.*) But only if I'm right. Only if Kafka isn't a saint and you are just an ordinary father and son.

Hermann K You are right. And I'll prove it. Go fetch the little scallywag.

> *Sydney goes off, leaving Hermann alone.*
> *Father enters, with his walking frame, hat and coat on.*

Father Do you know what the latest is? Besides the date and the name of the Prime Minister they ask you the name of a leading Czech novelist.

Hermann K Else what?

Father They take you away.

Hermann K You can't be expected to know that.

Father Of course I know it. Franz Kafka.

Hermann K My son's even more famous than I thought! What about his father?

Father You're not supposed to know about his father?

Hermann K Of course. Everybody knows about Kafka's father.

Father Kafka wrote books.

Hermann K A book is a coffin and in it is your father's body.

Father I'd better go and swot it up. The buggers. Every time you're ready for the examination they change the syllabus!

Father exits.

Hermann K Now. This is my chance to come over as a Normal Parent. (*He opens his arms, rehearsing his first embrace for his son.*)

Kafka enters, pursued by Linda carrying food; they are followed on by Sydney.

Linda You'll love it. It's kiwi fruit and satsuma segments. Didn't they have kiwi fruit in Prague?

Kafka No.

Linda How did they manage?

Hermann K (*waiting for Kafka, arms outstretched*) Look at him. Don't you just love him. Come, give your Dad a kiss.

Kafka Who? Me? What is this?

Hermann K Baby. You've been rumbled.

Kafka Rumbled? What? Who? Don't touch me. What do you mean?

Hermann K What do I mean? I love the boy. Forget his faults, I love him.

Kafka Dad.

Linda It seems the affection is not returned.

Hermann K I know. I *know*. Lady, you are so right. That's what it seems. But, as your clever little hubby has found out, things aren't always what they seem. Until this moment everybody thought I hated my son. They thought he hated me. (*He bursts out laughing.*) The truth is, we're devoted to each other.

    He embraces the shrinking Kafka.

Love me, dickhead. Do as I tell you.

Linda Leave him alone. Just because you're his father doesn't mean you can kiss him. He hates his loved ones, we all know that. You don't believe this?

Sydney Why not?

Linda You're pathetic.

Sydney All the evidence about Kafka's father comes from Kafka. The only son who ever told the truth about his father was Jesus Christ – and there are doubts about him.

Linda But this is a mean cheap person. Can't you *see*? He's a fraud.

Hermann K (*kissing Kafka*) Is this a fraud? Or this?

Kafka Father. You hate me, then all of a sudden you love me. What did I do?

Hermann K Listen, you teetering column of urine, this clown is writing an article about you.

Kafka I know.

Hermann K So. Don't you see? It's our big chance. We can be nice people. I love this kid, this is someone really special.

Kafka Our big chance? Your big chance. I am nice people already.

Hermann K Yes. Thanks to me. Thanks to me being the shit. Bless him.

Sydney Look at that. Do you know what this is, Linda? That is a breakthrough in Kafka studies.

Linda It looks more like somebody getting their arm twisted.

Sydney You used to be proud of me, Linda. You used to trust me.

Linda Sydney. I've talked to him.

Sydney I know. He's scarcely talked to anyone else. I've never had a look in. I love him.

Hermann K So do I.

Kafka I don't want to have this conversation.

Linda You told me you couldn't stand one another. You blamed him for everything.

Hermann K Lying.

Linda No.

Hermann K Tell her. Tell her it was all your fault. Or else.

Kafka Else what?

Hermann K Or else, you two-faced pisspot, I tell the world the one fact biographers never know. I reveal the one statistic every man knows about himself but which no book ever reveals. You see, sir, it's as I say, we're just a normal father and son. My normal. (*He indicates about eight inches.*) Your normal. (*He indicates about three inches.*)

Kafka No, Dad. You wouldn't.

Hermann K No? There is one fact about my son and his . . . old man that has never got into print . . .

Linda Stand up to him. Come on.

Hermann K The long and the short of the matter is . . .

Brod enters.

Kafka I was a terrible son. A dreadful son. A real father and mother of a son. And yet my father loved me.

Brod I don't believe what I'm hearing.

Hermann K Here's the real culprit. The original biographer. The man who led posterity up the garden path in the first place.

Kafka Max. Help me.

Brod Suddenly I'm forgiven. So what's the problem?

Hermann K You're at it again. The same old game. Coming between a father and son. Well, not any more. Now for the first time the truth is going on record. Say it again, my son.

Kafka My father loved me. It was all my fault.

Brod Brilliant. And your lips didn't even move. What's he got on you this time?

Kafka Nothing. Honestly.

Brod Listen. Max is back. We're friends again. The old team. Tell this gorilla to get lost.

Kafka No, Max.

Brod Are you saying you lied to me?

Kafka Yes.

Linda And you lied to me?

Kafka I lied to everybody.

Brod Why?

Sydney Because he was a writer. Writers do lie. They exaggerate because they always think they're the injured party. That's one of the things you learn in insurance: the injured party always exaggerates.

Hermann K Yes. You boys of art, you're all the same. I want to hear it again. How much did I love you? (*Indicating three inches.*) A little. (*Indicating eight inches.*) Or a lot.

Kafka I can't tell you how much.

Brod I'm nauseated.

Linda You're hiding something?

Kafka No. It's just that there were faults on both sides.

Hermann K We sparred a little, sure, but who doesn't?

Brod Sparred? 'Eat your meat or I'll get a long spoon and cram it down your throat like they do in prisons.'

Hermann K That's me. And you say I was wrong. Dr Spock says I was wrong. The *Cambridge History of Literature* says I was wrong. Does he say I was wrong?

Kafka You were right, Father. Parents love their children so they make them eat.

Hermann K True?

Linda I don't know. We have no children.

Hermann K So what do you know about anything?

Brod You tried to stop him writing. You even hid his ink.

Hermann K What time was it?

Kafka Three in the morning.

Hermann K What time did you have to go to work?

Kafka Seven. You were right. A boy needs sleep.

Brod He tried to stop you writing altogether.

Hermann K Of course I did. That's how clever I was. If I'd said 'Stick to the writing' he would probably have ended up a chartered accountant. Hermann Kafka didn't fall off the Christmas tree yesterday. Right, my son?

Kafka nods unhappily.

Kiss? Mmm. Yours a little kiss. Mine a big kiss.

Linda I think you might have told me. I told you about Sydney.

Sydney What?

Brod I'm the one he should have told. I wrote his biography. I gave him to the world. I'm nauseated.

Sydney What about me?

Linda I told him I wasn't very happy.

Sydney That's you. You said you'd told him about me.

Kafka How long do I have to keep up this charade?

Hermann K Until people start liking me more than they like you. Until they realize what a handful you were. Until I get into the books in a proper light and posterity has finally got to hand it to me, that's how long.

Kafka It will never happen.

Hermann K So should I tell them your little secret . . .

Kafka No.

Hermann K Then cuddle me, you soiled bandage. Snuggle up.

Kafka *Cuddle* you. I'm Kafka. I never cuddled anyone in my life.

Hermann K So you've just made a breakthrough. And not gingerly. If there's one thing I can't stand it's gingerly cuddling. Hey, just look at this boy. Someone take a picture.

Brod I am nauseated by this. Sick to my scrotum. The shrinking hypocrisy of it. Seen here embracing his son, one of the most notorious shits in literary history.

Hermann K (*gleefully*) I *know*.

Brod What is it you're hiding?

Kafka *Nothing*, honestly.

Hermann K Go into the garden, son. Get some fresh air. But remember, I love you.

Brod is about to follow.

No. Sorry. I think my son would prefer to be alone, wouldn't you, son?

Kafka Yes, father.

He exits.

Brod You make me sick.

Hermann K I know.

Brod exits.

Hermann K So. I'm going to come well out of this article?

Sydney An ordinary fellow.

Hermann K Well, don't think I'm not grateful. Anything you want in the soft-furnishing line, high-quality fancy goods, you only have to ask. Curtaining materials, rufflette, those little mats you put under glasses to stop them making a nasty ring on a nice polished table . . . A man wants to show his gratitude, exonerated after all these years. I feel sorry for my son, naturally, pushed off his pedestal, but the truth had to come out.

Sydney You were found guilty on false evidence.

Hermann K I was. Trial. I never had a trial. This is the joke: my son writes a book about someone who's had up for a crime he didn't commit and everybody thinks the book's about him. It's not. It's about me. In fact, if I weren't so fond of my son I'd say he's the one who should be put on trial.

Linda In what way?

Hermann K No, no. Forget I said it. Fundamentally this is a good boy.

Linda Try him for what?

Hermann K Perjury. Bearing false witness against his father.

Sydney It isn't only that. There are other charges. Other questions.

Linda But you admired him.

Sydney I did. I do . . . though he's not the man I thought he was. Still there's no question of you trying him: you're his father.

Hermann K You're in insurance. Investigation and assessment, it's right up your street.

Linda There's a difference between a man's reputation and a scratch on the bodywork. Sydney's no judge. He's . . .

Sydney What?

Linda He's nobody.

Sydney I married you.

Linda That proves it, probably.

Sydney Well, I may be a nobody, Linda, but what I am is a reader. And writers are tried by readers every time they open their books. Fetch him. He trusts you.

Sydney places the walking frame to act as a makeshift dock and draws the curtains.
The stage darkens.

Linda Sydney. This is persecution.

Sydney No, it's not. It's biography.

Brod My biography never put him in the dock.

Sydney I know. That's what was wrong with it.

Linda exits.
After a moment, Kafka creeps in. He sees the dock waiting.

Kafka Max, Father . . .

Hermann K Don't look at me.

Kafka What have I done?

Sydney (*taking the frame and putting it in front of Kafka*) You are famous. Fame is a continuing offence. It leaves you open to trial at any time.

Kafka But I didn't want fame.

Brod I know. It's all my fault. But I bet you still expect me to defend you.

Linda Why don't I defend you?

Sydney You?

Kafka How? You know nothing about me.

Linda I like you. Nobody else seems to.

Sydney I do, given the chance.

Linda Then why the trial?

Sydney I just want to cut him down to size. If I do that I might make my name. Don't you want me to make my name?

Linda No. Not at the expense of his.

Sydney Do you, Sydney, take this bottle of hydrochloric acid, Linda, to be your lawful wedded wife? Splendid. Would you, Linda, take your stiletto heel and force it up the groom's nose. Excellent. I now pronounce you man and wife. *All right.* You defend. I prosecute, and we'll see who wins. Right?

Linda Right.

Kafka (*in the middle*) Oh dear.

Sydney Very well. Let's kick off with this question of your name. While every other writer one can think of wants to make his name, you want to unmake yours. So you unravel your name until there's only one letter left: K. You sign your letters K, you refer to yourself as K. What was it you disliked about Kafka?

Linda What is it you disliked about Sydney?

Sydney I dislike Sydney because it carries within it the unhatched threat of Syd. And if you can't do any better than that I'd leave it to him (*he indicates Brod*). What was it you disliked about Kafka?

Kafka It means jackdaw. A thief. It also means me.

Sydney Can I suggest another reason? The name Kafka. Treat it like an equation in algebra. Take the F to one side of the equation and what are we left with? F equals Kaka. Franz is shit. Is that why you disliked it?

Linda Better than Syd.

Brod And T. S. Eliot is an anagram of toilets so does that make him a closet? This isn't biography. It's not even literary criticism. It's the only thing the English are good at . . . crossword puzzles. He denies it. He denies everything.

Kafka F equals Kaka. Truthfully, it hadn't occurred to me, but now you point it out it's not a bad idea.

Brod What do you do with this man?

Kafka My name, it was like a tin can tied to the tail of a cat. I wanted rid of it.

Sydney Quite, and though you get the credit for trying to lose your name, you never do lose it. You make it famous. And the person who does lose his name gets no credit for it at all.

Hermann K Who was that?

Sydney You.

Hermann K Me? Exactly! Was it?

Sydney Yes.

Brod Him?

Hermann K That's right. In Prague in 1919 stop any passing housewife and say Kafka and she'd direct you to my shop by the Town Hall. Cheerful service, high-quality goods, value for money. Kafka's is the place.

Sydney And what happens if you say you're Kafka now?

Hermann K 'You Kafka?' people say. 'Kafka didn't have a moustache for a start. Kafka is the skinny guy with the big ears on the back of the Penguins.' Suddenly I don't exist. So, Mr Name-Dropper. I'm the one who loses his name. Gets de-nominated. Mr Hermann Kafka. Only I didn't lose it. It was taken. By my son.

Brod All sons take their father's name.

Linda Not only sons. (*To Sydney.*) You took my name. When I married you.

Sydney And?

Linda Why is it when a woman gets married we say she takes her husband's name? What we mean is he takes hers. Takes it and buries it.

Hermann K All right, so you lose your name too, dear. The point the gentleman is making, precious, is that the one person who didn't lose his name is the person who claimed to want to lose it, and the person who got the credit for losing it: my son.

Linda And whose fault is that? (*She points at Brod.*)

Brod He was in two minds. He was always in two minds. I did him a good turn.

Sydney I've never understood that.

Brod It's called friendship.

Sydney Did he ever do you a good turn?

Kafka I made him famous.

Sydney But that's not a good turn, is it? When Kafka was alive, of the two of you who is the better known?

Brod I'd published several novels. He'd published almost nothing. I was a poet, a critic. Me, no question. With a comparable reputation in Czechoslovakia today I'd probably be a well-known dissident.

Sydney And what was Kafka when you knew him?

Brod A friend of Max Brod.

Sydney Whereas today . . .

Brod It's the other way round.

Linda That's nothing to be ashamed of. The great man's friend. That's all a woman gets. That's all a wife would have got.

Brod But I wasn't his wife. I was someone in my own right.

Kafka And my best friend. Rather nice I should have thought.

Brod If not to exist is nice. And since you do think not existing is nice, maybe it is.

Kafka Don't you exist?

Brod Not any more. I go on publishing novels after you die, notching up steady sales. Only then I start publishing yours. Result: as soon as they read yours they don't want to know about mine. (*He takes out some clippings.*) This is my last novel. It was about the Arab–Israeli War. This reviewer found in it 'a trace of Kafka's imagery but' (here it comes) 'none of that simple fascinating prose style that makes Kafka readable.' You readable! You may have been a genius, but you were never readable. You finished me as a novelist. All I could do was go round lecturing about the Kafka I knew. 'Kafka as I remembered him.' Or Kafka as I remembered remembering him. What you were actually like I'd forgotten till now. I had no life of my own any more.

Linda You *were* his wife.

Brod No. I was his widow.

Linda Even better.

Sydney Would you say your friend was good-looking?

Brod Yes. Yes, I would.

Kafka No.

Hermann K There has to be something about him, hasn't there? He's my son.

Sydney You think he's good-looking, don't you?

Linda In comparison w– yes.

Kafka My body wasn't satisfactory. I couldn't bear to look at it.

Sydney Your diaries show you looked at it all the time.

Kafka Only in disgust.

Sydney Do you grumble about your physique to your friend here?

Brod Does he ever!

Kafka Do I? I don't remember.

Brod When don't you? Every imperfection of the body tormented you. Constipation, a toe that wasn't properly

formed, even dandruff. Toes and dandruff. I wished I'd
had your problems.

Kafka Why?

Brod Why? You prick in a bottle. You turd in a hat. *Why*?
Did you never look at me? My spine was twisted. You're
complaining to me about dandruff. I was a *hunchback*.

Linda He's not a hunchback now.

Brod There's not much to be said for death, but it is the
end of disability.

Sydney Your sensitive friend.

Linda Say something. Defend yourself.

Kafka What for? Nobody can reproach me with failings
for which I have not reproached myself. List my
shortcomings now. I listed them all half a century ago.
Find fault with me now, what is the evidence: my own
fault-finding then. I stand here self-examined, self-
confessed and self-convicted.

Hermann K Self, self, self.

Kafka Nobody ever believed what I said about myself.
When I said I exaggerated they thought I was
exaggerating. When I said I lied, they thought I lied. I said
I was an agent of the devil, they thought this meant I was a
servant of God. When I said they must not believe me,
they did not believe me. But now you believe me. Only
now when at last you find I was telling the truth about
myself you call me a liar.

Linda I don't think you're a liar.

Kafka But you'd agree I was a terrible human being?

Linda No. Pretty average, if you ask me.

Brod Average? Kafka is average?

Sydney And now as in some Czech village wooing Kafka pauses with his rucksack at the garden gate, asks for a lemonade and our brisk Shavian heroine reads him a lesson on life and generally pulling his socks up.

Linda When I first saw you I thought here's somebody different. I can talk to this man. And what's more peculiar he listens. He notices. I also thought what nice hands.

Kafka And now?

Linda I still like your hands.

Kafka But I'm a terrible human being.

Linda No.

Kafka No?

Linda No. You're a man, that's all.

Sydney Oh no.

All the men except Kafka groan.

Kafka Not much of a man.

Linda Every inch.

Hermann K sniggers.

Kafka Dad.

Linda You're a man, because, although you despair, at the same time like all men you believe your despair is important. You think you're insignificant but your insignificance is not insignificant. Oh no.

Kafka That's because I'm a writer.

Linda No. It's because you are a man. Whatever happens or doesn't happen to you matters. You may not want the world to think you're somebody, provided it recognizes you are nobody.

Kafka But I am nobody.

Linda Why *tell* us? Women can be nobodies all the time and who cares? All these letters to your girlfriends . . . Letters to Milena, letters to Felice. Saved. Published. Where are their letters to you? Lost. Thrown away. That's a man.

Kafka I was born a man.

Linda What excuse is that? You changed into a beetle, a dog, an ape, the one thing you never transformed yourself into was the lowliest creature of all . . . a woman.

Sydney Good try, but you're wrong. One of the last stories he wrote is about a female, Josephina, a singing mouse.

Kafka You're defending me now.

Brod Against her? Of course he is. We have to stick together. Anyway, why save your girlfriends' letters? Are they literature?

Hermann K Women.

Linda Are you disappointed in me?

Kafka No. I always expect to be disappointed. If I'm not disappointed, then I'm disappointed.

Linda I always feel I want to mother him.

Kafka No. Once was enough.

Kafka tries to leave the dock.

Sydney One last point. You never saw fascism, communism, the totalitarian state.

Kafka No. By that time I was safely tucked up in my grave.

Sydney Your work suggests you would not have been happy under such regimes.

Kafka Does it? I can't say.

Sydney Oh, I think so. Your reputation today, at least among those who know your name but haven't read you (which is the measure of literary reputation after all) . . . your reputation stands high as a man who protested (though don't ask in what respect precisely), a man who shook his fist (helplessly, no doubt) against authority, officialdom, the law. You were, if not an enemy of the state, a friend of the enemies of the state. Is that reputation justified, do you think?

Kafka I have told you. Any reputation is a burden.

Sydney Where could you have shed that burden? Where would you be happiest?

Kafka It's not a place that exists in the world.

Sydney Why?

Kafka It would be a place where I am read only by vermin, the outcasts of the community, the convicts and exiles. I would be read by untouchables, furnacemen, sweepers of roads. Furtively, with discretion and behind locked doors. It would be a place where I am read, but not named, known but not spoken of, studied but not taught. That would be my ideal state.

Sydney There is a place like that.

Kafka Where? It must be wonderful. I'd like to live there.

Sydney You did. It's called Prague. (*He takes the frame away, and puts it offstage.*)

Kafka Is the trial over?

Sydney For the time being. (*He takes his manuscript.*) The process goes on, of course, I've no need to tell you that. Articles, books . . . every day is –

Kafka – a day of judgement. I know.

All clear, leaving Hermann K alone on the stage as Father comes in, either with his frame, or a makeshift version of it, like a chair.

Father Don't go. I want you to test me. Ask me any question you want about this Czech novelist *or* his father. I think you'll find it's all at my fingertips.

Hermann K What was his father like?

Father Dreadful. And a shocking bully. Made his son's life a misery. The root of all the trouble. Is that right? It is. Ten out of ten. Father goes to the top of the class. Now at last I can reveal the name of the Prime Minister . . .

Hermann K Sorry.

Father What?

Hermann K You're wrong.

Father I never am. I looked in all the books.

Hermann K The books are wrong. Kafka's father was a normal parent.

Father A normal parent? How am I expected to remember a normal parent: I'm a normal parent. Nobody remembers me.

Hermann K He was an average father.

Father But the world's full of average fathers. Average fathers are two a penny. An average father? I'm never going to remember that.

Father goes off leaving Hermann K pensive.

Hermann K Hermann Kafka, you want your head examining. You're trying to come over as a nice parent and get into all the books. What for? Nice parents don't get into the books. With nice parents there are no books.

Kafka enters.

Listen, son. A change of plan. I want you to do as I tell you.

Kafka Haven't you finished torturing me? You've destroyed my character, lost me my best friend . . .

Hermann K And now I'm going to do you a good turn.

Kafka No, please. Not that. Not a good turn.

Hermann K Can I have your attention please? That's everybody.

Father returns to the stage.

No, not you.

Father You said everybody.

Hermann K I mean everybody who matters.

Father exits again as Linda, Sydney and Brod enter.

Linda Do we matter?

Sydney (*with his manuscript*) We certainly do. This isn't just an article, Linda. It's going to be a book. And when it's finished I shall dedicate it to you.

Linda Yes? To the wall on which I bounced my ball. To the tree against which I cocked my leg.

Sydney Linda. I shan't be an insurance man any more. I shall be a literary figure. You'll be the wife of a famous man.

Hermann K (*gleefully*) Oh no she won't.

Sydney Well, not famous exactly, but . . .

Hermann K Not famous *at all*. Because there isn't going to be an article. There isn't going to be a book.

Sydney But . . . why not?

Hermann K Because I've decided to come clean. I'm every bit as bad as the books make me out. Worse.

Sydney I don't understand.

Hermann K You're an insurance man. You must be familiar with false claims. This was a false claim. Both parties were lying.

Kafka Father.

Hermann K Shut your face, you wet dishcloth.

Linda I knew you were lying.

Sydney But why deceive me?

Hermann K I'm human. Just. I wanted to be liked.

Linda But why did you lie?

Hermann K Blackmail.

Kafka Dad!

Hermann K Don't you Dad me, you dismal Jimmy. Do you want to know how I made him toe the line?

Kafka You promised!

Hermann K You know me: I'm your terrible father. When did I ever keep a promise? Besides, I owe it to posterity. I don't know how to put this delicately . . .

Brod It's never been a problem before.

Kafka puts his hands over his ears.

Hermann K The long and short of it is: my son is ashamed of his old man.

Brod We know that. That's what all the books say, starting with mine.

Hermann K No, not me. He's ashamed of his old man.

Kafka Don't listen. Please don't listen.

Hermann K Putting it bluntly: his old man doesn't compare with his old man's old man. His. Mine. (*He makes an unequivocal gesture.*)

Sydney But I know that. Everyone knows that.

Linda Even I know that.

Kafka You? How?

Sydney (*finding the book*) *Dreams, Life and Literature*. A study of Kafka by Hall and Lind, University Press, North Carolina.

Linda So you see, your private parts have long been public property.

Kafka He's won again. When will it ever stop?

Hermann K Stop? Stop? Mr World Famous Writer with the Small Dick, it won't ever stop. Literature goes on. You are one of its big heroes and I am one of its small villains.

Linda I'm a little confused.

Brod That's nothing fresh.

Linda You didn't like your son?

Hermann K No.

Linda But then you said you did.

Hermann K Yes.

Linda And now you say you didn't.

Hermann K Yes.

Linda Sydney. (*Pause.*) Is that what they mean by Kafka-esque?

Hermann K I thought I wanted to be a good father.

Linda Yes.

Hermann K Now I don't.

Linda Why?

Hermann K Because, *snowdrop*, a good father is a father you forget.

Brod You had a good father. You haven't forgotten him.

Hermann K I have.

Brod But he could . . .

Linda and Hermann K (*together*) . . . lift a sack of potatoes with his teeth.

Hermann K Yes. But that's *all* I can remember about him. Whereas bad fathers are never forgotten. They jump out of the wardrobe. They hide under the bed. They come on as policemen. Sons never get rid of them. So long as my son's famous, I'm famous. I figure in all the biographies, I get invited to all the parties. I'm a bad father, so I'm in the text.

Brod Same old Hermann.

Hermann K Anyway I couldn't change things now. My accountant would never forgive me.

Hermann K goes.
  Father enters, just missing Hermann K.

Father Has he gone? Damn. I was wanting to bring him

abreast of the latest turnaround in Kafka studies. Whereas we have all been brought up to suppose that Kafka and his father were at daggers drawn, recent research has been revealed that they both got on famously.

Brod Wrong.

Father You can't have me taken away when I'm in touch with the latest developments in Kafka studies. What did you say?

Linda You're wrong.

Father No. No. You're trying to confuse me. They were like you and me – friends.

Sydney No, Dad. They couldn't stand one another.

Father I give up. Put me away. My limited studies of Kafka have convinced me that being a vegetable is not without its attractions.

He retires.

Kafka Thank God I was never a father. It's the one achievement nobody can take away.

Brod You don't need to have children in order to be a father. You were so dedicated to writing, so set on expressing yourself even if it killed you, which it eventually did, that, like the best and worst of fathers you have been an example and a reproach to writers ever since. (*Meaning Sydney.*) Take him. He loves you. He hates you. So do I.

Linda You're not sorry?

Brod How should I be sorry? If I hadn't been Kafka's friend I wouldn't have been in the play.

Sydney If you hadn't been Kafka's friend there would have been no play. There would have been no Kafka.

Kafka is about to speak.

Brod Now don't say it.

Kafka puts his hand on Brod's shoulder and smiles.

Be content. We will meet at that posthumous cocktail party, posterity.

Brod goes.

Kafka Shall we see you there?

Linda Who says we'll be invited?

Sydney (*picking up the manuscript*) This is our invitation.

Linda Is it? Fifteen thousand books and articles about Kafka. What's one more? Poor Sydney. Anyway you hate parties.

Sydney This one might have been different.

Linda That's what one always thinks, every, every time.

Kafka You are so like Dora.

Linda Enjoy yourself. Be miserable.

Kafka I will. You know me.

*They touch fingers as they touched before.
Kafka vanishes.*

Sydney You see, try as we will, we can never quite touch Kafka. He always eludes us. We never do know him.

Linda I know him better than you.

Sydney Really? So what's this? (*He takes the quiche out of the bookcase.*)

Linda (*hurt*) His lunch. My quiche. Oh, Sydney.

Sydney (*consoling her*) I'll eat it.

They share it.

Linda Who was Dora?

Sydney His last girlfriend. The only one who made him happy. She got him to eat, wrap up warm. Nursed him, I suppose. She wasn't interested in his work at all. When he told her to burn some of it, she did. (*Pause.*) You'd better burn this, I suppose.

Linda Are you sure?

Sydney Yes.

She gathers it up briskly and is going.

Wait. What do you think?

Linda Since when does it matter what I think? (*She is going again.*)

Sydney Linda. Do *you* think I should burn it?

Linda How do I know? I haven't read it.

Sydney Will you read it?

Linda That depends. I may not have time. Now Father's off our hands I'm going back to nursing. (*Pause.*) Anyway I couldn't have burned it.

Sydney is touched. She hands back the manuscript.

We're in a smokeless zone.

Sydney You're not stupid.

Linda No. After all, I know that Auden never wore underpants and Mr Right for E. M. Forster was an Egyptian tramdriver. Only some day I'll learn the bits in between.

Sydney (*a cry of despair*) Oh Linda. There's no need. This is England. In England facts like that pass for culture. Gossip is the acceptable face of intellect.

Linda What I don't understand, she said, like the secretary in the detective story when the loose ends are being tied up, what I still don't understand is why people are so interested in a writer's life in the first place.

Sydney You like fairy stories.

Linda If they have happy endings.

Sydney This one does, every, every time. We are reading a book. A novel, say, or a book of short stories. It interests us because it is new, because it is . . . novel, so we read on. And yet in what we call our heart of hearts (which is the part that is heartless) we know that like children we prefer the familiar stories, the tales we have been told before. And there is one story we never fail to like because it is always the same. The myth of the artist's life. How one struggled for years against poverty and indifference only to die and find himself famous. Another is a prodigy finding his way straight to the public's heart to be loved and celebrated while still young, but paying the price by dying and being forgotten. Or just dying.

During the following the Lights concentrate on Sydney and music starts in the distance.

This one is a hermit, that one a hellraiser but the myth can accommodate them all, no variation on it but it is familiar even to someone who has never read a book. He plunges from a bridge and she hits the bottle. Both of them *paid*. That is the myth. Art is not a gift, it is a transaction, and somewhere an account has to be settled. It may be in the gas oven, in front of a train or even at the altar but on this side of the grave or that settled it must be. We like to be told, you see, that you can't win. We prefer artists to die poor and forgotten, like Rembrandt, Mozart or Beethoven, none of whom did, quite. One reason why

Kafka is so celebrated is because his life conforms in every particular to what we have convinced ourselves an artist's life should be. Destined to write he dispenses with love, with fame and finally with life itself so that it seems at the last he has utterly failed. But we know that in the fairy story this is what always happens to the hero just before his ultimate triumph. It is not the end.

> *Sydney and Linda go.*
> *As the Lights come up we are in Heaven, which is a big party going on offstage.*
> *Kafka enters through the french windows, which have become the Pearly Gates, and finds the Recording Angel, played by Brod.*

Kafka I don't know what I'm doing here. I shouldn't be in Heaven.

Angel Good. That proves you're in the right place.

Kafka I don't feel I deserve it.

Angel That proves you do. The worse you feel, the better you are, that's the celestial construct.

Kafka Will I be allowed to be as despairing here as I was on earth?

Angel You can be as gloomy as you like so long as it makes you happy. Look at Ibsen. He can just about manage a smile for Strindberg but nobody else. Now who don't you know? The gentleman over there with the shocking beard, that's Dostoevsky. Who's he talking to? Oh. Noël Coward! They've got a lot of ground to cover. There's Wittgenstein and Betty Hutton. Got it together at last! There's Proust (Hi, Marcel!) trying to con one of the waiters into making him a cup of tea so that he can do his act. (Kissy kissy!) Oh, and there's the Virgin Mary.

Kafka She looks sad.

Angel She never got over not having grandchildren. I say to her, well, look on the bright side. What about Gothic architecture? With two thousand years of Christianity to your credit what are grandchildren? But, as she said to me in a moment of confidence, 'You can't knit bootees for the Nicene Creed.'

Kafka Are there Jews here?

Angel *Mais oui!* In droves.

Kafka And there's no quota?

Angel Not officially. Though God is quite keen on them, naturally.

Kafka I was fond of animals. Are they here?

Angel Sorry, love. No animals. Well, they don't have a moral life.

Kafka No mice, beetles or birds?

Angel No. But if St Francis of Assisi can get used to it, I'm sure you can. You didn't really like them anyway. They were only metaphors. No metaphors here. No allegory. And nobody says 'hopefully' or 'at the end of the day' or 'at this moment in time'. We're in a presence of God situation here, you see. Talk of the Devil here comes God.

God (who is, of course, Hermann K) enters.

God My son!

Kafka Who are you?

God Well, I'm all sorts of things. The BBC, Harrods. The *Oxford English Dictionary*. The Queen. The Ordnance Survey Map. Anything with a bit of authority really.

Kafka You're my father.

God Of course. What did you expect? Enjoying yourself?

Kafka No. It's like a terrible party.

God It is a party. And I'm the Host. (*He should plainly be itching to dance, looking over his son's shoulder and waving at other (invisible) guests, all the time he's talking.*) There's Gandhi. Go easy on the cheese straws, Mahatma! You're going to have to watch that waistline! Can you dance?

Kafka No.

God I can. Mind you, I can do everything. Nuclear physics, the samba . . . it's all one to me.

Kafka Oh God.

God Yes? Come on. Just be happy you're invited. I bet you never thought you'd see Leonard Woolf doing the cha-cha.

Sydney crosses.

Sydney I'm not doing the cha-cha. It's Virginia. She's just put a hot cocktail sausage down my neck.

God (*calling after them*) You could have fooled me, Len. He couldn't of course. I know it all.

Kafka Father. Did you ever get round to reading my books?

God Are you still on about that? No, of course not. No fiction here anyway. No writing. No literature. No art. No need. After all what were they? Echoes, imitations. This is the real thing. Son. Try not to disappoint me this time. And there's no shortage of time. We're here for ever, you and me.

Kafka Yes, Father.

God Listen, unless I'm very much mistaken (and that's a theological nonsense) that sounds to me like the rumba and I've promised it to Nurse Cavell.

Linda comes on in a nurse's costume but with a Carmen Miranda headgear.

Kafka Nurse Cavell didn't look like Carmen Miranda.

God I know. Why do you think they shot her?

Father has come on playing the maracas.

And now, as the magic fingers of Bertrand Russell beat out a mad mazurka on the maracas, I must go and move in my well-known mysterious way. *Ciao*, son.

Kafka *Ciao*, Father.

The music swells as God and Carmen Miranda dance.
The stage is suddenly dark and Kafka comes forward.

I'll tell you something. Heaven is going to be hell.

Curtain

THE INSURANCE MAN

Diary: July–August 1985

The Insurance Man is set in Prague. It begins in 1945 with the city on the eve of liberation by the Russians, though the main events of the story, told in flashback, take place before the First World War. The film was shot in Bradford, where every other script I've written seems to have been shot, and also in Liverpool, a city I didn't know and had never worked in. Bradford was chosen because among the few buildings the city has elected to preserve are some nineteenth-century warehouses behind the cathedral. From the nationality of the merchants originally trading there this neighbourhood is known locally as Little Germany. The trade has gone but the buildings remain, the exteriors now washed and sandblasted but the interiors much as they were when the last bolt of cloth was despatched in the 1960s. Liverpool likewise has many empty buildings and for the same reason, and there we had an even wider choice. I found both places depressing, Liverpool in particular. Work though it is, a play, however serious, is play, and play seems tactless where there is no work.

Tuesday, 9 July, Connaught Rooms, Bradford
These masonic chambers on what's left of Manningham Lane serve as part of the Workers Accident Insurance Institute, the office in Prague where Kafka was a conscientious and well-thought-of executive. It is only the first day of shooting and already I feel somewhat spare. We are filming scenes in the lift, which is just large enough to contain the actors and the camera crew. There's no hope of hearing the dialogue so I sit on a window sill and read,

wishing, after writing nearly a score of films, that I didn't still feel it necessary to be in attendance at the birth. Just below where we are filming is Valley Parade, Bradford City's football ground where two months ago dozens of fans perished in a fire. Glance down a back street and there is the blackened gateway.

Wednesday, 10 July, Holcraft Castings and Forgings, Thornbury
Periodically between 1911 and 1917 Kafka helped to manage an asbestos factory set up by his brother-in-law. The hero of *The Insurance Man* is Franz, a young man who contracts a mysterious skin disease, seemingly from his job in a dyeworks. As a result he is sacked and comes to the Workers Accident Insurance Institute to claim compensation. He fails, but Kafka, anxious to do him a good turn, offers him a job in his brother-in-law's asbestos factory. The story is told in flashback thirty years later when Franz, now an old man, comes to his doctor to be told that Kafka's good turn has sealed his death warrant. Kafka describes in his diary the dust in the original asbestos factory and how, when they came off shift, the girls would dash it from their overalls in clouds. Even so I feel the design department has overdone it: dust coats every surface and lies in drifts against the machinery. I mention this to Richard Eyre, wondering if it's a little too much. It turns out we have had nothing to do with it: the forge, shut down six months ago, is just as it was.

The offices too have not been touched, a ledger open on a desk, records and files still on the shelves. In a locker is a cardigan and three polystyrene plates, remnants of a last takeaway and taped to the door a yellowing cyclostyled letter dated 12 June 1977. It is from a Mr Goff, evidently an executive of the firm, living at The Langdales, Kings Grove, Bingley. Mr Goff has been awarded the OBE in the Jubilee Honours and in the letter he expresses the hope 'that the People, who are the Main Prop in any endeavour, many with great skill and ability, will take Justification and Pride in it and will', he earnestly hopes, 'feel that they will be sharing in the Honour conferred on me'.

Thursday, 11 July, Downs, Coulter and Co., Vicar Lane, Bradford
Another empty factory, this time an ex-textile manufacturers, which we fit out as the office and medical room of a dyeworks. On the wall is a list of internal telephone numbers: Mr Jack, Mr Ben, Mr Jim, Mr Luke. It has evidently been a family firm and sounds straight out of The Crowthers of Bankdam. No wonder it did not survive long into Mrs Thatcher's England. Also on the wall is an advertising calendar sent out by Chas Walker and Sons, Beta Works, Leeds, and headed *Textile Town Holidays 1974*. From big cities like Leeds and Manchester down to the smallest woollen and cotton towns like Tottington and Clayton le Moors, the calendar lists the different fortnights in the summer the mills would close down. If they hadn't closed down for good already, that is. The artwork is a fanciful drawing of a toreador watched by elegant couples under Martini umbrellas but the obstinate echoes are of men in braces sat in deck chairs, fat ladies paddling at Bridlington and Flamborough and Whitley Bay. For most of them now one long holiday.

Tuesday, 16 July, Bradford
A boy of sixteen, hair streaked and dressed in the fashion, leads an old lady down Bridge Street. In this town of the unemployed he is probably her home help or on some community care scheme so it's not just the spectacle of youthful goodness that makes it touching. But not yet of an age to go arm in arm he is leading her by the hand. He little more than a child, she a little less, they go hand in hand along Hall Ings in the morning sunshine.

Night Shoot, Little Germany
In the original script the first scene was set in the doctor's
surgery in Prague at the end of the war. Old Franz is let in
and mentions there is a body hanging from the lamp-post
outside. Richard Eyre thought that a more arresting
opening would be of Franz picking his way down the
bombed street and hanging in the foreground the man's
body.

The corpse is played by an extra, who is perhaps sixty.
It is a complicated shot, done at night and involves water
flooding down the street, the camera on a crane and high
above it another much taller crane, a 'cherry-picker', from
which (since the lamp-post is false) the 'corpse' has to be
suspended. There is no dialogue and nothing for me to do.
It's too dark to read and too cold to be standing about. We
have done the first shot when I notice that a placard has
been hung round the corpse's neck saying TRAITOR. I
think this is too specific and ask Richard if we can do a
shot without it. There are other technical problems to be
sorted out before we do a second take and those not
involved hang around chatting and drinking coffee. As so
often on a film the atmosphere is one of boredom and
resignation, troops waiting for the action. Or the 'Action'.

Suddenly there is a commotion at the lamp-post. The
hanging man has been sick, is unconscious. There is a rush
to get him down, many hands reaching up, the scene, in
our carefully contrived light and shade, like a Descent
from the Cross. Thankful at last to have something to do
the duty policeman briskly calls up an ambulance while
the make-up girls (odd that this is part of their function)
chafe the man's feet. At first it is feared that he has had a
heart attack but soon he is sitting up. We abandon the
shot and Mervyn, the production manager, calls a wrap.
The water is turned off, props begin to clear the rubble
from the street as an ambulance arrives and the patient
gets in under his own steam. There is some discussion

whether anyone from the unit should go with him, as someone undoubtedly should. But it is 3.30 a.m. and he goes off in the ambulance alone. I note my own reluctance to assume this responsibility. I could have gone, though there is no reason why I should. Except that it's my play. I'm to blame for him hanging there in the first place. (Though it seems fairly obvious to me, in the finished film the meaning of this hanged man puzzles some people. The doctor has heard the man running down the street the previous night, trying to find a refuge from his pursuers. He bangs on a door and it is opened – by his pursuers. His refuge turns out to be his doom. This kind of paradox is one associated with Kafka and it's also the paradox at the heart of the play. Kafka does Franz a favour by giving him a job in his factory, but since the factory turns out to make asbestos this good turn leads in the end to Franz's death.)

Wednesday, 17 July, Peckover Street, Little Germany
Dan Day-Lewis, who plays Kafka, has a stooping, stiff-necked walk which I take to be part of his characterization. It's certainly suited to the role and may be derived from the exact physical description of Kafka given by Gustav Janouch. Even so I'm not sure if the walk is Kafka or Dan since he's so conscientious he seldom comes out of character between takes and I never see him walking otherwise.

We film the scenes between Kafka and his father (Dave King), the Kafka family home set up on another floor of the same empty warehouse. When I first worked on the script with Richard Eyre he wondered whether these scenes of the Kafka household were necessary, feeling that the film is really the story of Franz to which Kafka is only incidental. I pressed for them then, the producer Innes Lloyd agreed, so here we are in the Kafka apartment. Any doubts are resolved by a scene in which Hermann Kafka gets into his son's bed, then stands on it (an image taken from one of Kafka's stories) and begins to bounce up and down, the sound that of the sexual intercourse Kafka could often hear from his parents' bedroom when he was struggling to write.

(Richard's instinct proves right, nevertheless: in the editing the scene is cut as it seems to hold up the story.)

The Bradford sequences over we now have three days off before moving to Liverpool.

Tuesday, 23 July, Fruit Exchange, Victoria Street, Liverpool

This is a great rarity, a location that exactly matches the scene as I imagined it. A small steeply raked auditorium with a gallery done in light oak and lit by five leaded windows. It was built in 1900 and is as pleasing and nicely proportioned as a Renaissance theatre. Each seat is numbered, the numbers carved in a wood that matches the pews and facing them a podium on which is the hydraulic lift that brought up the produce to be auctioned. Ben Whitrow stands on the podium now as we wait to rehearse a scene in which, as a professor of medicine, he uses Franz in a clinical demonstration for his students. The students are played by fifty Liverpool boys, some of whom are given lines to speak. ('What is this word?' asks one. 'Origin.' 'What does that mean?') One is tempted to think that this auditorium and another that adjoins it should be rehabilitated and used as theatres. For revues possibly. Seeing it for the first time Vivian Pickles remarks, 'Look out! I feel a song coming on.' Yet if it was a theatre it would straightaway lose its charm, part of which lies in its being unwanted, a find. We do our little bit to hasten its decline by cutting out one section of the pews to accommodate a gallery. Pledged to restore it to its original state, our carpenters will patch it up but it will never be quite the same.

In the scene Robert Hines, who plays Franz, has to stand naked on the podium under the bored eyes of fifty medical students. As the day wears on the extras have no problem simulating boredom, often having to be woken for the take. I never fail to be impressed by the bravery of actors. Robert is a striking and elegant figure, seemingly unselfconscious about his nakedness. Did I have to display myself in front of a total stranger, let alone fifty of them, my part would shrink to the size of an acorn. Robert's remains unaffected. I mention this to John Pritchard, the sound supervisor. 'I see,' he says drily. 'You subscribe to the theory of the penis as seaweed.' It later transpires that Robert's seeming equanimity has been achieved only after drinking a whole bottle of wine.

Wednesday, 24 July, St George's Hall, Liverpool
We film a long and complicated shot that introduces the Workers Accident Insurance Institute, the office where Kafka worked for most of his life. I had written this shot in several scenes but Richard Eyre combines them into one five-minute tracking shot. An office girl is making her rounds, collecting on behalf of the retiring Head of Department. The camera goes with her as she moves from office to office, calling in turn on the three clerks who figure in the story, finally ending up in Kafka's office, where he is dictating to his secretary.

The WAI office has been built in the St George's Hall, the massive municipal temple on the Plateau at the heart of Liverpool. Ranged round the vast hall are statues of worthies from the great days of the city and on the floor a rich and elaborate mosaic, set with biblical homilies. 'By thee kings reign and princes decree justice,' say the roundels on the floor. 'Save the NHS. Keep Contractors Out,' say other roundels, badges stuck there at a recent People's Festival. 'He hath given me skill that He might be honoured,' says the floor. 'Save the pits,' say the stickers. It is a palimpsest of our industrial history. Peel and George Stephenson look down.

Most of the units are staying in the Adelphi, a once grand hotel and the setting of the thirties' comedy, *Grand National Night*. More recently the vast lounge figured in the television version of *Brideshead Revisited* as the interior of a transatlantic liner. One gets a hint of its former grandeur in the size of the towels but the service is not what it was. At breakfast I ask for some brown toast. The waiter, a boy of about sixteen and as thin as a Cruikshank cartoon, hesitates for a moment then slopes over to the breakfast bar and riffles through a basket of toast. Eventually he returns with two darkish pieces of white toast. 'Are these brown enough?' It is not a joke.

Friday, 26 July, St George's Hall
At the centre of the gilded grilles on the huge doors of the St George's Hall is the motto SPQL – the senate and people of Liverpool. There isn't a senate now and the building serves no civic function, the courts, which once it housed, transferred to less noble concrete premises down the hill. As for the people, they occasionally figure at rallies and suchlike and marches seem to begin here, but the portico stinks of urine and grass grows on the steps.

In front of the St George's Hall is a war memorial, a stone of remembrance inlaid with bronze reliefs. The inscription reads: OUT THE NORTH PARTS A GREAT COMPANY AND A MIGHTY ARMY. The panels, soldiers on one side, civilians on the other, are vaguely Vorticist in inspiration, the figures formal and angular and all inclined at the same slant. It was designed by Professor Lionel Budden of Liverpool University and the bronze reliefs done by H. Tyson Smith. These aren't notable names but it is a noble thing, far more so than Lutyens's Whitehall Cenotaph.

Behind the war memorial one looks across the Plateau to the Waterloo Monument and a perfect group of nineteenth-century buildings; the library, the Walker Art

Gallery and the Court of Sessions. Turn a little further and the vista is ruined by the new TGWU building, which looks like a G-Plan chest of drawers. A blow from the Left. Look the other way and there's a slap from the Right – the even more awful St John's Centre. Capitalism and ideology combine to ruin a majestic city.

Tony Haygarth plays Pohlmann, the kindly clerk in Kafka's office. In his period suit he is hanging about the steps at lunchtime wanting company. 'I'd like to go over to the pub, you see, but in this outfit I'd feel a bit *left-handed*.'

Sunday, 28 July, Cunard Building
Kafka was once standing outside the Workers Accident Insurance Institute watching the claimants going in. 'How modest these people are,' he remarked to Max Brod. 'Instead of storming the building and smashing everything to bits they come to us and plead.' We film that scene today with the injured workers thronging up the steps. Most of them are made up to look disabled but a couple of them genuinely are – a fair young man with one arm who plays one of the commissionaires and a boy with one leg and a squashed ear, who like the lame boy in the Pied Piper comes limping along at the tail of the crowd. Without regarding the disabled as a joke I have put jokes on the subject into the script. 'Just because you've got one leg,' shouts an official, 'doesn't mean you can behave like a wild beast.' Though the intention is to emphasize the heartlessness of the officials and the desperation of the injured workpeople the presence of these genuine cripples shows one up as equally heartless. I can't imagine, have not tried to imagine, what it is like to have a limb torn off or have half an ear. 'You say you understand,' says Franz in the film, 'but if you do and you do nothing about it then you're worse than the others. You're evil.' This is an echo of Kafka's own remark that to write is to do the devil's work. And to say that it is the devil's work does not excuse

it. One glibly despises the photographer who zooms in on the starving child or the dying soldier without offering help. Writing is not different.

Monday, 28 July
It is nine o'clock and still light and I go looking for a restaurant to have my supper. I walk through the terrible St John's Centre. It has a restaurant, set on a concrete pole (may the architect rot); now empty, it boasts a tattered notice three hundred feet up advertising to passing seagulls that it is TO LET. I pass three children, the eldest about twelve. They are working on a shop window which has CLOSING DOWN painted on it. Spelling obviously not their strong point, they are standing back from it puzzling how they can turn it into an obscenity when I pass with my book. The book takes their eye and there's a bit of 'Look at him. He's got a book.' 'What's your book?' I walk on and find myself in an empty precinct. The children have stopped taunting and seem to have disappeared. I look round and find that the trio are silently keeping pace with me. In an utterly empty square they are no more than three feet away. I am suddenly alarmed, stop and turn back to where there are more people. I have never done that in England and not even in New York.

Tuesday, 30 July, St George's Hall
Bob the gaffer is giving one of the sparks directions over a faulty lamp. 'Kill it before you strike it,' he says. It is a remark that could be called Kafkaesque did not the briefest acquaintance with the character of Kafka discourage one from using the word. But he lives and goes by public transport: at a bus-stop today the graffiti: HOPE IS FUCKING HOPELESS.

Wednesday, 31 July, St George's Hall
Happy to be drawing towards the end of the shoot, I have

come to dislike Liverpool. Robert Ross said that Dorsetshire rustics, after Hardy, had the insolence of the artist's model and so it is with Liverpudlians. They have figured in too many plays and have a cockiness that comes from being told too often that they and their city are special. The accent doesn't help. There is a rising inflexion in it, particularly at the end of a sentence, that gives even the most formal exchange a built-in air of grievance. They all have the chat and it laces every casual encounter, everybody wanting to do you their little verbal dance. One such is going on at hotel reception tonight as I wait for my key. 'You don't know me,' says a drunken young man to the receptionist, 'but I'm a penniless millionaire.' You don't know me, but I'm a fifty-one-year-old playwright anxious to get to my bed.

Thursday, 1 August, Examination Schools, University of Liverpool

In St George's Hall we have been insulated against noise. The vastness of the building meant that even a violent thunderstorm did not interrupt filming, the only problem the muffling of its huge echo. This final location is different. Outside three roads meet and the bus station is nearby so that traffic makes filming almost impossible. As chairman of the tribunal Geoffrey Palmer has a long, passionate speech, his only scene in the film. Traffic noise means that we go for take after take before we get one that the sound department thinks is even passable. Then, between buses, we re-record the scene sentence by sentence, sometimes even phrase by phrase. It is an actor's nightmare as all feeling has to be sacrificed to achieve consistency of tone. Entitled to get cross, Geoffrey Palmer remains good-humoured and in complete control and when the speech is edited there is no hint of the conditions under which it was recorded. A splendid actor with an absolutely deadpan face, he is an English Walther Matthau.

Monday, 5 August
The guard, an elderly and distinguished-looking West
Indian, announces over the Tannoy that this is the 16.45
from Leeds to Kings Cross, the estimated time of arrival
19.15. He adds 'May the presence of the Lord Jesus Christ
be with you and keep you always if you will let him.
Thank you.' Nobody smiles.

Friday, 9 August, London
Dr McGregor sends me for an X-ray to UCH and I go
down to Gower Street to make the appointment. I stand at
the Enquiry Desk while the plump, unsmiling receptionist
elaborately finishes what she is doing before turning her
attention to me.

'Yes?' She glances at my form. 'Second floor.'

I long to drag her across the counter and shake her till
her dentures drop out. 'Listen,' I want to say, 'you are as
essential to the well-being of this hospital as its most
exalted consultant. You can do more for the spirits of
patients coming to this institution than the most skilful
surgeon. Just by being nice. Be *nice*, you cow.'

I sit upstairs waiting for the next receptionist and realize
that this is what we have been acting out, playing at these
last two weeks in Liverpool. Here I am with my form,
queuing with my docket as we have filmed the claimants
queuing with theirs in Prague in 1910. I note that even
when we were filming and playing at bureaucracy we fell
into its traps. I never had much to do with the extras. I
mixed with the actors, who were known to me and who
played the officials, the named parts. I kept my distance
from the throng of claimants, none of whose names or
faces I knew. Indeed I resented them just as the real-life
officials must have done and for the same reasons: they
crowded the place out, mobbed the coffee urn and
generally made life difficult. Well, I reflect, now I am
punished.

It is a feature of institutions that the permanent staff resent those for whose benefit the institution exists. And so it will go on, even beyond the grave. I have no doubt that in heaven the angels will regard the blessed as a necessary evil.

The Insurance Man was first broadcast on BBC2 on 23 February 1986. The cast was as follows:

Franz (Old), Trevor Peacock
Doctor, Alan MacNaughtan
Franz (Young), Robert Hines
Landlady, Diana Rayworth
Old Man in Dyeworks, Teddy Turner
Workmen, Phil Hearne, Bernard Wrigley
Factory Doctor, Ronan Wilmot
Nurse, Jill Frudd
Beatrice, Katy Behean
Undermanager, C. J. Allen
Foreman, Fred Gaunt
Christina, Tessa Wojtczak
Christina's Father, Johnny Allen
Christina's Mother, Margo Stanley
Christina's Grandmother, Judith Nelmes
Christina's Sister, Fran O'Shea
Doorman, Bill Moody
Lily, Vivian Pickles
Inquiries Clerk, Guy Nicholls
Inquiries Official, Alan Starkey
Seamstress, Charlotte Coleman
Collecting Girl, Oona Kirsch
Pohlmann, Tony Haygarth
Gutling, Jim Broadbent
Jam Worker, David Miller
Culick, Hugh Fraser
Head-Bandaged Workman, Ted Carroll

Head of Department, Nicholas Selby
Head Clerk, Richard Kane
Kafka, Daniel Day Lewis
Miss Weber, Rosemary Martin
Butcher Boy, Lee Daley
Limping Client, John de Frates
Tall Woman, Richenda Carey
One-Legged Man, Sam Kelly
Man without Ear, Kenny Ireland
Attendant in Waiting Room, Ted Beyer
Bald Man, Iggy Navarro
Woman in Waiting Room, Rosemary Chamney
Man in Waiting Room, Peter Christian
The Angry Doctor, Geoffrey Palmer
The Thin Doctor, Ralph Nossek
The Fat Doctor, Roger Hammond
Woman at Tribunal, Joanne Ellis
Franz's Father, Derry Power
Lecturer in Medical School, Benjamin Whitrow
Man with Stomach Hole, Billy Moores
Young Woman in Medical School, Deborah Langley
Kafka's Brother-in-Law, Toby Salaman

Designer, Geoff Powell
Photography, Nat Crosby
Music, Ilona Sekacz
Producer, Innes Lloyd
Director, Richard Eyre

EXT. STREET. NIGHT

A foreign city. A body hangs from a lamp-post. In the distance the sound of gunfire and bombs falling. Franz (Old) walks down the street past the hanging body to ring the bell at a block of apartments.

INT. DOCTOR'S CONSULTING ROOM, PRAGUE. NIGHT. 1945

An X-ray plate of a pair of damaged lungs. The X-ray fills the screen. Over it we hear the distant sound of bombs falling. Superimposed on the screen over the X-ray plate: Prague, 1945. *We see as we pull out that the X-ray plate is being examined by an oldish Doctor in a once well-to-do consulting room. The Doctor is in an overcoat, and it is night. The state of the lungs on the plate obviously depresses him. He shakes his head. A doorbell rings.*

Doctor (*calling*) Lotte! Lotte! (*listens, calls again:*) Lotte!

> *When there is no response he gets up to answer the door himself. He goes out and we hear him open the outside door to admit a patient. The outside door closes again. Doctor and Patient ascend the stairs.*

(*Out of vision.*) My housekeeper must be in the cellar. (*Into vision.*) What is it like breathing?

Franz Well . . . we've been having some cold weather.

Doctor No pain?

Franz Not pain as you'd call pain. In peacetime you might

call it pain. These days illness is a luxury. They've hung
somebody from your lamp-post.

Doctor Last night. Still. We don't want to lose *you*, do we?

*The remark sounds absurd in the light of someone
hanged from the lamp-post outside and there is a pause.
The Doctor and Franz come into the consulting room.
Both are in their sixties.*

Sit down. Get your breath back.

*He gets him a drink out of a cabinet. From the way he
pours it, it is obviously precious.*

Franz (*indicating the drink*) Does this mean bad news?

The Doctor smiles.

Doctor We might as well drink it. Before the Russians do.

*The patient, Franz, is a plain-spoken man but he has
done quite well in life. The Doctor pauses.*

Franz Was it what you suspected?

Doctor (*lying*) Don't know. Never had the X-ray.
Infirmary got cut off. (*Shrugs.*) Still . . . I'm pretty sure it's
what I said it was, just a fibrous condition of the lungs.
Nothing malignant.

Franz So I'm not going to die.

*There is a loud crump in the distance as a bomb
explodes.*

Doctor You have to live long enough to be able to die.
No. You could go on for years. You could be lucky and
live to be hung from a lamp-post.

Franz Funny, you come along thinking this is the Day of
Judgement and it never is.

Doctor Or it always is. Tell me, out of sheer curiosity, what other jobs have you done, apart from the railway?

Franz Apart from the railway? Nothing. I started as a porter, I ended up stationmaster of the Central Station.

Doctor Nothing else?

Franz I was in a dyeworks once. For about five minutes.

Doctor A dyeworks?

Franz When I was young. We're talking about before the First War now. Terrible place. It's funny. I thought I was a goner then.

INT. A ROOM IN A CHEAP LODGING HOUSE. EARLY MORNING. 1910.

Franz as a young man lying in bed awake.

Franz (Old) (*voice over*) I'd just got engaged and I woke up one fine morning and found there was a strange patch on my skin.

He gets up and stands naked in front of the mirror, looking at something on his chest that we do not see. He frowns. There is a picture of a young woman on the dressing-table. There is a very quiet knock on the door. Franz clutches his clothes to him.

Franz (Young) Don't come in.

Landlady (*out of vision*) Why?

We see the door open and a cup and saucer appear round the edge of the door, followed by the Landlady, carrying a coffee pot in the other hand.

You can't show me anything new. My husband was in the armed forces. (*Pours the coffee.*) I'm not sure I like all this coming and going last thing at night. You'll need all your energy to get on in life.

She puts the cup down on the dressing-table.

Franz We're going to be married.

Landlady (*going*) This room used to be let to a fully fledged optician. He was quite alone. He had diplomas.

Back in the room Franz looks glumly in the glass. He moves the girl's photograph back a little, looks at it, then at his chest.

INT. A DYEWORKS. DAY

Franz (Old) (*voice over, across change of scene*) I didn't dare tell my fiancée and to begin with I didn't let on to anybody. I was just hoping it would go away. Only it didn't; it got worse.

Close-up of cloth being dipped in dye bath. Then reveal dyeworks. A Workman comes up to say something to an Old Man who is working at the dye bath. We track the Workman walking along the floor of the dyeworks, followed by an Old Man. They come through the works, and the Old Man goes into a lavatory while the Workman keeps cave *outside.*

Old Man (*out of vision*) Does it itch?

Franz (Young) (*out of vision*) No.

We stay outside until another Workman goes in for a piss. We follow him and see Franz with the top of his overalls rolled down, his shirt off and the Old Man peering at his skin and belly. All this is watched by the Second Workman, who is pissing.

Old Man Funny process, dyeing. Saw a lad once, scales from there down. Ended up spending the whole day in the bath. Slept in it. That were t'dye. Went to the board with it. They just pretended it was something in the family.

The Old Man touches the patch of skin with his dye-discoloured hand. The Old Man spits.

Have you reported it?

Franz shakes his head.

Factory Doctor (*voice over*) Dyeing won't do you any harm . . .

Cut from the noise of the dyeworks to the relative silence of:

INT. A CHEAP SURGERY OR MEDICAL ROOM, DYEWORKS. DAY

Four or five Factory Workers are waiting outside. One has his boot off, which he holds in his hand. Another holds a pad, made of his handkerchief, against some small wound. Others just sit. We follow a Foreman past them and into the surgery.

Factory Doctor (*voice over*) . . . Does it itch?

Franz No, sir.

Factory Doctor (*in vision, looking as ill as any of the patients*) Sore?

Franz No, sir.

Factory Doctor Have you been doing something that you shouldn't be doing?

Franz No, sir.

Factory Doctor (*mimicking him*) 'No, sir. No, sir.'

The Foreman is watching the examination.

Bit on your back. Take off your trousers. Come on.

The Nurse has been taking an interest, while bandaging another Patient.

Nurse (*pointing to Franz's legs.*) There's some.

Factory Doctor Oh, by God. We're all doctors now.

Nurse His proper skin's lovely.

Franz And it isn't to do with the dye?

Factory Doctor Well. Nobody else has it. Don't blame the dye. Blame yourself.

The Doctor exits.

Nurse He's only young.

Franz pulls up his trousers and turns to face the Foreman.

INT. UNDERMANAGER'S OFFICE, DYEWORKS. DAY

An office adjoining the factory floor. We are in the outer office and can see through a dusty window the inner office where the Undermanager is talking to the Foreman. The Undermanager is holding some papers. Franz sits in the outer office. A pretty secretary, Beatrice, enters with a bunch of cornflowers. She is conscious of Franz but wary of her boss next door.

Beatrice You're insured.

Franz looks up, not sure what she's said. She doesn't look at him.

(*putting flowers in vase*) These are cornflowers. I love blue. You're insured. Ask.

At which point the Undermanager and the Foreman come into the room, and she goes over to sit at her desk

and starts writing in a ledger.

Undermanager (*holding a docket*) Take this along to the cashier.

Franz I haven't done anything, sir. What have I done?

Undermanager We're not ungenerous. You've got your full bonus.

Franz is reluctant to take the docket.

Foreman There's generally a whip round.

Undermanager Something like that. I've got my other workpeople to consider.

Foreman (*easing him out*) Come on, lad. Have you got aught in your locker?

They go. The Girl's face is expressionless as she goes on working.

Undermanager I don't know what he's been doing. I'd've thought it was simple cleanliness.

Suddenly Franz comes back into the room with the Foreman trying to stop him.

Franz I want to ask about insurance.

Beatrice rises.

Foreman I never said anything.

The Girl has instinctively walked across to open a cupboard door to get a form and the Undermanager catches her movement.

Undermanager It doesn't apply. Beatrice. It doesn't apply.

She has her hand on the cupboard door. Franz and Beatrice look at each other.

INT. GYMNASIUM. DAY

Franz (Young) is in long trousers, and a singlet. He is exercising on some hanging rings. He checks his chest to see how much of the rash shows, then continues to exercise on the hanging rings. He does beautiful handstands and somersaults on the rings in the gym.

Franz (Old) (*voice over*) When you're young, you don't give your body a thought. Now I was thinking about nothing else, but yet it was as if it didn't belong to me. I wasn't myself any more.

INT. CHRISTINA'S PARENTS' APARTMENT. NIGHT

A formal supper. Franz (Young) and his fiancée Christina with her Parents. The atmosphere is strained. Nobody is talking. The family is obviously socially one jump above Franz. Any conversation is in undertones. An incongruous note at the dinner table is an Old Lady who has to be fed. Another Daughter puts food into the Old Lady's mouth. Franz is trying to hide his diseased hand and so is trying to eat with just his fork. Christina notices this just as he crams an overlarge piece of meat into his mouth because he cannot cut it.

Father I'm enjoying this, Mother.

Mother Does Franz want some more, Christina?

Father I think he's old enough to speak for himself, Mother, don't you? One of the family now.

Franz (Old) (*voice over, above the following dialogue*) I had to keep my skin to myself – I felt like an animal and I hadn't told my fiancée I'd lost my job; I daren't.

Mother (*to the other Daughter who is feeding the Old Lady*) Don't rush her, Rosa. One mouthful at a time.

Father That's right. Just take your time. Take your time. It's like everything else. Just take your time.

Christina discreetly tries to get Franz to use his knife but he ignores her.

INT. FRANZ'S LODGING/TUNNEL. NIGHT

Franz's suit hung over the wardrobe mirror. Franz (Young) in bed, not asleep. We see him reflected in the mirror. Zoom into mirror and mix to: Franz (Young) in silhouette walking down a tunnel.

Franz (Old) (*voice over*) The girl in the office had given me a form. She said I had a claim. I had to take the form to the Workers Accident Insurance Institute on Poric Street. Gone now. Though the building's still there. That building!

EXT. OFFICE BLOCK, PORIC STREET, PRAGUE. DAY

A large nineteenth-century office block. The Town Hall clock is striking. The office has steps leading up to the doors. Franz (Young) comes out of the tunnel opposite and joins the throng walking up the stairs on their way into the building. There is one main door and smaller ones on either side. Before the main door is an imposing Doorman.

Doorman (*shouting to a man on crutches*) Just because you've got one leg doesn't mean you can behave like a wild beast . . . (*to other Claimants who approach him with forms and chits*) Look. I'm not interested in bits of paper. Wipe your feet, wipe your feet. You're not coming into the factory now.

Franz tries to go in the central door.

Oi, this isn't your door. That's your door.

The Doorman shoves Franz in the direction of the other door, while letting the Head of Department and Head Clerk pass through unhindered. He also lets through another official, whom we will later discover to be Kafka. He is treated very deferentially by the Doorman.

Morning, Herr Doktor.

INT. ENTRANCE HALL/CORRIDOR AND MAIN HALL, OFFICE BLOCK. DAY

We follow Franz into the building, where there is a good deal of bustle.

Doorman (*out of vision*) Out of the way. Out of the way.

We see Clerks arriving for work, Workmen, some of them maimed, and Kafka threading his way through and going up some stairs in the background. Among those entering we should see a Butcher's Boy with a bandaged hand and other injured parties who will figure later in offices and corridors upstairs, including a man who is utterly bald, a man with one leg, and a woman with a scarred face. They all teem along a corridor and enter a huge hall. We follow Franz as a uniformed official points him to a bench just outside an inquiries window. The door of this should go up and down like a rat-trap. Any odd Alice in Wonderland *features like this should be emphasized. One or two people are sitting waiting outside the inquiries window. Next to Franz is a middle-aged woman, Lily.*

Franz Am I in the right place?

Lily They like you to wait.

The trap suddenly goes up and a Clerk rings a bell. The first person in the queue goes up to the window.

(*to Franz*) He's slipped up. You never want to be first. You're better off in the middle. Try and be routine. (*Pause.*) I don't even wear my glasses. You don't want a face anybody remembers. These are my documents.

She is holding a folder.

I crocheted the cover myself. I shall be all right today. (*indicating the official at the window*) My friend's on. He's very refined, I've seen him in a café. There's the Tribunal.

While Lily is talking, Three Distinguished Figures pass through the hall.

That coat's cashmere.

Clerk Next.

Lily is so absorbed in watching the Tribunal arrive, she doesn't hear.

Next.

Franz nudges her and she rushes to the window and hands in her folder. Most of the following sequence is seen through the inquiries window. The Clerk opens Lily's folder and goes through her papers.

Don't want to see that. Don't want to see that. I've seen that. Well? Nothing else?

Lily says nothing. The Clerk thrusts the folder at her, and it falls on the floor.

Next.

As Franz steps up to the window, Lily is at his feet, gathering up her documents.

Lily (*looking up apologetically*) He's got mistaken. He's confusing me with someone else.

The Clerk studies Franz's paper, clips a docket to it,

makes a note, all the while carrying on a conversation with an unseen Official behind him.

Clerk Why Vienna?

Official I fancied a change.

Clerk Don't we all?

INT. INQUIRIES OFFICE. DAY

We cut to inside the inquiries office. The Clerk shows Franz's paper to the Official. The Official sits on a chair which is on castors, which enables him to slide down his desk towards the clerk.

Official Dustbin job.

Clerk Quite, but which one? The fourth-floor dustbin or the second-floor dustbin?

Official Who are we not friends with?

Clerk 404?

Official 404. Anyway, they're supposed to like work, Jews.

The Clerk stamps the docket and hands it back to Franz through the window. We see Lily and Franz through the inquiries window.

Lily (*looking at Franz's docket*) That's this way.

INT. MAIN HALL/CORRIDOR TO LIFT, OFFICE BLOCK.
DAY

Franz leaves with his paper and docket, and follows Lily upstairs into a corridor.

Lily (*to Franz*) Come along. (*to Passers-by*) Good morning.

Franz follows Lily into a lift. She nods to everybody, but particularly to Officials, though they do not respond.

INT. LIFT/CORRIDOR, OFFICE BLOCK. DAY

The gates of the lift clash to.

Lily Good morning.

The Man operating the gates has a gloved hand and works the gates with such abandon he could well have lost the other in the operation. The shot should emphasize the machinery of the gates, and any item (like scissors) we happen to see that is capable of inflicting an injury. There should also be an impression as the lift goes up of a large building, so that we hear the sounds from the various floors as the cage slowly ascends. In the lift is a young girl, a Seamstress, with her hand bandaged. The Seamstress is talking to her neighbour in a low voice.

Seamstress They said was I sleepy. I wasn't sleepy. I don't get sleepy. Lift and push, lift and push. How can you get sleepy? It's a skilled job. Then they made out the safety guard wasn't in position. It was in position, only I've got little hands. The guard is meant for a man's hands. (*Shows her bandaged hand and her whole hand to her neighbour.*) The spindles go in and out, in and out, stitching the pattern into the cloth. So naturally it stitched me to the cloth.

Lily and Franz come out of the lift.

Lily Good morning.

Franz follows Lily through a door and into a corridor. It is lofty with various doors off it and could be a corridor in an art gallery or a concert hall. Once through one of the doors the atmosphere is more

*muddled and intimate. The topography of the offices in
general is intricate and illogical, rooms oddly located,
sudden staircases, like the topography of a dream. The
topography of* The Trial *is that of a dream (and not a
nightmare particularly) and the office should be similar,
though without losing touch with reality. Franz fails to
close the door he and Lily have come through.*

Attendant Door! Door! Door!

*Franz walks up to the Attendant and shows him his
docket. He indicates for them to sit in the waiting area.
Behind the Attendant is a corridor lined with offices,
partitioned off from the corridor and each other by a
wall. The upper part of the wall is glass, divided into
panes, like the partitions in nineteenth-century schools.
It is therefore possible to see from the corridor into the
offices and from one office into the next. The glass
dividing screens have small sliding panels through which
one office can communicate with the other, another odd
dream-like feature.*

INT. OFFICE AREA. DAY

*In the office are three clerks, Gutling, Culick and
Pohlmann. Gutling is a large, fastidious creature, Culick a
bit of a Romeo and Pohlmann placid and plump. We see
an Office Girl go through into Pohlmann's office with a
cigar box. Pohlmann is interviewing a workman.*

Pohlmann Now it's possible that your firm will try to put
the blame on you.

The Workman holds up his bandaged limb.

Workman Me?

Pohlmann Yes. Just because you're the injured party, it
doesn't mean you are not the guilty party.

Very low under the following Pohlmann dialogue, we hear Gutling and the Jam Workman in the next office.

Gutling (*out of vision*) I can't find the form, of course, but we're assuming your employer is up to date with the premium. If he isn't I'm wasting your time and what's more important you're wasting mine. It says here you were scalded. What with?

Jam Workman (*out of vision*) Jam.

Gutling (*out of vision*) Jam?

The Gutling dialogue now becomes predominant.

Jam Workman (*out of vision*) Jam. You have to understand, sir, jam is not like water. It's syrup. It sticks.

Gutling (*out of vision*) I know jam.

Pohlmann (*seeing the Girl with the cigar box, in mock despair*) Oh no, not me. You haven't seen me. I'm not here.

The Collecting Girl waits.

Collecting Girl Your grade are putting in five.

Pohlmann My grade.

He puts a peeled boiled egg in his mouth, whole.

Pohlmann groans and puts a note in the box. The Collecting Girl goes, and we go with her as we hear Pohlmann continuing with the questionnaire. Faded down under Gutling's conversation.

Now, degree of incapacity.

We go with the Collecting Girl as she goes along the corridor to the next-door room, but pauses with her hand on the handle of the door of Gutling's office as she sees another Girl coming down the corridor. They chat, and we see beyond them into Gutling's office. A middle-aged Man is telling Gutling the story we have already half heard. The following conversations take place simultaneously.

Jam Workman I have two vats. The foreman said, 'I'm going to give you two vats. Normally it would be one, but I'm going to give *you* two.'

Gutling How long is the scar? (*He takes out a ruler.*)

Collecting Girl I don't know whether I'm coming or going this morning. When are they going to have a whip round for me, that's what I want to know? Is your hair different?

Friend I washed it.

Collecting Girl No. It looks different.

Friend You're just not . . .

The Collecting Girl is still poised, her hand on the door knob chatting. This annoys Gutling who keeps glancing at her. Suddenly he jumps up, runs across the room and wrenches open the door.

Gutling Do you want me or not? Some of us are trying to work.

The Jam Workman looks round at the Collecting Girl and we see his scar.

Collecting Girl Everybody's putting in. It's for the Director.

Gutling How much?

Collecting Girl It's optional.

Gutling Rubbish.

Collecting Girl Five marks.

Gutling Here's four. I'm not like these other fellows. I have to look after my money.

The Jam Workman has got up and is looking at the Collecting Girl.

Jam Workman Excuse me, but aren't you a friend of my daughter?

Collecting Girl No.

Jam Workman Didn't she invite you to go on a cycling holiday in the mountains?

Collecting Girl No.

Jam Workman So the name Rosa means nothing to you?

The Collecting Girl shakes her head.

Gutling It seems rude to interrupt but we appear to be losing sight of the job in hand . . .

Gutling guides the Jam Workman back into the room and we follow the Collecting Girl down the corridor into the next office. In the next office Culick, the youngest and best-looking of the clerks, is filling out a form. A Man with his head bandaged sits by the desk.

Gutling (*out of vision*) . . . Are you interested in compensation or aren't you?

Culick (*shakes his head*) Your employer pays. The government pays.

Head-Bandaged Man The shop said they are not responsible.

Culick (*still writing*) Well, they normally do. (*Pause.*) What did you do with the ear? Did you save it?

Head-Bandaged Man No.

Culick It's not important.

The Collecting Girl has come in. Culick gets up to talk to her.

You realize you're taking a risk, being alone in a room with me?

The Collecting Girl is only slightly embarrassed and looks at the Head-Bandaged Man.

Women can't keep their hands off me, do you know that?

Collecting Girl It's only a gesture.

A Man in a dust coat enters. He looks enquiringly round the office, spots an artificial leg leaning in a corner and goes and gets it. Culick squeezes the Collecting Girl's breasts.

Culick So's that.

Collecting Girl Not now.

Culick goes back to talk to the Workman.

Culick Does it incommode you in any way? Only having one ear? Do you wear glasses?

We follow the Man in the dust coat as he leaves, and pick up Gutling showing the Jam Workman out, fading up their conversation.

Gutling . . . Can you or can you not lead a normal life? Since it's perfectly apparent that you can, I advise you to go away and lead it.

The Head of Department, just arriving for work, comes along the corridor. He is with the Head Clerk.

Head of Department I was at the opera last night and it occurred to me . . .

Gutling Good morning, Head of Department.

The Head of Department ignores him.

Head of Department The motor car.

Head Clerk Head of Department?

Head of Department Potentially a significant accident statistic or not?

Head Clerk No is my instinctive answer. Still, I'll give it some thought.

Head of Department Do.

They stop. The Head Clerk now withdraws.

Head Clerk (*as he goes*) Oh, and Head of Department. Congratulations.

The Head of Department nods complacently and departs as we follow the Head Clerk to Kafka's office. He opens the door and puts his head round. Kafka is staring out of the window dictating to his secretary, Miss Weber, who is taking it down in shorthand.

(*mouthing at Miss Weber*) Busy? Come back later.

He withdraws and by the time Kafka has turned from the window he has gone.

Kafka (*faded up*) . . . Although an extremely cautious operator would take care not to allow any joint of his fingers to project from the timber, the hand of even the most careful operator was bound to be drawn into the cutter space if it slipped. In such accidents usually several joints and even whole fingers were severed. Amen.

During the above, Kafka has taken up a letter he has opened.

My brother-in-law tells me he's starting a factory. Can I help him? (*Glances at Miss Weber.*) Ear-rings today.

She fingers them.

Do they go right through?

She smiles and nods.

You had a hole dug in your ears! What courage!

Miss Weber It's my body.

*Cut to the waiting area where Franz is sitting in line
with Lily. Lily nudges Franz and indicates Kafka, who
has come down the corridor.*

Lily This is the fellow you want to see.

*Franz rises and goes towards Gutling and Kafka who
are talking to a Butcher Boy with a bandaged arm.
Gutling has taken the boy's folder and is studying it.*

Kafka You've been in the wars.

Boy Yes, sir.

Gutling (*consulting the folder*) Our old friend the mincing
machine. (*Reads the account of the accident.*) You stupid
fool, putting your arm down.

Boy The throat was too long. The truncheon wouldn't
reach. You have to put your arm down.

Kafka Wasn't there a guard on the worm?

Boy I took it off, sir.

Gutling Well, then it serves you right, then, doesn't it? In
any case you don't belong here. You should be downstairs
in 272.

Boy I've just come from there.

Kafka Go back, and if they try and send you somewhere
else say Doctor Kafka says to say you're not a football.

This is the first time we hear Kafka's name.

Boy Yes, sir.

Gutling (*as they walk back down the corridor*) So, having fed himself into his machine, we now feed him into ours. Ha!

Franz follows them down the corridor trying to attract Kafka's attention.

Franz Sir.

The Attendant pulls him back and Kafka ignores him with a smile.

Kafka Have you noticed how often when claimants are telling you about their accidents, they smile? Why do they smile? They're apologizing. They feel foolish. Utterly blameless yet they feel guilty.

Gutling goes into his office and we go with Kafka into his, where the Head Clerk is looking at a report on Kafka's desk.

Head Clerk Bricks falling on someone's head. Do they ever do anything else? I say, do they ever do anything else?

Kafka moves over towards his desk.

Kafka Yet another firm trying to make out the fact they had an accident was sheer accident. Accidents, as we well know, are never an accident.

He sits. The Head Clerk peeps into the next office through the partition and finds Culick staring into space, with Gutling and Pohlmann beyond him, eavesdropping. The Head Clerk opens the panel in the partition.

Head Clerk Get on. Get on. (*Culick jumps to it but now it is Kafka who is staring into space.*)

Kafka I thought of Japan.

The Head Clerk looks askance.

Bricks don't fall on people there. They have paper houses.

Head Clerk They do, they do. Doctor Kafka . . .

Kafka Why is everything so heavy? This chair. This desk. The poor floor, carrying the burden. The sheer weight of Prague.

Head Clerk Doctor Kafka. It's no secret we're losing our Head of Department. Elevated to the fifth floor. Higher things. A chance for a modest celebration. A presentation. A speech perhaps?

Kafka Excuse me, Head Clerk, but you have a small smut on your chin. Don't be alarmed.

Kafka rubs the Head Clerk's chin with his handkerchief.

Head Clerk Well?

Kafka Help! I must go and put my head under a circular saw.

INT. SAWMILL. DAY

A large sawmill with lots of overhead belts. It is a dangerous and tricky looking place and there is a dreadful din. The Manager shows Kafka a large circular saw. Kafka examines the guard rails and looks under it, discussing it with the Manager, though all this is unheard through the din. Then Kafka goes to another machine some distance away. This has no guard rail. A Workman is standing by, watching. We see Kafka turn to the Manager and point this out, and ask him why, again unheard through the din. Mix through to:

INT. OFFICE AREA. DAY

Franz is still waiting, though now he sits by Pohlmann's desk. Pohlmann and Gutling are stood in front of an open filing cabinet. Both are searching through the files.

Pohlmann is eating a sandwich as well as looking up the docket. He places the sandwich on top of the open drawer. Culick is standing next to Franz with his foot on the desk – he is mending his shoe with glue.

Culick Is it my imagination or do we get more shit than anybody else?

Gutling Of course. There are four hundred people working in this company. Since only two of them are Jews and one of them happens to be Doctor Kafka we get sent a lot of shit. It's only natural.

Pohlmann looks askance and then walks away from the filing cabinet and, leaving his sandwich there, goes back to his desk where Franz is sitting opposite. Gutling removes the sandwich from the file with an expression of distaste and puts it on Pohlmann's desk.

Pohlmann I don't seem to be able to trace it. When did you have this accident?

Franz It wasn't exactly an accident.

Pohlmann Ah.

Franz I'm ill through work.

Culick (*still mending his shoes*) Well, I'm ill through work. We're all ill through that.

Gutling, having found what he was looking for, sits down on the desk – on some paper which Culick has been wiping his glue on.

Franz My skin's broken out. Look . . .

Pohlmann (*hastily*) No. We deal in accidents. You haven't had an accident.

Franz I get splashed with the dye. That's an accident, it happens all the time.

Gutling So it's not an accident, is it?

He goes back to his desk where his Client is waiting, the glued paper stuck to his trousers.

Franz But it's fetched my skin out.

We cut to Gutling returning to his office.

Gutling Look. This number here means that your firm has a policy that covers factory premises. It isn't a comprehensive cover for the firm's employees outside those premises.

Culick enters.

Culick He doesn't want a rundown on the filing system.

Culick has put his foot up on Gutling's desk and taken Gutling's scissors to cut off some fraying strands from the bottom of his trousers.

Gutling Why don't you put your foot on your own desk?

Culick Because I haven't any scissors.

The lunchtime bell rings.

Lunchtime!

Gutling (*getting up*) I'm going to have to refer you back.

Client It was their barrel.

Gutling You're not our pigeon.

Culick goes.

Client (*who is limping*) And I ruined a perfectly good umbrella.

We follow him as he goes and end on Pohlmann and Franz in Pohlmann's office.

Pohlmann It may clear up.

Franz It's spreading all the time. Somebody said I should see Doctor Kafka. If he's a doctor he might know.

Pohlmann Ah! He's not that sort of doctor.

Franz It must be the dye. What else could it be? I've just got engaged to be married.

Pohlmann takes the folder and goes in search of Kafka, but his office is empty. Miss Weber comes in.

Miss Weber Whatever it is, the answer's no. Anyway he's gone to look at a sawmill. (*Takes the papers and glances at them.*) No. No. You should know better than this.

She starts to touch him up, rubbing her hand over his thigh.

Pohlmann It's a borderline case. He may be interested.

Miss Weber Don't be ridiculous. Of course he'd be interested. He's got enough on his plate.

Pohlmann and Miss Weber are seen from Franz's point of view through the glass partitions.

He remarked on my new ear-rings. You haven't.

Pohlmann grasps her breasts.

Pohlmann What lovely ear-rings.

As Pohlmann kisses Miss Weber he slips the folder on to Kafka's desk. A telephone rings and Miss Weber goes to answer it. Cut back to Pohlmann's office and Franz who has been watching them kissing. Pohlmann returns.

I've put it on his desk. Come back tomorrow.

Franz What I want is an independent medical examination. By a specialist. It must be the dye.

Pohlmann I've put it on his desk.

Franz I just got engaged.

Pohlmann So you keep telling me. Come tomorrow.

Franz goes. Lily is waiting for him and they go together.

INT. GYMNASIUM. NIGHT
Franz (Young) exercising at night on the rings in the moonlight.

Franz (Old) *(voice over)* I'd started going to the gym at night. I didn't want anybody to see my skin. At the Institute where I did want somebody to see my skin, nobody would look. I went again and waited.

Mix through to:

INT. OFFICE AREA. DAY
Petitioners waiting, including Franz and Lily.

Lily *(looking straight ahead)* Do you hear that? Because I can hear a river. I never used to be able to hear a river. They say, 'Well, a river's nice to hear.' Not in your own head it isn't. The first thing I'm going to get is some new chair covers. Delayed concussion.

Pohlmann and Culick are already in their offices, when Gutling storms in, in a towering rage. He wrenches open the glass partition between his and Culick's office.

Gutling How long have I been in this department?

Culick I thought it was five years.

Gutling I thought it was five years, but it can't be. Because when the Head Clerk wants someone to make a presentation to the Director does he ask me? No, he doesn't. He asks Doctor Kafka who's only been here one year. So maybe I haven't been here five years. Maybe it only seems like five years. Maybe I only came here yesterday. Maybe I don't work here at all. Well, we'll see about that. Because I am now going to start making my presence felt.

He goes out of the office down the line of waiting Claimants.

Docket. Show me. Come on. Docket. Docket. Docket. (*Examines one.*) Well, you don't belong here for a start.

Claimant I was told . . .

Gutling You mustn't believe what you're told. Not in this place. I was told this was going to be a job with prospects. I don't care what you were told. This is a P48. It is not our pigeon. Out. Out. Out. Out. (*To Claimants in turn*) You've no business here either. Out. Out.

Then it is Franz's turn.

Out.

Franz I'm supposed to see Doctor Kafka.

Gutling Doctor Kafka is a busy man. Doctor Kafka has factories to inspect. Doctor Kafka has a speech to prepare. Out. Out. Out. Out. Out.

Gutling pushes Franz and the others out.

INT. LIFT. DAY

Kafka's calm face coming up in the lift.

Gutling (*voice over, screaming*) Out. Out. Out. (*many times*)

Cut to high shot of the lift coming up.

INT. OFFICE AREA. DAY

Cut back to Gutling expelling the rest of the Claimants.

Gutling Back, madam, back to where you came from. Out. Out. Out. Out!

He shoves the last of the Claimants out and turns to face the audience of Clerks and Secretaries who have come out of their offices to watch his mad behaviour. Nervously they go back to work as Gutling barges through them to his office.

INT. CORRIDOR/STAIRS OUTSIDE ROOM 404. DAY

Kafka walking towards the office, puzzled by the stream of Claimants leaving.

INT. OFFICE AREA. DAY

Miss Weber, in the process of handing out coffee to the Clerks, walks down the corridor between offices and meets Kafka.

Miss Weber Someone's on the war path.

Kafka sees Gutling fuming at his desk and approaches.

Kafka Charles.

Gutling rises to meet Kafka at the doorway.

I want to see this young man. He's a dyeworker. Some sort of eczema.

He has been looking in a folder.

Gutling Gone. I've just sent him away.

Kafka Ah.

Gutling He wasn't our responsibility.

Kafka I'm sure you're right. You're always right. Incidentally . . .

(*Kafka draws Gutling aside. They move off down the*

162

corridor.) I've been landed with a speech of farewell to the Head of Department, I was wondering . . . could you give me a pointer or two?

It is an exercise in pure charm. They stop.

Gutling Happy to.

Kafka How's mother?

Gutling She's well. Very well.

Kafka (*going*) Good. Good. About this dyeworker. Can you . . . retrieve him?

Gutling Ah!

He is nonplussed but Culick, coming out of his office, saves Gutling's face.

Culick I think I fancy a bit of a promenade myself.

INT. MAIN HALL, OUTSIDE INQUIRIES OFFICE. DAY

The Inquiries Clerk stamps Franz's docket. Franz now has another piece of paper clipped to his growing sheaf of documents.

Inquiries Clerk 452 . . . next!

Franz is walking across the large hall, when a Man runs down the steps and through the hall.

Man (*shouting*) I've got it. I've got my claim. I've got it. I've got my claim. I've got it. I've got it. I've got it . . . My claim . . . I've got it, I've got it, I've got it. I've got my claim. I've got it.

Franz shows his docket to an Attendant.

Attendant 452!

Franz moves off.

INT. CORRIDOR. DAY

Franz walks away from a stairwell and along a corridor. He passes a gents lavatory and goes in. We hold on the corridor as Culick rounds the corner and strides straight past the gents.

INT. TALL WOMAN'S OFFICE/CORRIDOR. DAY

A Tall Woman stands in front of a mirror. She sees how she looks with a bundle of assorted documents. She is still gauging the effect of this when Culick comes in.

Tall Woman (*still looking at herself*) To what do we owe this pleasure?

Culick We've lost a claimant. Inquiries said they'd sent him up here.

Tall Woman I haven't seen him (*Turns towards him.*) You're talking to someone who's just received a summons to the fifth floor.

They go out into the corridor and she locks the door.

Culick If he surfaces, point him back upstairs, would you? I'll do the same for you sometime.

Tall Woman Can I have that in writing?

The Tall Woman and Culick go along the corridor and exit. The corridor is empty for a second then a Child with a broom much too large for it comes out of a door and plays at sweeping. Franz coming along the corridor sees the Child just as the door opens and a hand pulls the Child inside again. The Child screams 'Ow'. We hear a slap. Franz tries the door of the Tall Woman's office (452). It is locked. Franz now begins to wander about the Workers Accident Insurance Building.

INT. CORRIDOR/WAITING ROOM. DAY

Franz walks down a wide corridor, through some strange wooden barriers, towards the Tribunal waiting room.

One-Legged Man (*voice over*) They were very pleased with me at the hospital. The doctor said, 'You got that fast in the loom?' He said, 'Well, you're lucky.' He said, 'If I'd had to take it off in the theatre I couldn't have done it cleaner than that.' And he said, 'You're fortunate in another respect'; I said, 'Yes?' He said, 'You're an extrovert.' He said, 'You've got the right attitude of mind.' I said, 'I have.' It's a bit unsightly, but I'm not incommoded. In some respects the reverse. More room in the bed; more scope for manoeuvre. I haven't noticed the wife complaining. (*Laughs.*) Mind you it's a wonder I didn't lose more than a leg. I pointed out there was no cradle on the shaft. After I'd had my accident I said to the foreman, 'You haven't got a leg to stand on.' He said. 'You can talk.'

By now, Franz has come upon a long line of people sitting waiting outside a pair of double doors. A uniformed Attendant guards the doors. We now see the One-Legged Man whose voice we've been hearing.

He said, 'They'll claim you were drunk.' I said, 'Drunk? Pull the other one.' He said 'What other one?' I said 'Precisely.' (*Guffaws.*) You have to laugh. Anyway, last lap.

Man Without Ear End in sight.

One-Legged Man Where will you go tomorrow? Eh? Where will you go? Won't know you're born.

Man Without Ear It's a way of life. (*Addressing the Attendant*) You're used to it, people coming and going. It's our big day.

Attendant Keep it down, keep it down.

Franz sits down next to the One-Legged Man.

One-Legged Man Here you are. Sit this side. More leg room. Ha ha. (*Takes Franz's dockets and looks at them.*) I say. This brings back memories.

Shows it to Man Without Ear.

Man Without Ear Eh?

One-Legged Man I say, 'This brings back memories.'

Man Without Ear Oh my goodness me!

Franz I'm wanting a certificate to see the doctor.

Man Without Ear What doctor?

Franz Their doctor.

One-Legged Man You haven't seen the doctor? Hey. He hasn't even seen the doctor!

Man Without Ear He hasn't seen the doctor.

This information passes down the line and Franz becomes an object of scrutiny. They should be reminiscent of characters in Alice in Wonderland.

Attendant Keep it down. Keep it down.

One-Legged Man How long have you been coming?

Franz Today.

One-Legged Man This is your first day? Listen, it's taken me six months to get this far.

Bald Man (*taking off his wig and rubbing his totally bald head*) It's taken me a year.

Franz Not every day?

Maimed Woman All I want is to be a normal person.

Attendant Keep it down. Keep it down.

One-Legged Man I went three months and never heard a thing.

Man Without Ear You haven't assembled any documents. You've got to assemble documents.

Franz I just want to see the doctor.

One-Legged Man Well, this isn't the doctor. This is the Tribunal. It's the Panel is this. You don't belong here.

Franz What should I do?

One-Legged Man Don't ask me. We don't want them upsetting. You've no business here. Now clear off. Go on, clear off. We want it all plain sailing. Bugger off. Go on.

Man Without Ear (*simultaneous with above*) Go on. Go on, get out.

Their attention is distracted by the door opening. A Claimant comes out. Sudden silence.

Attendant Next.

A Girl goes into the room while the others question the Claimant who has just come out.

Maimed Woman Well?

Claimant I made a good impression.

Maimed Woman How many are there?

Claimant Three. One doesn't speak. Just looks.

Maimed Woman Looks?

Claimant I was missing my birth certificate. One of them said could I give them my word that I had been born.

The others laugh.

They all laughed.

Maimed Woman Laughed?

Claimant They said now to try and lead a normal life.

Attendant All right, all right.

He ushers the Claimant out. Man Without Ear shakes his head.

Man Without Ear Disallowed. They always tell you. In the last stage, they always tell you.

Attendant Now make sure you've all got your documents. And that they're in the right order.

They all look through them like Alice *characters. Franz goes up to the Attendant to show him his docket. The Attendant waves it away.*

Are you on this list? Not interested. Not interested. List only. Out! (*He pushes Franz out.*)

INT. UPSTAIRS CORRIDOR/ROOM. DAY

Franz comes along another upstairs corridor, less grand, more attic-like than the other. Lily is sitting on a chair outside a door.

Lily Where do you want? (*Looks at Franz's docket.*) They'll take that in here, yes. My documents have just gone in. They're studying them now, possibly.

A Girl comes along the corridor carrying a mug and a comb.

Hello, Teresa.

The Girl ignores her.

Their dog's poorly. She's got a lot on her mind.

Franz is increasingly dubious of this woman.

Franz I'm not sure I shouldn't tell them I'm here.

Lily No. You'll go to the bottom of the pile. (*Pause.*) The girl said last week my file was taken out by the Assistant Manager. Of course I know them all here, I'm like one of the family.

Another Girl passes.

Sheila . . .

(*to Franz*) Sheila. I'd liked to have worked in a place like this. A sedentary occupation but with some coming and going. Banter. Whip-rounds. Relations between the sexes. Sat at home, it's no game, is it?

Franz listens at the door. She gets agitated.

Come away. They're just digesting the facts.

Franz Get off.

Lily No, you're young. You don't understand.

Franz Look. I could be stuck here all day.

He pushes Lily back into the chair quite violently. He knocks on the door. Quietly. Then louder. He opens the door. There is a broom. A bucket and some newspapers on the floor.

There's nobody here. Come and see.

Lily No. I'll wait till I'm called.

Franz There's nobody there. Look.

He drags her towards door.

Lily Don't shout. There's offices everywhere. Leave off. I'm a woman. I've had a head injury.

Franz It's an empty room.

He pushes her into it violently.

Lily Stop it.

Franz It's empty.

Lily (*simultaneously with the above*) You've just got to be . . . patient.

Franz Look at it.

Lily (*on her hands and knees*) You've no business . . .

Franz . . . empty!

Lily (*picking up the old newspapers*) Look, these are important.

Franz They're not important. They're rubbish.

Franz hits her with some newspaper.

Lily That's wicked, wicked. You're not supposed to hit women, everybody says.

Franz runs up the steps leading up out of the room.

Franz You're mad. You're wrong in the head.

He throws some papers on to her head.

Lily These are important – these are to do with my case.

Franz You're mad.

Lily You're young. You don't know.

Franz is running up a winding staircase littered with papers. We see Lily far below him. He then runs along a high, narrow corridor.

(*voice over*) Papers, facts, they all come into it, possibly.
You've got to keep track. You . . . you don't understand.

INT. SMALL HALL/BALCONY. DAY

*Franz climbs a poky staircase, which we see from above as
if it is a vortex. He comes through a door and on to the
balcony of a hall, like a small concert hall where the
Tribunal is sitting. Three Men are sitting behind a table on
a platform. Standing before them is a Girl naked.*

Thin Doctor (*reading out a report*) . . . breaking the left
arm and causing widespread abrasions to the chest and
abdomen the scars from which you can plainly see.

Angry Doctor Well, not all that plainly, surely?

Thin Doctor Quite plainly. Look. Raise your arms again.
Yes.

Fat Doctor Yes.

Thin Doctor (*sweetly*) Go on, shall I? She reports some
loss of feeling on her left side.

Angry Doctor 'Course she does. She's not stupid. Some
dozy general practitioner has probably said to her, 'Do
you have any loss of feeling on your left side?' and lo and
behold she suddenly finds she's got some loss of feeling on
her left side.

Thin Doctor (*patiently*) Her doctor reports there to have
been some personality change.

Angry Doctor Probably the same doctor.

Thin Doctor She is subject to violent changes of mood,
incapable of sustained attention.

Angry Doctor I don't believe any of this.

There is a silence.

Thin Doctor I beg your pardon?

Angry Doctor Has it ever occurred to you that everyone who comes before this panel has, prior to their accident, been of a sunny and equable disposition, capable of long periods of sustained attention, unvisited by headaches or indeed any infirmity at all, the mind alert, the body in perfect order, a paragon of health. Take this young woman. Previously a cheerful soul, she is now said to be anxious and depressed. So? Previously an optimist she is now a pessimist, is that such a bad thing? One could say that this accident has brought her to her senses rather than deprived her of them. She now takes a dim view of the world. So do I. She can't keep her mind on the matter in hand. Nor can I. She winces when she looks in the mirror. So do I.

Thin Doctor She's crying.

Fat Doctor So am I.

Angry Doctor We cannot compensate people for being cast out of Paradise. All these sheaves of reports are saying is 'I didn't know how lucky I was till this happened.' So? Now they do know. They have achieved wisdom. And a degree of self-knowledge. They should be paying us, not we them. We appear to have a visitor.

The Angry Doctor has spotted Franz. The Thin Doctor stands up, angry. The Woman covers herself up.

Thin Doctor What are you doing here?

Franz I want someone to tell me what's wrong with me.

Thin Doctor You've no business here. This is outrageous.

Fat Doctor stands.

Fat Doctor The idea.

Thin Doctor Get out.

Franz Not until somebody tells me where to go.

Fat Doctor Call someone. Call the doorman.

Thin Doctor Doorman!

The door springs open and the Attendant rushes on to the balcony and seizes Franz. He drags him down to the Tribunal.

Mad. Mad. Mad, sir, mad.

Franz struggles with him.

Angry Doctor (*to the Attendant*) Stop it, you animal. You're not in a farmyard.

Attendant Yes, sir. Thank you, sir.

Angry Doctor Let me see that paper.

Franz gives him his docket.

(*to Franz*) Come with me. (*Rises.*) Any excuse to get away from this collective idiocy. (*Shouts back at the panel.*) Idiocy. Come along.

INT. WAITING ROOM OUTSIDE TRIBUNAL. DAY

Franz follows the Angry Doctor, the Claimants are lined up outside.

Angry Doctor I hope you're all word perfect on your personality changes. (*Strides at great speed along the corridor, talking to himself.*) It's a wicked world. It's a wicked, wicked world. I have lost my faith. Doctor loses faith. Doctor goes way of other doctors.

He and Franz stop.

It just needs one person, just one to come before that panel and say, 'Doctor, since suffering this grievous affliction I am a new man, a better person.'

They move off.

'The loss of my hand has been an education. Blinded, I can now see.' Instead of which it's 'How much is it worth?'

One-Legged Man Doctor!

The One-Legged Man stands up, supported by his crutch.

Angry Doctor How much do you think this is worth, eh?

He takes the crutch and hurls it down. Without the crutch the One-Legged Man falls over. The Angry Doctor turns to Franz.

How much is whatever you've got worth? (*As they continue walking*) I'm not a doctor any more. I'm an accountant.

INT. CORRIDOR OUTSIDE TALL WOMAN'S OFFICE. DAY

The Angry Doctor and Franz arrive outside the Tall Woman's office.

Angry Doctor This it? (*Looks at Franz's docket*) Yes. Journey's end.

The door opens and the Tall Woman comes out.

Tall Woman Ah! The lost sheep.

Angry Doctor Blessed are the maimed for they shall be compensated.

The Angry Doctor goes.

Tall Woman Come on.

She goes down the corridor and round the corner, followed by a confused Franz.

Miss Weber (*voice over*) Don't you sometimes just long to see one . . .

INT. OFFICE AREA. DAY

Pohlmann and Miss Weber in Pohlmann's office.
Pohlmann eating as usual, sandwich in one hand, the other hand on Miss Weber's bottom, though she betrays no sign of this on her face except for a slight wavering in her voice.

Miss Weber (*reading from a file*) . . . single able-bodied person. Someone who doesn't lack an arm here or a finger there, who doesn't pull up their shirt without wanting to reveal some frightful burn. Somebody normal?

The door opens and the Tall Woman shows Franz into the office. Pohlmann hurriedly removes his hand from Miss Weber.

Tall Woman Your lost sheep.

She goes.

Pohlmann Oh, take a seat.

Franz doesn't.

Franz I was here this morning . . . I've been all over. I was supposed to see Doctor Kafka.

Miss Weber Doctor Kafka has gone home. His hours are eight until two.

Franz Does that mean I have to come back?

Pohlmann You have reached the beginning. You are about to start. You have been allowed to enter the race.

Franz Look. I'm covered in scale.

He shows them his hands and a shower of scurf falls on the desk.

Miss Weber You're not. Your face is perfectly normal. Don't exaggerate.

Pohlmann (*filling in a form*) This gives you an appointment with the Institute doctor. They're having public clinics on Thursdays. He will look at you and decide if he thinks this skin complaint is anything to do with an accident at work.

Franz I've told you. I haven't had an accident.

Miss Weber So why go on? Stop now. Before it's too late.

Pohlmann No new process? No new chemicals? Nothing new in your life.

Franz I've just got engaged.

Miss Weber (*drily*) Any accident there?

INT. CHRISTINA'S PARENTS APARTMENT. NIGHT

Franz and his fiancée, Christina, are sitting awkwardly in the formal parlour. The Old Lady in a wheelchair is there also. Christina tries to kiss him. Franz looks unhappy, and indicates the Old Lady as an excuse. Christina rises, then turns the wheelchair round so that the Old Lady is facing the wall. She closes the doors. She slowly unbuttons her dress to reveal her breasts. Franz looks away, tears in his eyes. Christina turns away, angry.

INT. RAILWAY STATION/PLATFORM, PRAGUE. DAY

A steam train has just arrived at the platform. From the other side of the train we see Franz standing looking at his Father who has just got off a train. He is a peasant and is much smaller than Franz. He embraces his son.

Franz (Old) (*voice over*) I'd written to my father. He was a peasant. The family were in . . . well, it's now Germany . . . he came to Prague. I think of my father then as an old man. But he was younger than I am now. He had remedies of his own.

INT. STATION LAVATORY. DAY

Franz and his Father are in a cubicle. Franz has his shirt open. Franz's Father spreads out some kind of leaves, presses them to his son's chest. We see Franz's face. He is touched by his Father's love but he has no faith in this remedy.

INT. FRANZ'S LODGINGS. NIGHT

Franz is asleep. His Father is sitting in a chair by his bedside, his hat on. He takes it off.

INT. MEDICAL SCHOOL ENTRANCE. DAY

Kafka rushing in, late, confronted by several staircases, and trying to find his way into the auditorium.

Lecturer (Senior Doctor) (*out of vision*) All in all it's a pretty mixed bag, but slanted on the whole in the direction of injury at work. Plus some teasers for the . . .

INT. AUDITORIUM, MEDICAL SCHOOL. DAY

Sitting at the back of the auditorium, Franz's Father watches.

Lecturer . . . people in the fourth year and also some interesting examples of occupational disease. Increasing industrialization means this field of medicine is bound to expand. I imagine that's why many of you are here.

Some laughter. We follow Kafka in, to reveal the Senior Doctor standing before the auditorium full of Students. Kafka sits down.

Physical conditions, some of which you will see, take time to declare themselves and I would ask you to remember that we are seeing today casualties of conditions in the industry of twenty, even thirty years ago, conditions which . . .

This speech continuing under, we cut to a group of patients, sitting on benches at the side of the auditorium all made ready in linen gowns. Among them, we note Lily. An Attendant sits next to them. Franz, gowned, and ready, is sitting waiting.

Man I'm a miracle. I have a hole in my stomach. They watch the food passing through.

Young Woman He's had an article written about him. Show him your article.

Lecturer (*out of vision*) . . . in all likelihood have since been improved. Industrial safety is bound to lag behind medical knowledge . . .

We now cut back to the Lecturer.

Lecturer . . . and doubtless in thirty or forty years' time when I hope I shall be safely tucked up in my grave . . .

We cut back to the Patients as the speech goes on under.

The Man begins to show his article to Franz.

Young Woman He's famous with doctors. Somebody came from Paris to see him. And they pay.

Attendant Ssh!

Cut back to Lecturer.

Lecturer (*out of vision*) . . . my hapless successor will still be stood here. Legislation is after all only a net.

Lecturer Nowadays the mesh may be wide. But if you believe in progress, which I do not, the mesh will get smaller and the number of people suffering from industrial injury will dwindle. But it won't, of course: because there will be new industries and new industries mean new diseases. You have chosen a wise profession, gentlemen. Doctors will never be unemployed. Now could we have our first conundrum please.

The Attendant signals to Franz.

Attendant Come on.

Franz walks on to the stage, watched by Kafka. Franz is standing in a pool of light on the stage.

Lecturer (*to Franz*) Disrobe.

Franz does so, and stands naked. We see his scaly chest, and as the Lecturer indicates for him to turn round, his back also.

(*to Students*) Well? (*Seeing Student raise his hand.*) Yes.

First Student Is it a form of psoriasis?

Lecturer Wonderful. Anybody got any brilliant ideas about the aetiology? Patient is in no discomfort. Affected areas don't itch, not sore. Well, come on, come on. What sort of question should we be asking?

Second Student What age is the patient?

Lecturer (*to Franz*) How old are you?

Franz Twenty-six.

Lecturer Twenty-six.

Third Student Married or single?

Franz Single.

Fourth Student Is it venereal in origin?

The Lecturer looks at Franz, who he thinks has not understood.

Lecturer Did you get it from a tart?

Franz (*passionately*) No.

Lecturer Patient says no. Patient probably right.

Fifth student raises hand.

Well?

Fifth Student Could it be nervous?

Lecturer Are you asking me or are you asking the patient?

During the next section we see Kafka watching intently.

We know what he does. He works in a dyeworks. But what sort of a fellow is he . . . is he nervous, highly strung, cheerful, not cheerful? Look, what are we supposed to be doing here? Who are you? I thought you were supposed to be medical students.

Franz (*shouting*) What is it? What have I done? Give me something. Give me something for it. Stop it. It's all over my body. Why? Why?

We see Franz's Father, tears running down his face. He leaves.

INT. MEDICAL SCHOOL ENTRANCE. DAY

We leave with Franz's Father. He sits at the bottom of the ornate staircase in the entrance hall.

Lecturer (*voice over*) Gentlemen will note agitation of patient and need to assess degree of proper agitation due to patient's physical condition as distinct from evidence of neurotic instability. Next patient, please.

INT. AUDITORIUM, MEDICAL SCHOOL

The Lecturer standing on the stage. Lily is sitting beside him in a pool of light.

Lecturer Some of you might say that there is nothing wrong with the patient. Once upon a time she met with a slight accident at work.

INT. MEDICAL SCHOOL ENTRANCE. DAY

Franz, once more in his own clothes, comes down the steps to meet his Father. They leave.

Lecturer (*voice over*) A box fell on her head. She took a few days off and she felt none the worse. But then she heard that in this enlightened age there is compensation for those that suffer injury at work.

INT. AUDITORIUM, MEDICAL SCHOOL. DAY

The Lecturer and Lily, on the stage in the auditorium.

Lecturer 'Is she entitled to this?' she wonders. And the wondering turns to worrying as she begins to lie awake at night suffering from headaches. She is increasingly unhappy.

Kafka listens intently to this.

And so begins her quest for compensation but for what?

Not the injury, for she has scarcely suffered one. And she is not malingering for the headaches are real. And to those of you who say there is no injury therefore there can be no compensation she can say, 'But I was not like this before my accident. I had no quest. Looking for what is wrong with me *is* what is wrong with me!'

INT. ENTRANCE TO RAILWAY STATION. DAY

Franz is seeing his Father off. They embrace. Franz, weeping, runs off down the steps as his Father turns to go.

INT. OFFICE AREA/CORRIDOR. DAY

A cake on a trolley is pushed along the corridor by two Secretaries. Gutling and Culick and others follow it along the corridor. In Kafka's office, seen from the corridor, Kafka is dressed up and is trying to tie his bow-tie. Pohlmann is sitting at his desk, working. Miss Weber comes in with a bottle of wine and a plate of food.

Miss Weber The good doctor didn't want you to feel left out.

Pohlmann And the cigar?

Miss Weber goes.

INT. OFFICE. DAY

The party. Kafka is speaking. The room is crowded. The Head of Department in the place of honour. We see Kafka's colleagues, the Head Clerk, all the staff.

Kafka In my four districts people fall off the scaffolding as if they were drunk, or they fall into the machines, all the beams topple, all embankments give way, all ladders slide, whatever people carry up, falls down, whatever they hand down they stumble over.

Laughter through much of this from Gutling.

And I have a headache . . .

INT. OFFICE AREA. DAY

During this speech, cut to the empty office area, where Pohlmann is alone. Franz enters.

Kafka (*out of vision*) . . . from all those girls in porcelain factories who incessantly throw themselves down the stairs with mountains of dishware.

Hoots of laughter.

I say this only because in making this speech, I fully expect to fall on my face . . .

Fade down sound.

. . . and when I do, Herr Head of Department, please remember that it has been in the proper course of my duties and I shall expect to be compensated.

More laughter.

INT. POHLMANN'S OFFICE. DAY

Pohlmann is working. Franz comes in slightly drunk. Kafka's speech continues under, but inaudible.

Franz Why do you work here? This is a terrible place. It's a place of torture.

Pohlmann One has to do something.

He holds out his hand for Franz's papers out of shot.

I need your papers for your file.

Franz I don't want money. I want it to be given a name. How can I ever get rid of it if it doesn't have a name?

Suddenly he picks up the bottle of wine and flings it through a window.

INT. OFFICE. DAY

Cut back to Kafka speaking at the party. The sound of shattering glass is heard.

Kafka *Voilà*. An accident.

More laughter.

Our thanks then to the benign ruler of our topsy-turvy world. This kingdom of the absurd, where it does not pay to be well, where loss determines gain, limbs become commodities and to be given a clean bill of health is to be sent away empty-handed. Our world, where to be deprived is to be endowed, to be disfigured means to be marked out for reward and to limp is to jump every hurdle. The Director guards us, the workers of the Workers Accident Institute, against our own institutional accidents. And I don't mean falling over the holes in the linoleum on the bottom corridor (Maintenance please note).

Laughter.

INT. OFFICE AREA. DAY

Pohlmann sitting at his desk with Franz sitting opposite him. An Old Mailman trundles his carriage along the corridor and past the office.

Kafka (*out of vision*) I mean blindness to genuine need, deafness to a proper appeal and hardness of heart. These are our particular professional risks for which there are no safety guards, no grids, no protective clothing. Only a scrupulous and vigilant humanity.

INT. OFFICE. DAY

Cut back to the party.

Kafka A toast then to the benevolent umpire in our absurd games, our firm but kindly father to whom without fear we can always turn, as we do now and say, Herr Director.

They toast him – 'Herr Director' – and people applaud.

INT. OFFICE AREA. DAY

The office staff are coming away from the party.

Culick He can certainly talk.

Gutling Of course he can talk. But I can talk. You haven't heard me talk.

Culick Haven't I?

Gutling Not in a formal situation.

Culick Does that make a difference?

Gutling I'd have told him. I'd have used the opportunity to let them know exactly what's wrong with this place.

Culick Yes.

They disappear into their respective offices. Kafka is in his room, still dressed up, when Pohlmann brings in Franz. Miss Weber is filing away papers.

Kafka Yes?

Pohlmann The dyeworker.

Miss Weber Not again. Really.

Kafka (*fiercely*) Silence. (*Pause.*) Please. Sit down.

Franz does so.

Franz I've been told you are kind. I've been told you are the one to see. They say you are a human being.

Kafka No. I do a very good imitation of a human being.

Franz You are harder to see than anybody.

Miss Weber There has to be a procedure. A system. Is that so terrible?

Kafka What did you want to say to me?

Miss Weber There is nothing to say. It is a hopeless case. People coming in, wanting money.

Franz I don't want money.

Miss Weber Nobody ever does. I sometimes wonder what they think they're doing here, it comes as such a shock. 'You mention money to me when I've lost my precious fingers.' 'All my treasured auburn hair gone up in smoke and you ask me how much it's worth.'

Pohlmann Some things are beyond money.

Miss Weber Really? I've yet to find them.

Pohlmann We'd all rather have our health than the money.

Miss Weber Correction. We'd all rather have our health *and* the money.

Kafka You are asking for a justice that doesn't exist in the world. And not only you. More people. More people every year.

Kafka is looking through the files on the table and finds one.

A man works in the carding room of a cotton mill. Dust everywhere. The air dust. Taken ill. Examined by the company doctor. Unfit for work. Discharged. Nothing unusual in that. Except somebody decides to put in a P48, a claim for compensation, just as you did.

Miss Weber Not applicable. Either of them. Not accidents.

Kafka Quite. But bear with me. Take this millworker. No beam has fallen on his head. No bottle has exploded in his eye. He has not got his shirt caught in the shaft and been taken round. All that has happened is that he has been inhaling cotton dust for some years. And day by day this cotton dust has crept into his lungs, but so slowly, so gradually that it cannot be called an accident. But suppose our lungs were not internal organs. Suppose they were not locked away in the chest. Suppose we carried our lungs outside our bodies, bore them before us, could hold and handle them, cradle them in our arms. And suppose further they were not made of flesh but of glass, or something like glass, not yet invented, something pliable. And thus the effect of each breath could be seen, the deposit of each intake of air, calculated, weighed even. What would we say then, as we saw the dust accumulate, the passages clog, the galleries close down, as cell by cell these lungs hardened, withered, died. Mm?

Pohlmann But that still wouldn't be an accident. You can't conduct an insurance company on suppositions like that, can you?

Kafka And if we were able to magnify each inhalation, see under the microscope each breath, capture the breath that killed the cell, register the gasp that caused the cough that broke the vein that atrophied the flesh. Wouldn't that be an accident? A very small accident? This man has no claim because he is suffering from a condition. But isn't a condition the result of many small accidents that we cannot see or record?

Pohlmann But so is living. Or dying. There is no alternative but to breathe.

Kafka And this man. A young man. So regularly doused in dye he has begun to grow a second skin. Isn't that an accident? A long slow accident?

Miss Weber People will be wanting compensation for being alive next.

Kafka looks as if this might not be a bad idea.

Kafka I do understand.

Franz What good is that to me? You can't do anything. You're worse than them, not better. You say you understand; well, if you understand and you don't help, you're wicked, you're evil.

Miss Weber Don't speak like that to Doctor Kafka. He has a university degree.

Kafka begins to take out his wallet.

Franz I don't want money.

Franz rises. Kafka follows him.

Kafka I am not offering you money.

They leave the office. Kafka gives Franz a card.

I know of a factory that is starting. It will be in a month or two.

They move off down the corridor which runs between the offices.

Franz This is a terrible place.

Kafka Is it? I always forget that. I find it . . . almost cosy. But then I'm just an official. I am accustomed to office air.

They stop at the end of the corridor.

If you cannot find a job I may be able to help.

Kafka shakes hands. When Franz has gone Kafka removes some small bits of skin that have adhered to his hand.

INT. AN EMPTY FACTORY. DAY

The high ornate door of an empty factory, with a huge rose window. Inside the factory there is a rope hanging down attached to a sack. We hear Kafka's brother-in-law before he enters.

Brother-in-Law (*out of vision*) Don't expect anything too wonderful. It's very rudimentary. Well, one factory is very much like another.

Kafka enters the factory with his Brother-in-Law.

But why am I telling you? You've got expertise. You know about factories. You've seen plenty. (*Pause.*) It's not as if I'm asking you to go into something blindfold.

They are now up on a higher floor.

And here; shipments could come in and out. You see, you see. It's ideal. I know I can succeed, Franz. Do you ever have that feeling?

Kafka Only when I'm very depressed.

They walk down steps and out of shot. Mix through to:

INT. CHRISTINA'S PARENTS' APARTMENT. NIGHT

Franz sits awkwardly in the formal room with his fiancée Christina, and the Old Lady in the wheelchair. Christina reaches out to him. Franz says nothing, then stands up and to Christina's horror starts to remove his clothes. The Old Lady watches. The Girl is horrified by the disfigurement of his skin. She runs out of the room.

Christina Mother! Father!

Franz stands there, naked, looking at the Old Lady, who looks at him without emotion. Christina's Mother looks in, shrieks and closes the door. Christina's Father opens the door, stares wordlessly, and closes the door. Then Christina very nervously opens the door, and gets hold of the wheelchair and takes the Old Lady out. Her Sister closes the door. There is silence. Franz sits down. He seems quite tranquil. There are whisperings and muttered conversations outside the door. Finally the door opens and Christina comes in and throws something on to the sofa, next to where Franz is sitting. Franz picks it up. It is the engagement ring. Mix through to:

INT. NEW FACTORY. DAY

Kafka at the new factory. A busy atmosphere and noticeably dusty. Kafka coughing, handkerchief over his mouth, as he supervises the work. His Brother-in-Law comes up to him with a message.

Brother-in-Law Franz, Franz, some people to see you in the office.

We track Kafka and Brother-in-Law through to:

INT. FACTORY OFFICE. DAY

Brother-in-Law (*as they enter the office*) Coughing still?

Kafka No.

Brother-in-Law (*jubilantly*) This is something to cough about. Three more orders this morning. I'm run off my feet.

He exits up the stairs. Franz is waiting in the office. Kafka smiles and shakes hands.

Kafka So you're still interested in the job?

Franz Yes. Very much so.

Kafka You look well.

Franz Yes, I'm better. My skin cleared completely. (*Shows him his hands.*) A miracle.

Kafka Why is that, do you think?

Franz I don't know. I've never been so well.

A Girl is sitting in the background.

This is my fiancée, Beatrice.

The Girl moves towards them and we see it is not Christina, but the girl from the dyeworks office, who, at the start of the film, told him to ask about insurance.

Kafka Let me show you.

The three of them go through into the factory.

Franz So what is it you're producing here?

Kafka Building materials. Mainly asbestos.

Franz shakes hands with Kafka.

Franz Thank you. You saved my life.

Mix through to:

INT. DOCTOR'S CONSULTING ROOM, PRAGUE. NIGHT. 1945

Franz (Old) and the Doctor are standing by the X-ray.

Franz It's so long ago. But you think it may have been that factory?

Doctor It's possible. Who knows?

They walk through to the consulting room.

Franz (*on their way out*) I was happy working there, though it was only for a year or two. The place went bankrupt. They say no good deed goes unpunished. He worked there too, Doctor Kafka, part-time, so I suppose the same thing could have happened to him.

They stop by the door.

Doctor You weren't to know. He wasn't to know. You breathed, that's all you did wrong.

Pause. They move off down the stairs.

You breathed in the wrong place.

Franz I've a feeling he died. But he was a Jew, so he would have died anyway.

Doctor Mmm. I know the name. The father had a shop. He sold fancy goods. I bought some slippers there once.

He and Franz are now at the outside door. He opens it and we see on the road the shadow of a corpse hanging from a lamp-post.

I wonder how long they're going to leave that body up there. (*Shakes his head.*) I heard him battering at some door last night, begging to be let in. Somebody was after him. Then the door was opened and he thought he was safe. But they were there first. Take care.

They shake hands. Franz goes out into the street and the Doctor closes the door. Then exits up the stairs. Hold on the closed door for the credits, seeing the corpse shadow through the glass.

THE OLD COUNTRY

To Mary-Kay

The cast consists of three married couples:

Hilary
Bron

Eric
Olga

Duff
Veronica

The Old Country opened at the Queen's Theatre on
Wednesday, 7th September 1977. The cast was as follows:

Hilary, Alec Guinness
Bron, Rachel Kempson
Eric, Bruce Bould
Olga, Heather Canning
Duff, John Phillips
Veronica, Faith Brook

Directed by Clifford Williams
Designed by John Gunter
Lighting by Leonard Tucker

The play was presented by Michael Codron

Act One

*A broad verandah above a garden, which is not seen. It is
a ramshackle place, a kind of open lean-to put together at
various times suggesting one of the 'down at heel riding
schools, damp bungalows in wizened orchards' described
in the text. The furniture is simple and includes a rocking-
chair. There are plenty of books about, standing on and
under tables and in piles on the floor. The impression
should be that the house is so full of books that they have
overflowed on to the verandah. The colour and tone of
these books is important. They are a library put together
in the 1930s and 1940s and should have the characteristic
faded pastel colours of books of that period. Many of
them are still in their original dustwrappers. There is a
piano offstage.*

*Hilary and Bron are in their early sixties, their colour
and tone rather like that of the books, shabby and faded.
Hilary is in a stained linen jacket, old flannels and carpet
slippers. Bron is dressed in a vaguely artistic way,
distinctive but not elegant.*

As the curtain rises Hilary is asleep in the rocking-chair.

*The sound of Elgar on the gramophone drifts through
from an adjoining room. A very English scene. The music
stops.*

*Hilary, sleeping, suddenly shouts out. It is a terrible cry
of guilt and despair. He wakes. Sits. Hears the record has
ended and leaving the chair rocking goes out to take it off.*

*For a moment the stage is empty, the chair rocking, then
Bron comes up the stairs from the garden as Hilary comes
back.*

Hilary I went to sleep.

Bron Do you wonder? Elgar!

Hilary I was at home at Hookham. I was alone in the house when suddenly all the lights came on. I knew it was burglars; I could hear them whispering outside. I got everybody into one room . . .

Bron I thought you said you were alone?

Hilary I was . . . but there were other people there. Somebody started to open the front door so I got behind it with a hammer. I was just bringing the hammer down on his head when he looked up at me and smiled. It was Pa. Then we were all somehow at a garden party. (*He has been reading a bookseller's catalogue, which he picks up again.*) Anyway I *like* Elgar.

Bron You don't like Elgar.

Hilary I do like Elgar.

Bron I don't see how anyone can like Elgar. I would prefer anything to Elgar.

Hilary starts to get up laboriously.

Except Vaughan Williams.

Hilary sinks back.

I looked up that pretty yellow flower. It's a weed apparently.

Hilary I like it.

Bron I don't dislike it. It's just getting a bit big for its boots. I think a blitz is in order.

Hilary Is it native to these parts?

Bron 'A determined little creeper' the book says.

Hilary Botanically at least the world hasn't shrunk.

Bron Has it shrunk?

Hilary When it comes to airports and architecture one place may look very much like the next but at least vegetation hasn't gone international. Plants still stay more or less put.

Bron Have to. Don't have a choice. It's a kind of primrose. Smells fractionally of cat. Anyway that's not true. These trees could be anywhere.

Hilary goes to one of the piles of books, with his catalogue.

Hilary People are insane. Thirty pounds. I paid . . . eight-and-six.

Bron When? In nineteen thirty-three? You never buy any books. You're never going to get rid of the ones you've got. Why go through catalogues.

Hilary They collect anything now. Even fakes. Here's a special section in which every item is an authentic guaranteed forgery. In which context a fake would need to be the genuine article. Like a woman at a drag ball. By being exactly what she seems she is the imposter. Soon, one imagines, forgeries *of* forgeries. However.

Pause.

Bron I'm terrified I'm not going to see any of the jokes.

Hilary Who says there'll be jokes? You want help?

Bron With the jokes?

Hilary With the lunch. I wonder what we've got in store for them in the way of weather. Doesn't look too promising. Dull but I imagine there'll be a spot of sunshine later. No dramatic change: just a light rational breeze with a promise of gradual improvement. A day for Burke, not for Hobbes. Empirical weather.

Bron That's not what it said on the forecast. The forecast said thunder. Have you nothing to do?

Hilary No. I thought I might write to *The Times*. I never have.

Bron What about?

Hilary Anything. Everybody else does. That seagull. Sir, Am I right or merely sentimental in thinking that in the old days one saw seagulls exclusively by the sea? Here we are, miles from any shore and there is a seagull.

Bron Aren't you going to wear a tie?

Hilary Seagulls on the land, starlings by the shore. Perhaps Nature herself is becoming more liberal, embargoes are lifted, borders dissolved and birds as free to roam as we are.

Pause.

Bron You want to look nice. Spruce yourself up a bit.

Hilary No.

Bron I miss the sea. It's ages since I saw it.

Hilary Quite candidly I've never seen the point of the sea. Except where it meets the land. The shore has point, the sea none. Of course when you say you miss the sea that's what you mean: you miss the shore.

Bron I miss the sea. Chop, chop, chop. How do you know what I miss?

Hilary Lots of people seem to have died. I could write a note for the obituary column.

Bron Shall I look you out a tie?

Hilary Sir, Might I be permitted to pen a footnote to your (otherwise admirably comprehensive) obituary of Sir Derek (Jack) Clements.

Bron Is he dead?

Hilary Clem blew into my section sometimes in 'forty-two during those early Heath Robinson days when we still lived over the shop at the old Ministry of Supply. We must have seemed a pretty motley crew: a novelist or two, a sprinkling of dons. There was even a fashionable photographer. It was the sort of shambolic, inspirational kind of outfit that fetched the War Office out in a periodic rash. So when Clem came along with his one leg and Ronald Colman moustache it gave the proceedings a welcome air of respectability.

Bron He's not dead?

Hilary Soon after the advent of Clem the tempo quickened. Dieppe, St Nazaire, Arnhem . . . none of them successes in the orthodox sense of the word. But then Clem was never orthodox: that wasn't his way. Throughout his life and particularly in these last trying years he was sustained by the loving kindness of his wife, the famous Brenda. 'More than a wife' he used to say. 'A chum.' A few days before his death he was visited by a friend. 'I'm sorry,' he said, 'I've just pissed the bed. Still,' and his face broke into a grin, 'free country.' Ah Clem, with you, irony was never far away. The world is a colder place without you. However.

Bron Is he dead?

Hilary Years ago.

Bron You keep doing that. Who was it died the other day? Somebody. I can't remember. You should tell me when people die, otherwise I lose my bearings.

Pause.

He was the one with the ears?

Hilary That was Sillitoe.

Bron He's not dead?

Hilary No. He lives with his sister in Tewkesbury. Or did. He may be dead . . . I don't know. You can sort it out with Veronica. She'll have all the dirt.
    'Praise, my soul, the King of Heaven
    To his feet thy tribute bring'

He sings this snatch of a hymn and tails off into silence.

Bron Would you rather they weren't coming?

Silence.

Would you?

Hilary Where would you say this landscape could be? Other than here.

Bron Would you?

Hilary Where?

Bron Nowhere.

Hilary Because given the lie of the land I would have said Scotland.

Bron Scotland.

Hilary
    List characteristics, natural features,
    Available cover to safeguard retreat.
    A long fir tree plantation, heather handy for hide-outs.
    Odd birch trees give bearings and pinpoint the place.
    A house by the forest, the best of grid references,
    Smoke from a chimney, the first one for miles.

Scotland, darling. Caledonia, stern and wild. A smiling refuge on the edge of the moors: what the Scots call a policy. A patch of order. Peace amid the wildness of nature. Straight out of John Buchan. The moors baking in the sun of a pre-war summer. A line of beaters advance through the heather, as a single plane climbs slowly in the empty sky and a black car waits at the cross-roads. There is a crashing among the trees and a young man stumbles into the garden, incongruously dressed in a crumpled city suit. 'I say, you look about all in.' The young man eyes them warily. Who are they, this couple? They look ordinary enough. A country doctor perhaps. A retired professor and his wife. Dotty he decides, but harmless, and soon he is tackling a goodly meal of ham and eggs and fresh-baked bread, washed down with lashings of strong tea. In the spotless cottage kitchen he tucks in with a will, not knowing that elsewhere in the house a telephone call is being made. Did the young man but turn his head he would see beaters filtering through the wood as the black car creeps slowly up from the cross-roads. It is a trap, this haven: the place where they had meant him to end up all along. Or a reservoir, property of the East Midlands Water Board. That's where they plant forests like this. To cover something up. A blanket round dumps. Camps. An official forest.

Bron goes out.
    Hilary gets up and looks across the garden, singing another snatch of the same hymn:

'Ransomed, healed, restored, forgiven,
Who like me his praise should sing?'

(*He waves.*) Hello! Where've you been hiding yourself? You're quite a stranger. Nothing amiss, I hope? I was just wondering whether I dare venture forth. Doesn't look too promising, does it? Best not go too far afield. Still it's what

we need: the dahlias are dying on their feet. However.
Soldier on. Don't work too hard.

Bron comes back with three ties.
Hilary takes one, changes his mind and takes another
instead, say a Garrick Club tie.
Pause.

If one was a drunkard and one's name was Johnny Walker
one could form a society called Alcoholics Eponymous. Or
if there were two of you called Johnny Walker, Alcoholics
Synonymous. However.

Bron Are you going to be sitting around here all morning?

Pause.

What happened to your walk?

Hilary shrugs.
Pause.

Can't keep up with you. Five minutes ago you were
bubbling over.

Hilary Well now I've bubbled over.

Bron Pity you couldn't save it.

Hilary Save what?

Bron The bubbling over. Been bubbling over when they
were here and bubbled over after they'd gone. Or be like
me. Always at Gas Mark One.

Hilary And nothing in the oven. (*He stands up and*
stretches.) Oven/haven, given/Devon, leaven/lumpen, open/
heaven. Where do birds go when they fly across the sky?

Bron You've got birds on the brain.

Hilary Not all birds of course. Some just float around the
sky not doing anything in particular. But look, that one.

(*He hands Bron some binoculars.*) That's quite definitely off on an errand. It's got up early, done its stint in the dawn chorus, looked at its wrist watch and set off somewhere. Now where? I think it's late for an appointment with the headmaster of a good comprehensive school that might possibly be persuaded to admit its child on the strength of its slight proficiency on the cello and the prominence of its father in the field of communications. Whereas that one, flying round and round in seemingly aimless circles, is in some agitation over the proposed demolition of several quite pleasant, though not architecturally outstanding Victorian villas in order to make room for some old people's flats. Themselves an outmoded social concept. However. Do you know what that is . . . birds with wrist watches?

Bron Yes. Tripe.

Hilary The Pathetic Fallacy. The idea that animals behave as we do. Or feel at all. We have visitors.

Bron Already?

Hilary Other visitors. (*He is looking through the binoculars.*) Your friend.

> *Hilary hands Bron the binoculars. Hilary's movements should now be swift and precise. Both are getting ready quickly, removing any sign that they have been there very recently.*

Were a person to cut across the field to the trees that person could be seen instantly from the track.

Bron I can't. I can't.

Hilary Except if that person or persons were to wait until the last moment when the car has come through the gate and is coming round the back of the house there would be just enough time to reach the wood before they came in.

(*He opens the drawer of the table and takes out a revolver.*) The car has stopped by the gate. Eric is getting out to open it.

Hilary and Bron are now crouching down by the verandah steps. It ought to be tense and comic.

Bron I like him.

Hilary I like him.

Bron She's all right.

Hilary He's back in the car. She is a bleak bitch. They're just coming up to the corner. They are out of sight . . . NOW.

They both dash down the verandah steps across the garden. Pause. Sound of a car door slamming, twice.

Eric's Voice Hello.

Eric comes on. He is in his late twenties, a rather weak good looking young man. His wife Olga is older, has a faint mid-European accent, plainly dressed. Ankle socks.

Eric Knock knock. Got a visitor.

Olga comes on very slowly and stands waiting.

Don't say they're not here. No.

Olga sees the rocking-chair is still faintly rocking. She looks at Eric. He hasn't seen it. She stops it, without him noticing. She looks across the garden.

The car's here. They can't have gone far.

Olga What do you want to do?

Eric I don't know. What do you want to do?

Pause.

These chairs are nice. I always liked these chairs.

Olga What do you want to do?

Eric I said they're nice chairs. Do you like them? The chairs. Yes or no?

Olga Why?

Olga sits down. Eric gets up and looks in one of the rooms offstage.

Eric (*off*) Our place isn't like this?

Olga You don't have any books.

Eric Besides books. The things. Bits of wood. Things they find on walks. Pebbles. Bits of glass. Bones. (*He walks round touching objects, looking at books, meddling.*)

Olga The contents of a schoolboy's pocket.

Eric Treasures.

Olga We pick flowers.

Eric Bluebells! Kids pick flowers. That's nothing. She picks weeds. That's art. I could have done art. It was an option. Art or mechanical drawing. Trigonometry. You never hear of that now. Not that it was ever big news.

Olga We could call coming back.

Eric Who else do I see? I like them. Why don't you go on?

Olga What happens to your picnic?

Eric *My* picnic is it now? It was you that suggested it.

Olga You wanted to go. You behave like a child. We could wait all day. They are not here. Come on.

Eric No

Olga Why?

Eric What's wrong with just sitting. I like just sitting. I had two years on and off just sitting. Looking out. Allotments. Trucks shunted past. My personal piece of sky. Heaven.

Pause.

What could you see?

Olga Where?

Eric In prison, *dear*. Stir. The nick.

Olga If I looked, I could see a wall.

Eric That all? A wall?

Olga That, or the eye in the door. I forget. You should forget. Your little memories. Gosport. Wakefield. Your would-be souvenirs. They all have to be carried. So leave them. They are not important.

Eric That was always the refrain. 'It is not important.' 'Do not worry about it.' The box in the wardrobe, the pit in the floor. The ritual with the bathroom curtains. 'What are you doing?' 'It is not important.' 'Where are you going?' 'Never mind.'

The telephone rings. Eric waits a moment then goes to answer it.

Olga No.

Eric You then.

Olga No.

Eric Why not?

Olga What is it to do with us? Leave it.

Eric sits down and it stops ringing. There is a moment of relief, then it starts to ring again. Hilary comes in rapidly, revolver in hand. He ignores them and goes through into the inner room where the telephone is ringing. As he answers it, it stops. He comes back.

Hilary Sorry.

Eric We weren't sure what to do.

Hilary Well. You have a telephone. Sometimes it rings. It seems to me then that you have a very limited number of choices. I mean, I have been known not to answer the door were someone to call unexpectedly for instance, but I always answer the telephone. You didn't telephone?

Eric We just called on the off-chance. Only you were out.

Hilary Exercise, Eric. Stretching the old legs. Fleeing the spectre of coronary thrombosis.

Olga In your carpet slippers?

Hilary My brogues are at the menders.

Eric Why the gun?

Hilary I have been defending Elgar.

Enter Bron, breathless, with some grasses.

Bron Visitors! Eric! Goodness! Isn't this a surprise? (*She kisses Eric on both cheeks.*) And Olga. Well! Well! (*She shakes hands with Olga.*) Was it anybody?

Hilary It was a reverse charges call. A Mr Joseph Stalin is telephoning you from a Haslemere call box and wishes you to pay for the call. Will you accept the charge?

Hilary is restless, sensing there is something wrong with the room, something out of place. He roams round until he has located the (say) two objects Eric has (very slightly) displaced.

This place is upside down.

Bron Eric, some lemonade?

Eric I'll come.

Bron Stay and entertain Hilary. Olga, you don't, do you?

Bron goes out.

Hilary A lesson to us all. You don't drink. I'm not sure I've ever known you eat. Does she eat, Eric?

Eric Yes. We're just going on a picnic.

Olga Sandwiches in the woods, only.

Eric Well, a *picnic*.

Hilary The most I've ever seen you have is a few sips of water. And that was after a three-hour meeting when us lesser mortals adjourned for lunch. But not your good lady, Eric. She pours herself half a glass of very old water and keeps at it right through the afternoon.

Eric We thought we'd try out one of these specially designated picnic areas. In the forest by the lake. It's all laid out, apparently. There are big tree stumps for tables and little tree stumps for chairs.

Hilary I may be sticking my neck out on this one, but that sounds as if somebody in authority's been using their imagination.

Eric Boats, toilets, music. And it all blends in. What we wondered . . . I suggested . . . if it would be a good idea if . . .

Hilary We made up a foursome, you mean? That's a thought. So far as I know we've nothing on the agenda for today and in principle it sounds a fine idea. Still I'd better put it to the management. Don't want to take a unilateral decision on this one. (*He adjusts something else.*) This room looks as if it's been hit by an earthquake. What's been going on?

Enter Bron.

Bron. Mate o' mine. It appears our young friends are picnic-bound and we oldsters are more than welcome to tag along. What say? We've nothing scheduled have we?

Bron Stop being silly. You know we've got people.

Hilary smacks his forehead in a gesture of absentmindedness.

Hilary Dolt! Cretin! *Deceiver!* My sister Veronica is coming to lunch. Big occasion. The fatted calf. All the trimmings. And not only my sister but her newly knighted husband.

Eric Never mind.

Hilary Always the way. Days, weeks go by and nothing doing then treat jostles with treat.

Eric There'll be other times.

Bron Perhaps you and I could go on one of our little expeditions during the week.

Hilary Hear that, Olga? Little plots being hatched behind the backs of the workers.

Olga You will be pleased to see your relatives?

Bron Oh yes. Particularly Veronica. Her husband's a bit of a stick, but we're quite fond of him.

Hilary What's that, dear?

Bron Duff.

Hilary I don't think you'd like him, Olga. Duff, basically,

is just a nasty green bogey drizzling from the nose of art.
However.

Olga Is she older or younger than you?

Bron Younger.

Hilary Older. No Eric I don't think I'd want to be on the
roads today. Today is one of those days when the people,
God bless them, will be out in force.

Bron Why not?

Hilary Well to be quite candid because one sees quite
enough of them during the week. Come the weekend . . .
and I know this isn't everybody's cup of tea . . . come the
weekend I like to get right away from my fellow man,
plonk the old backside down in a field somewhere, get my
back up against a haystack, close my eyes and sit there
while the skylarks and the thrushes and the bees etc. do
their worst and Dame Nature weaves her healing magic.
That's how I recharge my batteries. You can keep your
leisure centres, your Costa Brava . . .

Bron Chuck it.

Hilary You can help us here, Olga. Before your somewhat
adventitious arrival we were talking, my wife and I, about
the alternative locations for this landscape.

Pause.

Say you had no means of knowing whereabouts you
were, where would you say this was? Eric? A
synonymous place. You are to imagine you have been put
on a train, Olga, your destination something of a
mystery. The train travels day and night for the best part
of a week, finally is shunted into a siding. You try and
see out. It is the middle of the night. Lights nearby.
Loudspeakers. At dawn the doors are slid back and you

fall out on to the platform, look round and see . . . (*He lifts his arms.*) this.

   Pause.

Where would you say you were? Because I would have said Aldershot. Or if not Aldershot exactly, Pirbright. You have the pines.

Bron Spruce in fact.

Hilary Sandy soil. Scrub. Bracken. The odd silver birch. It's the common at Pirbright as seen from the Salisbury train. Or half a dozen places in Hampshire.

Bron Pirbright's in Surrey.

Hilary Aldershot then. Were you ever in Aldershot?

Olga No.

Eric Yes we were. We had a Chinese meal there one Sunday afternoon.

Hilary That sounds as if it could be Aldershot. However, I'm afraid I must love you and leave you. We working girls. Olga, nice to see you in mufti, as it were. Eric be good. And Bronnie, don't keep them too long or they may not get a tree stump. (*He is going.*)

Bron Hilary.

Hilary What?

Bron Take that thing with you. (*She points at the revolver.*)

Hilary No. Put it back where it belongs. It lives in the drawer.

   He goes.

Olga Your husband does not like me.

Eric Olga.

Bron He likes his routine.

Olga He likes his routine. He does not like me.

Eric Olga.

Olga I embarrass you. It is in bad taste to say that. It is without irony. I make you uncomfortable.

Eric You don't even try. She doesn't try. Just be nice.

Olga Nice. Is that nice? The railway train? Was that nice?

Bron Never mind . . .

Eric Let's talk about something else.

Olga I say your husband does not like me and you are embarrassed. Why?

Eric groans.

Eric She was only trying to be nice. You should try to be nice.

Olga These little feelings do not matter. Nice. They belong to the past.

Bron They do matter, don't they? Otherwise everybody ends up feeling terrible. I do.

Eric It's different for Olga. She's had a different upbringing.

Olga It is not my upbringing. I had no upbringing. Feelings like that, feelings about feelings. Putting yourself in another person's place. These are luxuries for which there is no time any more. Making people *feel* better. What is the point in that? It does not last.

Eric Then why bother to tell us? Why not leave us to get on with it?

Olga They are the most embarrassed nation in the world, the English. You cannot look each other in the face. Eric can scarcely look me in the face, my *husband*. Husbands embarrassed by wives, wives embarrassed by husbands. Children by parents. Is there anyone not embarrassed in England? The Queen perhaps. She is not embarrassed. With the rest it's 'I won't make you feel bad so long as you don't make me feel bad'. Then everybody is happy. That is the way it works. That is the social contract. Society is making each other feel better.

Eric We'd better go.

Olga No. Stay. You enjoy it here. Eric likes you. He says you are his only friend.

Eric Olga. Why *say* it?

Olga I say your husband does not like me and you are embarrassed. I say my husband likes you and he is embarrassed. I do not understand it. I will go and sit in the car.

Eric Yes.

Bron No.

Eric Oh God.

Olga Do not hurry. We are not in the least pushed for time. I am not hurt. (*She goes.*)

Eric Clumsy cow. I don't talk about you. Not all the time. I . . .

Bron It doesn't *matter*. It's not important.

Pause. Eric wanders round touching things again. Picking up items.

Eric I wish I read. I want to.

Bron What's stopping you? Take something. He won't mind.

Eric No point.

Bron Then you don't want to read, do you? You just want to want to.

Eric No.

Bron It's like me. I used to think I wanted to leave Hilary. Then I realised I didn't want to. I just wanted to want to.

Pause.

Eric I tell you about Joyce? My sister.

Bron Joyce. No. Why?

Eric I had a letter. She's going in for one of these child care officers. I reckon she's quite brave to be branching out. Thirty-eight.

Bron Is that the one in Leicester?

Eric Nottingham.

Bron The one who's married to the personnel officer.

Eric Labour relations.

Bron That should be interesting.

Eric Apparently local government now you can't go wrong. They're on a sliding scale. Haven't *you* any news?

Bron is still staring after Olga.

Leave her.

Bron Hilary's father's in the bin again.

Eric Is that bad?

Bron Belsize Park.

Eric They're generally on the outskirts somewhere.

Bron What?

Eric Homes.

Bron Belsize Park is London.

Eric Belsize Park? It sounds like a country house.

Bron I suppose it was once. Robin's come out of the army.

Eric He the good-looking one?

Bron He doesn't know what he wants to do. He wondered about starting a safari park. He's got someone to put up the money but I think they may be going out now, safari parks. What do you think?

Eric I've only been to one and the animals were all asleep. It's the same as a cage only bigger: they'll soon know it inside out.

Bron Zoos seem to be full of people staring at animals that hail from the same countries as they do. Africans, Japanese. It's as if they've gone to the zoo because it's where they're sure to find a familiar face. Friends who just happen to be living abroad.

Eric Japan doesn't have any special animals though, does it?

Bron Doesn't it? I don't know.

Eric I wish I could see them.

Bron Who?

Eric Your visitors. I wouldn't talk. I wouldn't show you up.

Bron Eric.

Eric I'd keep out of sight.

Bron Peep through the bannisters.

Eric They've no need to see her.

Bron You're all she's got.

Eric What're they like?

Bron Not sure now. What are we like now? The same. Or even more the same. That's the difference.

Eric Maybe they could put a word in for me?

Bron I wrote. You know I wrote.

Eric But maybe if I met them. She might like me. Feel sorry for me. You like me. I'm good at making people like me.

Bron I'll see.

Eric So can I stay?

Bron Eric. You shouldn't ask. It's family. It's not fair on them.

Eric Why? Because I'm just a draughtsman from Portsmouth Dockyard. The sort of people you're reduced to.

Bron Eric. They're coming all this way to see us.

Eric Skip it. It will be boiling in the car because she won't have opened the windows. She won't even have noticed. It's not important. She sweats. There's no excuse for that, is there. Nowadays. I've told her. That's not important either. Because she once had it much worse nothing else counts. You'd think it might make her jump at all the little things. Perms, lipstick. Frocks. No. It's not important.

Hilary begins to play the piano offstage. It is the same hymn, 'Praise, my soul, the King of Heaven'.

Anyway, I'd better go for this picnic.

Bron Stay a bit longer. Go on.

Eric I wish she was dead. I wish I could go out to the car now and find her dead. That would be a real picnic.

Bron Eric.

Eric goes as Hilary begins to sing the words of the hymn.

Hilary (*off*)
'Praise him for his grace and favour,
To our fathers in distress.'

Bron Hilary.

Hilary (*off*)
'Praise Him still the same as ever,
Slow to chide and . . .'

Bron *Hilary*.

Hilary stops and comes on.

What gives you the right to be so bloody condescending?

Hilary Did you know they've scrapped the Holy Communion? They're experimenting with something called Series 1, Series 2 and Series 3. That doesn't sound like the Eucharist to me. That sounds like baseball.

Bron Who are we?

Hilary I am a snob. We know that.

Bron He likes you.

Hilary I imagine when it comes to the next prayer book they won't write He, meaning Him with a capital H. God will be written in the lower case to banish any lurking sense of inferiority his worshippers might feel.

Pause.

The C. of E. was my first love. Until the age of sixteen I had every intention of going into the ministry.

Bron Saved everybody a lot of trouble if you had.

Hilary Had I chosen orders I would have been a bishop by now.

Bron She's a lonely woman. What pass do you flip to allow you to behave like that?

Hilary One of the few lessons I have learned in life is that there is invariably something odd about women who wear ankle socks. Olga. Four letters. Anagrams Gaol and Goal. Eric. Rice. A pale flavourless substance consisting of millions of seemingly identical grains.

Bron He's just a lost boy.

Hilary This isn't Never Never Land.

Bron You could pretend. For half an hour.

Hilary I appreciate Olga has seen things she cannot forget. What is tiresome is that she will not let anyone else forget that she can't forget them. I get it every day at the office. They're a dismal couple and I see no reason why I should have them in my house.

Bron Your house. This *shack*.

Hilary My house. My country home. A doting frump with her silly little copper's nark of a husband. Who is he? A common criminal. What is she? A woman to whom the past is simply misery and horror. Not surprising she can't wait to get to the future. We have nothing in common at all.

Bron (*without emotion*) Except the one thing. You're all traitors.

Hilary goes and puts a record on the turntable and comes back. The next speech is over the slow introduction to a very grand Strauss waltz.

Hilary Considering this taunt was quite deserved and in substance true, he thought he kept his temper very well. The easiest accusations to bear are, after all, the ones of which one is innocent. To be accused of something of which one is guilty, that is the intolerable thing. Though I use guilt to mean responsibility. Not guilt. However.

Bron Your whole life is on the other side of the glass. And there is nobody watching.

Hilary If the past is anything to go by, we would normally sulk for the rest of the day. Then towards evening we'd make it up, get drunk and dance. But we haven't all day and we can't get drunk until the company comes so . . . come on, old lady.

Hilary and Bron dance immaculately, in best ballroom fashion. Occasionally he shouts instructions or the time. 'Two, three and turn. Two, three and reverse.'
He is also very easily puffed and almost has to stop and fight for breath, but goes on.
Bron stops suddenly. Listens. Goes to the gramophone and stops it. Listens again.
There is the sound of a car door. Voices off.

Bron I am terrified.

They wait.
Veronica, a slim, very chic lady comes on slowly, picking her way with a fixed smile, not sure whether she's come to the right place. Duff, her somewhat stouter husband, bringing up the rear.

Veronica Bron! Oh Bronnie, darling! Hugs, darling. Hugs, hugs, hugs. Such hugs.

Bron You found us, then?

Veronica And Hilary. Hilary. You look *well*. Doesn't he look well?

Bron Dear Duff!

Duff kisses Bron.

Veronica So trim. And so young.

Hilary holds out his hand.

Duff Put that careful hand away. We too shall kiss. And kiss properly. See, Veronica, the great man blushes. My dear, it is accepted now. Men can kiss. And remain men.

Hilary No, they kiss here too. No . . . I . . . we are very happy to see you.

Bron Oh yes. *Yes.*

Hilary Welcome to the Forest of Arden.

A slightly awkward pause.

Veronica This is heaven, Bron. Do admit. A Wendy House. And here you both are. Looking so young. Children.

Hilary You found it all right?

Duff We came in an embassy car. They seemed to know exactly where it was.

Hilary That's not surprising.

Veronica Darling. Is there somewhere I could wash my hands?

Bron You want to 'freshen up'. Then let me show you 'the geography of the house.'

They laugh.

Oh the heaven of jokes. That's our little garden.

Veronica Sweet. Duff. Look. The garden.

Duff The English garden.

Bron We'll go through.

Veronica (*off*) So cool here. Moscow was *boiling*.

Duff You live here in the summer? Charming.

Hilary It's hardly Hookham.

Duff Your books. A garden. Some distant prospect. *Dieser kleine Pavillon*. Paradise. How very clever of you. (*He mouths.*) Are we overheard?

Hilary Sorry?

Duff mimes someone listening.

Here? No. Why, what do you want to say?

Duff Nothing. Nothing. *Nothing.* Anyway, Hookham is now a diocesan conference centre. It's wild with bishops.

Hilary So I'm told.

Duff They've put in a sauna bath. What do bishops want with a sauna bath? You look *so* well.

Hilary Flourishing. Flourishing.

Duff Thoreau. A second Walden. The great, good place. How enviable. Listen to that silence! Delicious.

Hilary What are you lecturing about?

Duff Lecturing, lecturing? Lecturing?

Hilary I thought you were in Moscow to give a lecture?

Duff Oh *lecturing*! Forster. Forster. For my sins. And for my supper. For my sins and for my supper.

Hilary He died, I gather. Forster.

Duff I rather think so, yes. Yes, he's gone at last. That mild but steady glow put out. I was at the funeral. But not *Passage. To India.* My lecture. Not the evils, say rather the indignities of colonialism. That is what they are expecting but no. *Howards End.* I shall run up the flag of personal relations for ever and ever. That should set the cat among the pigeons. Beard the Wilcox in his den, be it Stock Exchange or Palace of Culture.

Hilary That's bold. I've got a first edition of it somewhere. (*Begins to look.*) I'm not sure it's not inscribed.

Duff Only connect, comrades. Only connect.

Hilary I never quite understood what that meant.

Duff Neither did I. But it is not important. It's all the things it might mean, the penumbra of half meanings, the nimbus of uncertainty. That's its power.

Hilary I don't know what it means at all.

Duff What do all such enjoinders mean? 'Grace under pressure.' 'Be generous and delicate and pursue the prize.' 'Only connect.' Forster. Hemingway. Henry James. All add up to the same thing. Be nice. Behave, or people won't like you. Neo-platonism diluted. The farewell at the mouth of the cave. Remember, be nice!

Hilary finds a copy and hands it to Duff who looks at it.

Hilary Cambridge.

Duff Cambridge. Love. Life.

Hilary I was waiting for you to admire our trees.

Duff Yes. Yes. I do.

Hilary Spruce, apparently.

Duff Indeed? And what happens beyond the trees?

Hilary 'Beyond the wild wood comes the wide world.'

Duff The freedom of the fields, the shelter of the woods. *Un vrai paysage moralisé.*

Hilary I must apologise for the birds. They do not do their stint so far as singing is concerned. When you consider most of them are only here for the summer, that winter finds them in Bournemouth, or even Amersham, it really is rather unfair. *I'd* sing.

Duff You're not happy?

Hilary Did I say that?

Duff Are you happy?

Hilary Well, Duff, shall I put it like this. I'm not sorry it's not Surrey.

Duff Yes. I see. The real tragedy with us lately has been the loss of the elm. Practically every single elm has gone.

Hilary Does that make a difference?

Duff A vast difference. We are only now starting to count the cost. Wiltshire is a wilderness. A spokesman in the Department was telling me that upwards of nine million trees have perished. One of the most characteristic elements of the English landscape cancelled out. A gap in nature. Constable. Cotman, Crome now documents. Invaluable evidence of the countryside as it was ten, even five years ago. The loss of an inheritance.

> 'Felled, felled, all felled.
> After comers cannot guess the beauty been.'

Hilary I'm sorry.

Duff *'Nous n'irons plus au bois. Les lauriers sont coupés.'*

Hilary I wonder what those girls can be up to?

Duff It is sad to find oneself so often striking the elegiac note when one is by temperament and inclination a modernist. One's whole nature yearns towards the new yet time and time again one finds oneself averting one's eyes from evidences of modernity. Pain. Pain. Too much pain. One thinks of Bath. Northampton. Leeds. Worcester. I too am an exile, and in my own country. From my own time. You should see Glasgow, that Grecian place. Edinburgh. And dear, dear Brighton. How much better off you are, Hilary. Amputated. Cut clean. Not to see the slow death of friends. And as the monuments, so I fear the institutions.

Hilary Yes. I was reading the other day that Lyons were closing down the teashops. That does seem to me to be scandalous. Where will people go?

Duff I don't know. I do not know. You must be rubbing your hands.

Hilary At the death of the teashop? No.

Duff All part of the prescribed withering away. Only what you've been tell us to expect.

Hilary Me, Duff?

Duff History delivering the goods.

Hilary Not me.

Duff Your team.

Hilary On the contrary the nice things about my people . . . how quaint to call them a team . . . is that they're very old-fashioned. Not at all forward looking. And whatever their shortcomings in point of the liberty of the subject very litter-conscious. Do I want the old place to change? I don't think so. I have left it. It must stay the same or there is no point in having come away. I certainly don't want things to improve. Though I remain, of course, firmly in two minds. Whereas ideologically I must count every sign of decay an improvement, so my personal inclination is to think of every improvement as decay. Certainly where the end of Lyons is concerned. Was that presented as an improvement? I imagine so.

Duff I forget. But it is paradoxical that it is the socialist regimes which are so bent on demolishing the institutions of the past that are the most scrupulous guardians of its monuments. One thinks of Dresden, doesn't one (every stone restored). Die Altstaddte: Prague, Warsaw. A hint of aspic. But does that matter? They remain. They survive.

Hilary Moscow, you can take tea on every street corner.

Duff The fact is, at this moment in our history I fear we flounder. And if one were asked, as indeed all too often one is asked (conferences, think-tanks, round-ups at the year's end) the inevitable question: 'Diagnose our predicament' 'Sort out some symptoms' 'Pin-point the problem' 'Name the culprit' (Ah ha!) In a word 'What's Up?' Then lamely I say that in the people I come into contact with . . . last week in Wiltshire, man laying us new cobbles, a genuine craftsman, stalwart figure (minded of Hardy) thirty-five, two children, set up on his own, £90 a week, doing very nicely thank you . . . *and no bad barometer* . . . in such people again and again one comes on this settled conviction that *things will turn out all right in the end*. And this conviction, this *common* sense not so different from the official philosophy here that, leave history to itself and one way or another all the eggs are going to end up in your basket.

> *While Duff has been talking he has been going round the room, looking at books, picking up objects and replacing them.*

Hilary (*pause*) What I think I would say, Duff, is this: people are the same the world over.

Duff (*sagely*) Absolutely.

Hilary rights the books and objects Duff has disturbed.

Hilary Of course the service is bad here. But then it always has been. Apparently one waited an age in a restaurant even under the Tsars. Nothing has changed.

Duff Quite. And do we differ? Not fundamentally. Because slow lane, fast lane, we all of us seem to be headed in the same direction. Where? Well, in the general direction of the millennium. But remember, no goals or grand arrivals. No end in sight. No fullness of time. Just dribbling along. Stop, go. Carriages in a siding. Shunted along, middle of the night. Where are we? Never mind. We're en route for the millennium. Not that we'll see it. The millennium's a place to go to not arrive at. Millenniums mean murder. Trials in football stadiums. Babies on bayonets and poets in prison, indignities offered ambassadors' wives. No. Amelioration. Improvement. As here. Not the best. Too soon for the best. Slow but sure. Slow but share. World wide amelioration. (*He winces.*) I'm being bitten.

Hilary Really? It's funny, they don't bite me.

Enter Veronica and Bron, giggling.

Veronica I'm just saying to Bronnie one of the delights of Moscow is that young men keep sidling up to Duff and saying 'Have you any jeans?' I mean Duff! Jeans! I shriek.

Duff In point of fact, Veronica, I have a pair of jeans.

Veronica Never. Oh yes, you do. They're a sort of tinned salmon colour. He bought them at Simpsons for when he does Saturday shopping down St John's Wood High Street.

Duff I'm not a complete fool, you know.

Veronica Listen, I haven't given you your stocking. (*She gets a bag.*)

Hilary How's Father?

Veronica Pa? Marvellous. Tip-top. What's this? Oh, the garlic crusher. (Is that the sort you wanted?) Gentlemen's Relish.

Bron Heaven. Two pots.

Veronica Your hymns record. King's College Chapel.

Bron Oh God.

Veronica Crossword puzzles.

Bron Bath Olivers.

Veronica The last Anthony Powell.

Duff I'm told it's very good. I think he's probably brought it off.

Veronica A *Times*.

Hilary I see that at work.

Veronica No. Pa is marvellous. Never better. Can't see him pegging out for years yet. He thrives.

Hilary He always does in the bin. Ordering everybody about. It's like old times.

Veronica Like, duck? It *is*. He's so confused. He thinks Ma is still alive, Duncan and Frank. Gussie with her bugle. Dozens from the trenches. All there. It's just like a wonderful cocktail party. No distinction of age, creed or class. Everybody.

Hilary The resurrection.

Bron The open society.

Duff It's actually a form of arteriosclerosis.

Hilary Now, how about a drop of the old nail varnish?

Veronica Whisky for me. I won't venture to say Scotch.

Hilary Duff?

Duff Not for me.

Hilary Oh.

Duff With the meal perhaps. Now, no.

Hilary Duff tells me Lyons have closed all their tea shops.

Duff I didn't tell you. You told me.

Hilary Where on earth do you go for a cup of tea now?

Veronica One seems to manage.

Hilary The nice thing about Lyons was that they cropped up at such regular intervals. Rather like lavatories in that respect. I suppose one could have spent the day hopping from Lyons to lav and lav to Lyons all the way across London. If one was so minded. But not any more. However. They still have lavs?

Duff Yes.

Hilary That's a relief.

Bron Here they're in rather short supply. One does tend to see people doing it in corners.

Hilary Only if you look. She looks.

Veronica I saw somebody peeing in Jermyn Street the other day. I thought, Is this the end of civilisation as we know it? Or is it simply somebody peeing in Jermyn Street?

Hilary And did you come to any decision on that?

Veronica No. But I saw a rat in St James's the next day. That seemed somehow an omen. These things add up.

Duff Well! Here we are. A country house. Wine. Talk. Friends.

Veronica Summer days.

Duff They seem to persist. Country houses. By dint of the turnstile. We open our gardens twice a year.

Veronica Rhododendrons are our strong suit. A riot of colour.

Hilary No kangaroos?

Duff Staff are prohibitive. Still, open prisons, homes for the aged, management training centres . . . museums or menageries they survive.

Hilary They must. The Big House as nutshell, the novelist's venue. Lose that and what happens to the detective story? On the sunlit lawn the empty rug, the open book and the faintly rocking chair compose a setting from which someone has suddenly departed, leaving a thriller open at the point where on a sunlit lawn the empty rug and the open book and the chair faintly rocking indicate someone has suddenly departed.

Bron (*quickly*) We haven't congratulated you.

Duff What on?

Bron *Sir* Hector.

Duff Hardly a surprise. One's definite due.

Veronica If you ask me, it's just a sharp nudge in the direction of the grave.

Hilary Well done thou good and faithful servant.

Duff Nobody more so. They search the ranks for someone

still fit for hard labour and I curse my stature that singles me out. Oh let me not be named, I think, when some fresh commission is mooted. Not me. Then comes the call. You, sir! Fall out! So chained and marched away. Another sentence to run concurrently with the others. Another room to sit in all those slow afternoons. Carafe and tumbler, blotter and sharpened pencils . . . the instruments of my martyrdom. Still, it is what I have to do. *Ich kann nicht anders.* But pity me. (*He raises his hands in a gesture of martyrdom and blessing.*) Pity my poor prickling piles. I am unfree. A slave. I am a servant at Liberty Hall.

Veronica What exactly do you do, darling? Or should I know better than to ask? Except you always knew better than to tell me.

Hilary Very dull. I have an office. I translate. My advice is occasionally asked and ignored. Not very different from the Foreign Office. However. Why is working for the party like a mushroom?

Veronica Why?

Hilary Because you're kept in the dark and every so often someone comes and throws a bucket of shit over you.

Veronica Actually I'd heard that, only in my version it was the BBC.

Hilary What are you writing down?

Duff I want to . . . just make a note of that . . . joke . . . I never remember jokes. Excellent memory for facts. But jokes just do not seem to stick. Why is that? Mushroom was it? And of course one does need them. Jokes. Very handy with the young. One must count oneself fortunate in numbering among one's acquaintance several Young People, whose intellectual and spiritual restlessness I find salutary. I come away refreshed. Invigorated. And they in their turn, feel that the world of decisions has a human face if only because they see it over a glass of beer.

Veronica Beer!

Duff The place where I find these contacts stand me in unexpectedly good stead is in Whitehall, of all places. *Dans les coulisses*. Royal Commissions, Arts Council, grant allocations and so on. One can be sitting there with a group of well-disposed people . . . intelligent, informed and above all *concerned*. The suggestion is that such and such a proposal will benefit young people. But will it benefit Stephen, the hospital porter? How will Trevor, a counter assistant at Dickins and Jones, fit into the scheme or Fiona, his girlfriend? And I'm afraid the answer I come up with is often very different from that of my esteemed colleagues. The result is I'm getting a name as a bit of a maverick. Duff, they say, Duff is *difficile*. But I must live with that. What I think is vitally important is not to let the young assume that middle age must necessarily mean the middle ground. There can still be jokes. Adventures. Irreverence. (*To himself as he writes.*) A bucket of shit. Good. Good.

Bron We don't see many young people.

Hilary Eric? Olga? Called only this morning, wanting us to bathe. We can bathe. Or stroll in these commodious woods. Tea under the trees. Every facility.

Veronica People call? Here?

Hilary All the time.

Bron They're a sad couple. He was the clerk in the dockyard at Portsmouth, though she was the real brains. When they swapped her she insisted on him being part of the package. Rather touching. I should feel very Hampstead bathing now. The Ladies Pond. My bathing days are done.

Hilary Do old gentlemen still hurl themselves into the Serpentine on Boxing Day?

Veronica No. That went out with Pathé News.

Duff As I understand it, bathing is now considered distinctly therapeutic. We've got some of our chronic arthritis people into the baths at the Middlesex Hospital and they go splashing around like two-year-olds.

Hilary takes the revolver out of the drawer.

Hilary Best bathing I ever had was in the war. North Africa. (*He takes aim at something across the verandah on the edge of the garden.*) Did you ever fly in a Sunderland? The old flying boats. (Don't move, sweetheart. That's beautiful.) Flew from Gibraltar to Crete in one once, during the war. (Head up a fraction.) Came down in the drink just off the coast of Tripoli. Engine trouble. (To your right a bit, darling.)

Bron Oh, leave it, Hilary, leave it.

Hilary Shut up. We sat on top of the water, opposite a brilliant white shore.

Duff has been getting quite nervous and stands up.

Sit down, man, for God's sake.

(*He puts the gun down.*) Bugger. We just slipped down into the sea and swam ashore. It was perfect.

Veronica The Mediterranean? Not any more, dear. It's the Elsan of Europe. And we tried Tripoli two years ago. It's the Costa del Tesco.

Duff The image of soldiers bathing has a long history in art. Does Berenson have an essay on that? Those armed and flexed for war, now relaxed, vulnerable. At rest.

Hilary It's my opinion, for what it's worth, that Berenson was a bit of an arsehole. Don't you agree?

Duff Oh . . . yes. On balance, I think, probably, yes.

Hilary An ancient American arsehole that anybody who was anybody had to stop and lick if they happened to be passing through Florence. Did you ever go?

Duff I believe we may have called once – purely out of politeness.

Hilary I didn't. I wasn't famous enough then. I could go now, of course, if he were alive. Now that I'm something of a celebrity. Instead people come and see me. Berenson at I Tatti, Max at Rapallo, Willie at Cap Ferrat. Me here.

Bron Except you're not an artist.

Hilary And always in the background some capable lady of either sex, tucking in the rugs, censuring his utterance, presenting the old boy to the world. Protecting him. Rationing him. The great man. Life is short. Art is long. Breakfast is prompt at eight o'clock.

> *Hilary suddenly brings up the revolver and fires. It should not be a loud noise. One of those long revolvers fitted with a silencer.*
>   *Bron goes.*

Jolly good.
   This is when I miss Shep. (*He goes.*)

Veronica Help! Help! Help!

Duff Nonsense. Running pretty true to form. Tiresome, but not more so than one remembered. Nice books. (*He wanders round the room, absorbed in its contents.*)

Veronica They're both so old. Aren't they?

Duff Oh *very* nice. I thought Bron was looking a bit *desséchée*.

Veronica She had a little cry upstairs.

Duff Such a slum. What about?

Veronica What about? The Scotch for a start. It's Jeyes Fluid. I would go mad. All this unnecessary countryside.

Duff It's true he was never overly rustic.

Veronica She'd come back like a shot. Have you said anything to him?

Duff Pretty. Very pretty. Wasted here.

Veronica The old fraud.

Duff And mostly first editions. You think he's being lazy, it's then he's working hardest. Suspect him and his fidelity will put you to shame. Trust him and he instantly betrays you. What sort of man is that?

Veronica Lyons! He never went into Lyons in his life.

Duff Are you sure?

Veronica I am his sister. And what about that gun?

Duff That's all silly. So silly. Still he seems not to go at the drink now.

Veronica I've been waiting for someone to say that about Berenson for years.

Duff It was actually a very ill-informed remark. Berenson was art-historian first and sage second. He didn't seek society. Society sought him. His exile was not less fruitful for being populous. Whereas who comes here?

Veronica You, for one. Look out. Home is the hunter!

Hilary enters with a dead hare, which he holds up by the ears.

Hilary Isn't he a beauty! Take him. Go on.

Duff No.

Hilary Why? He's dead.

Duff I know he's dead.

Veronica Darling, it's only a rabbit.

Hilary It's not. It's a hare.

Veronica I've always thought hares were simply rabbits writ large.

Hilary Not at all. They're quite far apart in the evolutionary chain. Further apart than a dog and a fox for instance, which are likewise deceptively similar. Rabbits are gregarious, slow-moving, leading a rich, underground life. Hares are swift, solitary, creatures of the open field. (*He waves the hare at Duff.*)

Duff NO!

Veronica Hilary, behave! Acting the fool!

Duff There's blood on my face.

Veronica It's only the tiniest spot. Oh and another bit here.

Hilary Sorry. Sorry. Should I apologize to Duff?

Duff Don't be absurd.

Veronica Yes.

Hilary Duff. I apologize.

Veronica I should think so too. There. All gone. What are we having for lunch?

Hilary Rabbit.

Duff Not this one?

Hilary Duff, how many more times? This is a hare. We shall have to hang you a while, won't we?

Bron (*voice off*) Food!

Duff We've had a big best seller about rabbits. Good rabbits and bad rabbits. I haven't got round to it yet. I suspect the presence of allegory, which is always a slight deterrent. Shall I stagger in? Rabbits are coming back in England now. (*He goes.*) Myxomatosis or no myxomatosis.

> *Hilary goes off with Duff carrying his record. Veronica remains, smoking.*
> *Hilary returns as a hymn begins on the gramophone.*

Hilary One advantage of living in Russia is that it's one of the few places where smoking doesn't cause cancer. At least the authorities don't say it does, so one must presume it doesn't.

Veronica Are you happy?

Hilary Why does everybody keep asking me that? No. I'm not happy. But I'm not un-happy about it. However.

> *Veronica goes.*
> *Hilary lifts the hare to show it to the watcher in the garden.*

Rather good, don't you think. Just bagged him. Bonny creatures. Still. One has to live. Popping in for a spot of lunch now. Old friends from way back. Broach a few bottles of the old vino rosso, have a natter about old times. Cheers.

> *Hilary goes off, the music continuing, as Bron enters*

with a tray. She lifts it high to show it to whoever is watching in the garden and just before she does so the music cuts out as Hilary takes the record off inside the house. Bron puts the tray down on the top step of the verandah and goes off.

    Curtain

Act Two

Bron and Veronica are talking. It is after lunch.

Veronica Such a pretty garden. Such a pretty house.

Bron We love it.

Veronica It is a knack. Making the place cosy. Newport Street was cosy. Tiny, but cosy.

Bron We nest. The books help.

Veronica Ye-es.

Bron And with the end of summer we walk out of here without even locking the door, come back next spring and nothing will have been touched. Where else in the world could you do that? (*She retrieves the tray with empty plate etc. from the top step of the verandah.*)

Veronica Wiltshire once. Not any more. There are muggers in Malmesbury.

Bron The Hebrides, I suppose. Coll. Tiree. He keeps pretending this is Scotland.

Veronica Heavenly rabbit. Like chicken used to be before they started locking the poor loves up in factories. Do they have those here? Battery farms?

Bron No.

Veronica How very sensible. You are lucky eating so simply. We would, but it's too complicated.

Bron I miss shopping.

Veronica Don't. London is a midden. Every street knee deep in filth.

Bron Moscow is clean.

Veronica Darling, spotless! Are those sweet peas?

Bron Beans.

Veronica How clever. Clever old Bron.

Bron You look younger.

Veronica To tell the truth, I did actually have a tiny op. Took up a bit of the slack. Why not? Free country.

Bron All that couldn't happen quickly enough for me. Getting older. The stroke of fifty I was all set to turn into a wonderful woman. You know what I mean by a wonderful woman.

Veronica Yes. I'm married to one.

Bron The wife to a doctor or a vicar's wife. Chairman of the County Council, a pillar of the W.I. A wise, witty, white-haired old lady, who's always stood on her own feet until one day at the age of eighty she comes out of the County Library and falls under the weight of her improving book, breaks her hip and dies, peacefully, continently and without fuss under a snowy coverlet in the cottage hospital. And coming away from her funeral in a country churchyard on a bright winter's afternoon people say, 'She was a wonderful woman.' That's what I wanted to be. Only here there's nobody to be it for.

Veronica Nobody to be it for anywhere nowadays.

Bron I shall die and they'll still not be able to pronounce my name. Just a coffin waiting on the tarmac to go on the night flight to Heathrow.

Veronica I've a feeling they don't have cottage hospitals now. I'm not even sure about county councils. There was some alteration, Duff was on the commission. Which only leaves the W.I. and that's not what it was. Talks on abortion and new trends in foreplay.

Bron But you need an audience. Character needs an audience or what are you? Here, who's watching?

Veronica Hilary.

Bron Hilary. Hilary is watching Hilary. Watching Hilary.

Veronica As ever.

Bron Slightly better if he were dead. Then I could come home and be his widow. So much more rewarding than being his wife. I wake in the middle of the night thinking: I know what this is: it's happily ever after.

Veronica It's not the place. Think of coming to in Wiltshire, beached beside my chosen piece of matrimonial software. Are we going to walk?

Bron Do you like trees?

Veronica I don't mind.

Bron There's this way. Or that way. East. West. Guermantes. Combray. Either way, trees.

Veronica Yes. They have rather overdone it.

Bron Each one the same height, the same distance from next. Line after line after line.

Veronica Duff's taken up embroidery, did I tell you?

Bron One day our first summer I took a picnic and went along the edge of the trees meaning to reach the corner of the plantation, see what was on the other side. I walked and walked, all day and when I eventually gave up the trees still went on in the same straight line. No break to the horizon. At any point here you might be at any other point. Any time any other time. The leaves don't fall. No spring. No autumn. Nowhere.

Veronica Yes. Well, I wasn't frantic to go. These are hardly the shoes.

Bron The one other place I felt the same was Los Angeles.

Pause.

Veronica Say we were to lure you to London. Any thoughts? Duff (Duff!) thinks it could be arranged. This is death. Come back.

Bron One gets used to it.

Veronica One gets used to it. I used to hate Walton Street until it became all antique shops. Is he happy?

Bron He never imagined he would have to join. Actually rub shoulders. He thought he would carry his secret to the grave.

Veronica The country churchyard. I don't believe it. He's just a tease. He'd have had to tell somebody. That's the way all good teases have to end. What fun. What wonderful lifelong fun. I am not what you all think I am. Just like when one was young and thought one had an inner life. Who's that brute in the garden? Is he watching you or protecting you?

Bron I don't know. I shouldn't think he knows. He's been there all summer.

Veronica The liberty! I'd soon get shot of him.

Bron I'm not sure I want to.

Veronica You should go straight out and say, 'Who is your immediate superior?' then get on the phone, and make a nuisance of yourself. I know it's different here, but it's not. Nag, nag, nag. Nag so much they realise it will be easier to do it than not. There is no other principle involved.

Bron What totalitarian institutions have you dealt with?

Veronica The worst. The North Thames Gas Board. I'd shift him.

Bron At least he's an audience. Watching me gardening, getting up in the morning. Hilary reading, feeding the birds. Like having a tortoise, you can't always spot it. Then you fall over him, asleep in the sun. I like it.

Hilary and Duff come in.

Hilary Did you ever come across Gaitskell?

Duff Many times.

Hilary I only met him once. Nice man. We had a long conversation about . . . hamsters.

Duff Hamsters?

Hilary Yes. Like what? You were saying you liked something.

Bron Here. I like here.

Duff Charming. It's charming. It's a poem.

Pause.

I just want to plant the seed. Take the temperature of the water. That's all I want to do at this moment. That's all I'm empowered to do. I'm not looking for a Yes or a No. I just want to slot the suggestion in at the back of your mind, then we can go on from there. But know that the possibility exists. The door is at least ajar.

Hilary Isn't that nice? So nice. Hear that, Bron. I think that's very . . . nice.

Pause.

Do you know what I've always wanted to do? *Desert Island Discs.*

Duff Well, why not? Why not? I am a governor of the Corporation. One word. The Chairman a personal friend. Bowled over.

Bron Elgar.

Hilary Bron has never liked music.

Bron I do like music. It's the appreciation of it I don't like.

Duff And . . . what is it . . . one book, apart from the Bible and Shakespeare.

Hilary *The Book of Common Prayer.*

Duff Yes! Yes! The last thing anybody would expect.

Bron Of course.

Duff I can't wait. The castaway. The castaway (I do not say prodigal) returned. Riveting.

Hilary Returned? (*Pause.*) I couldn't record it here?

Duff No. I think you'll find it's a studio job. Portland Place.

Hilary Portland Place.

Duff Tube to Oxford Circus.

Hilary The other thought that's been running through my head (you'll laugh at me now) is, 'Come on, Hilary, old boy. I know it's a bit late in the day but why don't you pull the old socks up and do what you've always wanted to do, deep down, namely, have a stab at Art.'

Duff I don't believe it. Veronica. I do not believe it. On the plane. Did I not say?

Veronica Pa does pretty paintings.

Duff We are talking of literature, Veronica, not therapy.

Hilary Art. The ineffable. The role of redeemer. Become an order out of chaos merchant. Novels, poems. A play.

Duff I could place your memoirs tomorrow.

Hilary Telling it all has become so respectable. Dirt. Treachery. Murder. Boys. My dear, who cares?

Duff Oh no. Boys are nothing nowadays. And memoirs make a mint.

Hilary Always at the head of the charts. Always at No 1. American Express, Diners Club. Art trumps them all. It's the other country. Betray anything for that. But not memoirs, quite.

Duff No? Art is memory.

Veronica Down, Proust!

Hilary I can't see yet how far from one's life one has to stand to make it art. You know? At what angle. It's not enough to tell the tale. One's private predicament. One man running naked through Europe.

Duff From a purely commercial point of view almost anything would have a ready sale. Except perhaps poetry. Poetry might be taken to indicate a certain weakening of the intellect.

Hilary Yes. A faint message in morse indicating the ship is sinking. No. It wants to be something more substantial than that. My testament. An edifice standing four square against the winds of dogma. Light streaming from every window. A mansion to which all my life has simply been the drive.

Veronica Or the garden path.

Hilary Is that the way to redeem myself? What do you say, Bron?

Bron Why not? It's where it's all supposed to make sense, isn't it? Death, disappointment. The joyful serenity of Mozart. Wagner's ineffable majesty. Art. I should stick to religion. At least that has no pretensions to immortality any more.

Hilary My wife.

Bron He's not serious, you know. You don't think he's being serious? He doesn't mean a word he says.

Hilary In England we never entirely mean what we say, do we? Do I mean that? Not entirely. And logically it follows that when we say we don't mean what we say, only then are we entirely serious.

Veronica Except we're not in England, darling.

Duff I see England now in grammatical terms almost as a tense, a mood. The optative. Would that this were so. Would it were different. But, of course, that will change. It will be different.

Hilary I am so out of it. Fourteen years. I am a stranger.

Duff Precisely. So who better. You return from exile with a new perspective. So fruitful, exile. But then all writers are exiles here, are they not? Exiles in their own country. Which is where (dare one say it) our friend Solzhenitsyn made his mistake. I'm afraid they were in some sense right: he does want his head examining. Here he was. Grand. Isolated. Attended to. A man as majestic and romantic as Byron. A torch. Drawing all eyes (all eyes that mattered. All *caring* eyes). And he throws it away. Switzerland. Connecticut. He should have stayed put.

Bron And gone to a camp?

Duff My dear Bron. Which is better, five years in a camp or three pages in the *Listener*? Fool. I thought (we had a reception for him at Chatham House). Fool. And a tendency already to button-hole. Sad. A talent betrayed.

Hilary He was never someone one came across. What you are saying . . . let us spell it out . . . he has gone into exile and betrayed his talent. I am to return from exile and fulfil mine. Is that it?

Duff Absolutely.

Hilary There is just one thing. I don't have any.

Duff What?

Hilary Talent.

Duff You are too modest.

Hilary Literary talent. None.

Duff You have a story to tell. You must tell it. My publishers have several very bright young people down from university. Tell it to one of them.

Hilary Isn't that cheating?

Duff Cheating? To tell it to the tape recorder, and let the editor do the rest: my dear, what else is film? There are no categories. Form is in the melting pot. My publishers have brought out several vivid and successful books by an ex-housemaid. Has she talent? Content is what counts. Style can come later.

Bron Don't take away his style or there'll be no content left.

Hilary And where are they, your publishers?

Duff Bedford Square.

Hilary Bedford Square. Is that handy for Portland Place? I suppose it is. No, I don't think so. Not really. Do you? Frankly Duff I don't think I'm cut out for literature. I don't know whatever made you think I was. The real artist confronts the world saying, 'Why am I not immortal?' 'Why am I second-rate?' is not the same question.

Duff My dear, dear man. You can be second rate and still be first class. Carve it above the door of the Slade. The Foreign Office. Oxford. The Treasury. Any institution you care to name. Draw the curtains. Pull up a chair. This is the family. Comfort. Charm. Humour. None of them negligible. What makes life worth living? None of that with jagged dirty genius on the hearthrug. No. The good is better than the best, else what does society mean?

Bron Dear Duff.

Hilary Dear Duff. You are so kind. (*Pause.*)

Veronica And when you bolted was it planned?

Hilary Not a bit. All very much on spec. It was a Friday. I got back to the Foreign Office after lunch to find a note on my desk. It was in a brown, government envelope marked Urgent, underlined and with two exclamation marks. How dare the writer even of a brief note in dramatic circumstances be so confident of my amazement as to add an exclamation mark? And here were two of the buggers! It was a literary reference. *Great Expectations*, it read; then, in parentheses (and somewhat condescendingly), Dickens. Chapter 44. Wemmick's Warning. And another *bloody* exclamation mark. My first thought was, 'Who is this . . . person, this . . . well-wisher, this *friend*, who knows me so little as not to know how cross the medium of this message would make me? To say nothing of the punctuation.

Duff I thought you liked crosswords.

Hilary I do. Provided they are set properly. The easier the crossword, the sloppier the clue. This was a sloppy clue.

Veronica Could you solve it?

Hilary No. We were put to Dickens as children but it never quite took. That unremitting humanity soon had me cheesed off. I prefer Trollope. So on that Friday afternoon I scoured Whitehall for a copy of *Great Expectations* finally running one to earth in the lending library at the Army and Navy Stores. Is that still there?

Duff The Army and Navy? Oh yes.

Hilary The lending library.

Duff No.

Hilary Is there no end to your lunacy? The lending library at the Army and Navy! Senseless.

Veronica And what is Wemmick's warning?

Duff Do not go home. A note left for Pip at the gate of his lodgings and read by the light of the watchman's lantern.

Hilary Do not go home.

Veronica That's straightforward enough.

Hilary On the contrary. It's riddled with ambiguity. Home? Which home? I had three. Hookham, Newport Street or Cadogan Square. I always called Newport Street Newport Street, Cadogan Square Cadogan Square. The only place I had ever called home (because it was where Pa lived) was Hookham.

Veronica So where did you go?

Hilary Hookham.

Bron I was sitting in the garden. I was reading a thriller. I

had just come to an intriguing part when Hilary arrived.
Within ten minutes we had left.

Veronica And who was it tipped you off?

Hilary It could have been anybody.

Duff Anybody brought up on Forster. 'If I had to choose
between betraying my country and betraying my friend I
hope I should have the guts to betray my country.'

Veronica The old boy must have had nice friends. I'd
plump for the old Union Jack any day.

Hilary All that's rubbish anyway.

Duff Hilary.

Hilary Nancy rubbish. You only have to substitute 'my
wife' for 'my friend' to find it's nothing like as noble. 'If I
had to choose between betraying my country and
betraying my wife I hope I should have the guts to betray
my country.' Well . . . yes. I should hope so too. Wouldn't
most people? And put the other way round it's sheer music
hall. 'If I had to choose between betraying my country and
betraying my wife I should betray my wife.' 'Your wife?'
'My wife.' 'Kindly leave the country.' If I had to choose
between betraying my country and betraying my children I
hope I should have the guts to betray my country. *Guts?*
Or. If I had to choose between betraying my country and
betraying . . . my brother-in-law . . . No, you see Duff.
Friend is what does it. My friend. That's what brings in the
cellos. My friend. Who is my friend? My friend is the
memory of the youth half of them were gone on at school.
My friend is True Love as it presents itself the one and
only time in their stunted, little lives in the shape of some
fourteen-year-old tart giving them the glad eye during the
service of Nine Lessons and Carols. And then of course
they did have a choice, if they had but known it. If only in

the matter of a kiss in the long grass behind the sightscreens. A choice between country, which is to say school, headmaster, government, club and class; and fidelity, which is to say friendship, honour, compassion and all the other virtues which, if they were going to get anywhere at all in the world they were going to have to betray anyway.

Bron They? You. Us.

Hilary No. That is their game and I never played it.

Bron But not wives. They never get a look in. Wives are part of the betrayal. Wives are part of the selling-out. Wives are settling for something. Do not go home. Do not settle down. 'Leave for Cape Wrath tonight.'

Veronica And your friend, whoever he was?

Hilary Unknown and unthanked.

Duff He certainly did you a good turn.

Hilary Possibly. Possibly. After all we weren't entirely welcome here either. Like the unlooked for arrival of a distant relative from Australia. Naturally they made the best of it. Kitted us out. Job. Flat. Not unpleasant. But a good turn would you say, Bron? Not entirely.

Veronica So come back.

Duff Let me come clean. There have been several occasions this last year (so different is the atmosphere nowadays) when one or two of us have been sitting around, powers that be in a mood of relaxation when quite independently your name has come up. And people have suddenly started scratching their heads and saying, 'What are we going to do about old Hilary?' You've been stuck here now for what, thirteen, fourteen years. Fourteen years *in partibus infidelium*, and the upshot is, some of us are now prepared to come out and say enough is enough. Now I can't quite say, 'Come home. All is forgiven.' There are still one or two people who feel quite strongly. Time dwindles their number but the fact remains, there were deaths, disappearances. People . . . died. Some of them first class. And I think you will probably be made to stand in the corner for three or four years, five at the outside, which with remission means three, which with parole would probably be two and in one of these open places (I'm on the board of a couple), more hydros than houses of correction. Librarian pushing your trolley round. Rather fun, I would have thought. Then once that's out of the way you can get a little place somewhere. Gloucestershire would be nice, handy for Bath. They've got a delightful festival now . . . and Bristol, the Old Vic, restaurants galore; England's changed since your day, all sorts of places now where you can get a really first-class meal. And financially, of course, no more problems. Television, the Sundays, people falling over themselves. You could even write this book you were talking about. Set up your stall in the open market. I guarantee you'll have plenty of customers. Granted some people are going to turn their backs, but we live in a pluralist society and what does that mean: it means somebody somewhere loves you. What do you say?

Bron You're wasting your time.

Veronica Did you know?

Bron No.

Hilary She never asked.

Bron Because I never dreamed. What had it to do with me? You think your husband is in central heating. You find out he is in refrigerators. A commercial traveller toting his cheap little case of samples round the suburbs. Little appointments. Rickmansworth. Ruislip. Dollis Hill.

Hilary Not Dollis Hill. Never Dollis Hill. I give you Ruislip, Pinner. But not Dollis Hill.

Bron What does it matter?

Hilary My wife has no sense of place. To her one spot is very much like another. It matters to me. It was my rendezvous. The top of my week. My epiphany. But hardly a double life. About as double as yours is double, Duff. The inner life of personal relations. The outer life of anagrams and Ongar. I say Ongar. Ruislip. Meetings at line's ending.

Duff At the station?

Hilary Thereabouts. I used to walk from the station. Always walked. I took my umbrella, strode out into the suburbs and really revelled in it. Priestley, Duff. Wells. A little man on the loose. Past the ideal homes and Green Line bus stops. Factory sportsfields lined with poplars. I was so *happy*. Is it still unloved, that landscape? I loved it. Boarding kennels, down-at-heel riding schools, damp bungalows in wizened orchards. The metropolis tailing off into these forlorn enterprises. And not inappropriate. Had my superiors been blessed with irony I might have thought the setting deliberately chosen to point up the folly of individual endeavour. As it was I grew fond of it. And just as well. Shacks, allotments, dead ground. So many places like that now. Here. Africa. Soon, already, Arabia. Well, it suits me. At home in one you can be at home in them all.

Duff Forgive me, but am I fanciful if I begin to see your defection, say rather your odyssey in terms almost of a choice of *setting*? The heart of the country. The edge of the city. Two worlds. Past. Future. Not difficult to betray your country in so drab a setting for that setting has already betrayed the country you stood for: the house in the park, the church in the trees. No? Well. Possibly not.

Hilary Is it a programme note that you want? Extracts from pertinent texts to point you in the right direction. Shots of the Depression, the upper classes at play. Injustice the impetus, the guilt of one's breeding. Neat. Good intentioned. The best motives gone wrong. Would that find favour?

Duff It's not unfamiliar. The road many took. Though few went so far.

Veronica I always knew you were a big Stalin fan.

Hilary You seem anxious to nudge me into some sort of credo.

Veronica Well what about this mess on the carpet, which we've had to live with for fifteen years? When you've lowered your pinstripes and carefully done your No. 2's right in the middle of the hearth-rug one is entitled to some explanation. It would be nice to think this turd had an infrastructure.

Hilary Talking of credos, do you know that in the latest recension of the creed one doesn't say 'I believe in God' but '*We* believe in God?' I've never heard such vulgar nonsense. The Archbishop of Canterbury should be shot. *We* believe. How am I to know what anyone else believes? But does one have a choice between systems? This mode or that, an institutional best buy? When? At Cambridge? Or before that? The nursery perhaps. (My first taste of an institution that was on the decline.) I don't count the family. I believe that's now suffering from planning blight. Done out of devilment, would that meet with sympathy? To be on one's own. Alone. If for no other reason than to be one's own worst enemy.

Veronica You were always that.

Bron Only just.

Hilary It's quite hard to be absolutely alone. I never have.
Though I have seen it. One particular afternoon I had been
on one of my little jaunts, kept my appointment. Nothing
unusual had occurred or was in the least likely to occur. It
was a routine Thursday and I strolled back to the station
across a piece of waste ground that I knew made a nice
short cut. I must have seemed a slightly incongruous figure
in my city clothes. I never dressed the part, even to the
extent of an old raincoat. At which point I came over the
brow of the hill and found myself facing a line of
policemen, advancing slowly through the undergrowth,
poking in ditches with long sticks, hunting for something.
It appeared there was a child missing, believed dead.
Clothes had been found; a shoe. It was a bad moment. I
had no reason at all for being there. I was a senior official
in the Foreign Office. What was I doing on a spring
afternoon, with documents in my briefcase, crossing a
common where a child had been murdered? As it was no
one thought to ask me any questions at all. I looked too
respectable. And indeed they already had a suspect waiting
handcuffed in the police car. I joined in the search and was
with them when they found the child about half an hour
later, lying in a heap at the foot of a wall. I just got a
glimpse of her legs, white, like mushrooms, before they
threw a blanket over her. She had been dead a week. I saw
the man as the police car drew away through lines of
jeering housewives and people cycling home from work.
Then they threw a blanket over him too. The handy
blanket. And I have a feeling he was eventually hanged.
Anyway it was in those days. I came back, replaced the
documents, had my tea by the fire in the Foreign Office. I
took in some parliamentary questions for the minister, had
dinner at the Garrick and walked home across the park.
And in a tiled room at Uxbridge Police Station there
would have been that young man waiting. Alone in a cell.
Alone in custody. Alone at large. A man without home or

haven. That is what you have to do to be cast out. Murder children. Nothing else quite does the trick, because any other crime will always find you friends. Rape them, kill them and be caught.

Eric enters.

Then there is no refuge, even in prison.

Eric There's a car at the end of the track. They looked at my papers. Has anything happened?

Hilary What sort of car?

Eric Security men. Have they been here?

Bron Here? Nobody's been here.

Hilary Apart from our visitors. This is Eric, Duff. Eric, Veronica. Our young friend.

Eric I'm sorry to spring myself on you. Only Olga wanted to call in.

Hilary Olga? Why? Perhaps we should stroll down.

Bron No.

Hilary Why not? Duff?

Duff I won't, if you don't mind.

Hilary It's always good for a laugh. V?

Veronica I'm game. I'm game for anything.

Hilary and Veronica go.

Bron Where is Olga?

Eric Down there.

Bron I'd better go too.

Bron goes. Duff looks at a book.

Duff Yes. Ye-es. (*Turning decisively into the room.*) Yes.

Eric Have you ever been here before?

Duff No. No, I haven't. I've never had a particular reason. I've never had the *yen*. I suppose if I were pressed for a reason I would have to say that I came to Slavonic art only comparatively recently. Yes. Art. That after all is what tempts us out of doors. Beckons us across the street. Across continents. Greece. Italy. Ceylon. Art is the magnet. That is why I have never been to Jersey. Or the Isle of Man. And very seldom to Wales. One can't see them from here?

Eric No.

Duff The museums here are stuffed with good things. The Impressionists are *staggering*. And most of them, one suspects, wasted.

Eric We've met before.

  Duff smiles.

At home.

Duff At home. And where is that? Home?

Eric Gosport. London.

Duff Gosport. No. I think it unlikely. You have seen my face in the press. I am on the Arts Council, a member of several working parties. Occasionally one creeps into the headlines.

Eric You took me back to your flat.

Duff Lately I have been active in promoting some new form of remuneration for the writers of fiction. The outlook for the novel has never been so bleak. I have no flat. I live in St John's Wood.

Eric You were very nice to me. I stayed the night.

Duff Novels. Poetry. One marvels they get written at all. You spent the night? I don't think so. I have a daughter at Warwick University.

Eric It was in the National Gallery one Sunday afternoon.

Duff Weekends invariably find me in Wiltshire.

Eric I don't understand all that. People trooping round. I never know which pictures to stop at. I end up looking at pictures I've seen pictures of because I think they must be the best.

Duff Why not? Why not? They probably are. Tried. Tested. I propounded a scheme not long ago (rejected solely on grounds of cost) for galleries to print little flags. Stickers. Of the sort . . . Skegness, Luxembourg . . . you see on Dormobile windows. Why not 'The Laughing Cavalier', 'The Hay Wain', 'We have seen the Wallace Collection'. On the lines 'We have seen the lions of Longleat'. We must not be afraid to take art into the market-place.

Eric Have you seen those?

Duff What?

Eric The lions of Longleat?

Duff No. No.

Eric We have. My wife and I. I'm married, too.

Duff Too? You are certainly thinking of someone else.

Eric I had a bit of a moustache then. You were thinner.

Duff One was always thinner.

Eric It was you.

Duff What can be keeping him? One hopes our host hasn't done anything foolish. The art form hardest to justify in cost-benefit terms is of course opera. On the board of the Royal Opera we are very much aware of this. I never go into Covent Garden, which of course I do constantly, without some feeling if not of actual guilt at any rate certainly of it not being entirely fair. Feelings somewhat allayed now that we have introduced our promenade evenings with tickets to fit the pocket of the office worker. The shop assistant. The bank clerk. In a word Young People. To be young, that is the privilege. What is a box at the opera? What is a seat in the stalls? A cushion. Part of the upholstery of life. What it is not is youth. Beauty.

Eric I thought you just wanted a go in the bogs. Instead you took me back and gave me some tea and I spent the evening sat in my underpants looking at *Country Life*. It was really civilised.

Duff That is something I never do, if I want to sleep at night. Look at the back numbers of *Country Life*. The properties. Palaces practically. Sold, for nothing. Ten, even five years ago. Had one but known. No. No. That way madness lies. As for this other I am not sure what is being required. Corroboration, is it? Or nostalgia. Hardly an idyll. And very Angus Wilson.

Eric Who's he?

Duff Angus Wilson is a . . . never mind. Have you the correct time? We have a car coming at five.

Eric It's just that I'd like to come home.

Duff I was warned against blackmail.

Eric Not blackmail. Old times.

Duff It is old times, all that. Cuts no ice nowadays.

Eric You could pull strings. You know people.

Duff What makes you think that? I am virtually a recluse.

Eric No.

Duff A lackey. A mere *fonctionnaire*. We are talking about the Law. Authority. The immutables. Here you are, and here, short of a radical alteration, you will have to stay.

Eric You're just a prick.

Duff I think I hear the party returning.

Eric It's not fair.

Duff It is a distasteful fact but I am fifty-six. You are in Russia. Neither of us can go back. We must both make ourselves at home.

Eric It's not the same.

Duff Why is it not the same?

Eric I don't know. Because . . . it's not my fault I'm here.

Duff Fault. Fault. It's not my fault I'm fifty-six. Time . . . just went. It dribbled away.

Eric You had your life. What have I had?

Duff We must both of us strive after resignation. We all have to be somewhere.

Eric Pisspot.

Enter Veronica.

Veronica I see we've broken the ice.

Duff What precisely is happening?

Veronica Nothing. A black car. Four men in overcoats looking like commissionaires. 'Have you any jeans?' Nothing very ominous at all. They talked to your wife.

Eric They would.

Duff What did Hilary say?

Veronica Big joke. What time is our car coming?

Duff Soon. On schedule. Our friend would like to go with us.

Veronica To Moscow?

Duff Home.

Veronica Why is that?

Duff It appears he is not happy here. He is homesick. I've told him he must buckle to. One can't be flitting about the world just because one isn't happy. One would never be still.

Veronica Anyway you wouldn't recognize London. London's frightful. So smelly. Onions. Fried chicken, that sort of thing. Your wife on the other hand seems at home here. Chatting.

Eric She was at home in Holloway.

Duff Was it Holloway? I know the Governor there. Delightful woman. And a lion in committee. I must find out if they ran across each other.

Eric I was in Wakefield.

Duff Yes. That's quite a small gaol, isn't it? I don't actually know it. I know the bishop. Splendid man. One of these train fanatics.

Hilary enters with Bron.

Hilary I should have been a bishop by now, if I'd taken orders.

Duff What of our friends? Were they forthcoming?

Hilary One gathers it's a routine visitation. In that line of work there's very little that isn't routine.

Veronica Including pulling finger-nails out.

Hilary I think you'd find that's rather old-fashioned. It's curious, isn't it, that whereas the man who gets pleasure out of his job will generally do it better, a torturer who gets pleasure out of it will invariably do it worse. It has to be routine. Though of course I don't believe it happens. Oh. Curiouser and curiouser. He's got a little friend.

Bron Hilary. What is happening?

Hilary We seem to be the object of some attention. Now why is that, Duffy? I hope you've been behaving yourselves.

Duff Our car is coming at five, and we're bidden to the ballet this evening so we have a fairly tight schedule. I must ask you again. As a friend. Will you come back? It isn't an idle question.

Hilary Oh, I thought it was. 'Slot it in at the back of your mind,' you said. However. I have to decide. Come down on one side or the other. And without recourse to irony. Which is not to decide at all but have it both ways. The English speciality. I wonder with the new European vogue that we don't have a referendum on it. Irony, is it a good thing? And on the voting paper two boxes, one to read Yes or No. The other Yes *and* No. The whole thing would have to be held under the auspices of an institution impervious to irony . . . the Egg Marketing Board suggests itself, or the Royal School of Needlework. Except there is the problem: no institution you can name but the choice is tinged with irony. Utterly absent, it is never more present. Irony is inescapable. We're conceived in irony. We float in it from the womb. It's the amniotic fluid. It's the silver sea. It's the waters at their priestlike task washing away guilt and purpose and responsibility. Joking but not joking. Caring but not caring. Serious but not serious.

Duff I am serious. It is serious.

Hilary Bron?

Bron Why ask me?

Hilary Weigh it all up. No Gamages. No Pontings. No more trains from Kemble to Cirencester. No Lyons. On the other hand I read of the renaissance of the small bakery; country breweries revive. Better bread, better beer. They come from Florence to shop in Marks and Spencer. It is not an easy decision.

Bron You never get tired of it, do you? Shoving your arse out of the car window. Pissing on the Cenotaph. Spitting on the graves. People died. And not merely died. Eventually died. Good people. Friends.

Hilary That is true. It isn't altogether fair, but it's true.

Duff (*blandly*) Dear Bron. To talk of guilt in a world where the purchase of an orange, for instance, is fraught with implications . . . the endorsement of tyranny, the sweating of labour . . . to talk of guilt in a world where the individual is incapable of calculating the economic consequence of his simplest action . . . is to talk of the air we breathe. Yes. There are germs in the air. Microbes. But how should they be eliminated? And if they should be, would we find ourselves to have been dependent on those microbes for the condition of our lives? We would. So let there be no talk of guilt at this juncture. As soon talk of cause and effect.

During this speech Hilary has been looking for a book.

Hilary Talking of microbes I was reading somewhere that there are more microbes *per person* than the entire population of the world. Imagine that. Per *person*. This means that if the time scale is diminished in proportion to that of space it would be quite possible for the whole story of Greece and Rome to be played out between farts.

Duff Hilary.

Hilary How can I come home? I am home. I am a Soviet citizen.

Veronica I didn't know that.

Hilary Duff did.

Duff A technicality. To do with ordinary people.

Veronica Since when?

Duff 1939. The Nazi-Soviet pact.

Veronica A curious time to choose.

Bron What do you expect?

Duff You see we could go today. Now. When the car comes. I think you'll find that there won't be any problem with your people here. Rather the reverse.

Hilary I see. Hence our friends in the garden. With Olga.

Duff It would be convenient. For everyone.

Hilary Have I a choice?

Duff You would be doing me a great personal favour.

Hilary But have I a choice?

Duff When has one a choice? I am your friend. If you felt you had it would be . . . nice.

Enter Olga from the garden.

Olga (*to Duff*) But they are not ready.

Bron We haven't quite decided yet.

Olga You had better get ready. There will be two cars. You will go in the first car. The others in the second car.

Duff I wanted him to feel it was his decision. I should have felt easier if it had been your decision. You would have felt better.

Olga We don't have time for any of that.

Duff One didn't want a scene.

Olga The British have someone we want. We have no one they especially want. But you will do.

Duff You and a disgruntled flautist who is also coming out. Denied opportunity to practise. Works on the roads. Sounds a little second rate to me.

Hilary It's funny that the word that best describes all these disaffected people is 'Bolshy'. I'll be of no use to you. I have no information other than what I read in the English newspapers. And if I had, who would believe me now?

Duff No, no. I'm sure. No. It's none of that. None of that at all. Just think of it as a gesture. A tidying up. Part of the spin-off of détente.

Olga Anyway you are sixty-five.

Bron Sixty-four.

Olga The age of retirement.

Veronica It'll be nice to have you home.

Hilary Home. The dustbin.

Duff That happens to us all. I did so much want it to be your decision.

Eric What about me?

Duff It makes everyone feel better. Me. You. People at home. Coming home to face the music, *sua voluntate* as it were. That will strike a chord. But willy nilly arrangements had to be made. Security are so tedious. You will be handed over on Tuesday at Vienna.

Eric What about me?

Duff I'm longing to see their new *Cosi* but I don't think that there'll be time. You don't care for opera, do you?

Hilary No.

Duff Pity. It's another world.

Bron Nobody really wanted us here from the start.

Veronica Well, you don't want to stay where you're not wanted.

Hilary I do. That's the only place I feel at home. And what about you, *liebchen*. When will they send you home?

Olga I have no home. Here is home.

Hilary For how long? Jewish bitch.

Duff On the contrary, this lady has been very helpful.

Bron What about Eric?

Duff That's not for me to say. We have this lady's feelings to consider.

Olga You should pack. If the cars are on schedule you have five minutes.

Veronica Is there anything I can do?

Bron No, I'm getting used to it. (*She goes off.*)

Hilary Did I tell you the joke about why is a mushroom like working for the party?

Pause.

I did, didn't I?

Veronica Yes.

Hilary wanders round among the books.

Hilary We've forgotten now . . . it's too recent to remember . . . that for a short period just after the war England seemed on the verge of a Christian revival. Eliot, Fry. The converted Auden. God was suddenly quite smart. The same people who'd felt vaguely benevolent towards communism in the 30's now felt as kindly, and as vaguely, towards its antithesis.

Veronica I hope you don't think I knew about this. Nobody tells mother.

Eric I wouldn't mind going back to prison. That wouldn't bother me.

Duff Do you know how much it costs to keep a man in prison? Something in the region of £150 a week. From a cost-benefit point of view prisons should be scrapped tomorrow and the prisoners put up in Trust Houses. Do them just as much good.

Eric You can talk. He's a puff!

Bron Eric.

Eric Who's embarrassed now?

Hilary If my hands were to be cut off and put in a bucket with a lot of other hands, and someone said, 'Now pick out yours,' I don't think I'd know them.

Pause.

Bron I would.

Hilary We shall be able to go to church. Although I gather they've got rid of the old Eucharist and are experimenting with something called Series 1, Series 2 and Series 3. That doesn't sound like religion to me.

Pause.

It sounds like baseball. Did you go to church, ever?

Eric A bit. But only for the ping-pong. The vicar used to lock up the bats. That's not Christianity, is it?

Hilary Moscow comes under the diocese of Fulham. Ever come across him, Duff? Barry, our Bishop. One of these ecumenical merchants. All join hands. Forget our differences. No fear.

Duff No sign of them?

Hilary A nice book would be the Anglican church in Europe. Riviera vicars. Embassy curates. A rich haul of eccentrics. Incidentally, does the embassy have a chaplain?

Duff No.

Hilary How on earth do they manage?

Veronica What happened to the ban on irony?

Hilary That's the dilemma. Its presence is intolerable, its absence inexcusable. Where you could set my mind at rest, Duff. Or you, Veronica, is whether (having paid the penalty, wiped the slate clean, whatever) I will still be in time to catch a decent afternoon tea. By that I mean tea, bread and butter, scones and jam. Not to mention Fuller's walnut cake.

Bron Oh stop it. Stop it. You've no need to keep it up now.

Hilary Nothing to keep up, as you should know by now. The best disguise of all is to be exactly what you say you are. Nobody ever believes that.

Duff No sign.

Olga No.

Eric If she really cared about me she'd want what I wanted.

Bron Eric.

Eric Don't keep saying, 'Eric, Eric.' That doesn't mean anything either. You're no different from her. What am I going to do?

Hilary Well, there's a pistol in that drawer.

Bron I don't know. Maybe you ought to get a dog.

Hilary I believe some people commit suicide out of sheer curiosity. Certainly if one were to cut one's throat I think the first thought as blood spurted through one's fingers would be, 'Goodness! It works!' Exclamation mark. Now Duff, what about my books?

Duff I foresee no difficulty. They will be home almost as soon as you are.

Hilary That's what I'm worried about. I think I ought to leave them here.

Duff It would please the British Council. The Embassy is barren of books.

Hilary I wasn't thinking of the Embassy. I was thinking of Eric.

Duff Eric?

Hilary Someone must. You see it's all here, Eric. *Horizon*, the parish magazine. *Scrutiny*, the school chronicle. All the nice distinctions, careful cross-bearings and distances on the pedometer. Relief maps of anxiety, the contours of small depressions. Get well cards and invites to funerals.

Notes under the general heading of amelioration. Deaths in vicarages and (Little) Venice. Bottles of Jordan water and basinfuls of the warm south. School and the trenches, good talk and good wine and the never-ending siege of the country house. Messages from an unvisited island. What would the Ambassador want with all that? He is a cultivated fellow. He can take it as read. But it's just what Eric wants.

Eric I don't read.

Hilary It will be something to do.

Olga He doesn't want the books.

Eric Yes, I do.

Bron Why? Crosswords, anagrams. Detective stories. English nonsense.

Hilary Why do you think I don't want them? It's Toad Hall.

Bron It's all very well never to do what is expected of you, but what do you do when the unexpected is what people have come to expect?

Hilary Then you do the done thing.

Veronica Make one person happy. Pa.

Duff I imagine the telephone is cut off, is it?

Olga Yes.

Duff Pity.

Hilary Here we are again. A country house. The telephone out of order. The road blocked. A group of disgruntled people waiting for . . . what? Deliverance, is it? Judgement?

Bron Will there be photographers at the other end? Press?

Duff I can't give you an absolute assurance on that. I hope not. I don't know.

Olga The cars are here.

Duff Good, good. This time on Tuesday we shall be in Wiltshire.

Duff shepherds Bron and Veronica out. Olga waits. A car horn sounds, two short notes.

Eric I don't want the books. I don't want the bloody books.

Hilary takes no notice. The car horn sounds again.

Hilary Poop-poop. Poop-poop.

The chair is still rocking as Hilary leaves, followed by Olga. Eric watches them from the verandah, the books still in his arms.
    Curtain

AN ENGLISHMAN ABROAD

Characters

Burgess
Coral Browne
Tolya
Tailor
Shop Assistant

An Englishman Abroad was first performed at the Royal National Theatre, London, on 1 December 1988 as part of a double bill entitled *Single Spies*. The cast was as follows:

Coral Browne, Prunella Scales
Guy Burgess, Simon Callow
Tolya, Paul Brightwell
Tailor, Alan Bennett
Shop Assistant, Edward Halsted

Director, Alan Bennett
Designer, Bruno Santini
Lighting, Paul Pyant

A projection screen hides the set. Stage right of the screen is a bentwood chair. The screen glows red and projected on it is the head of Stalin as we hear a record of Jack Buchanan singing 'Who stole my heart away?'.

The song fades as Coral Browne enters stage right. She is a striking woman, tall and elegant, and carries a luxurious fur coat.

Coral Stalin died in 1953. I was in *Affairs of State* at the time, a light comedy that had a decent run at the Cambridge. Stalin had had a decent run too, though I'd never been a fan of the old boy, even during the war when he was all the rage. It wasn't so much the cult of personality that put me off (being in the theatre I'm no stranger to that); it was the moustache. One smiles, but more judgements than people care to admit are grounded in such trivialities, and when you're just a fool of an actress like me you don't mind coming out with it.

After Uncle Joe's death they played with the understudies for a bit, then brought in a cast of unknowns in something called The Thaw. Soviet experts in the West (what nowadays would be called 'experienced Kremlin-watchers') thought that this show was going to run and run, predicting – poor loves – that the Iron Curtain was about to go up and stay up. Ah well. Incidentally, don't let any of this deceive you into thinking I took any sort of interest in Soviet affairs. Actresses are excused newspapers much as delicate boys used to be excused games; the only paper I see regularly is *The Stage*, and its coverage of the comings and goings in the Politburo is, to say the least, cursory.

Still, there were repercussions, even on me. When peace breaks out suddenly, as it did then, culture is first on the menu, actors and musicians sent in ahead of the statesmen like the infantry before the tanks. We had the Red Army Choir; they got the Stratford Memorial Theatre in *Hamlet*. Michael Redgrave was the eponymous prince, and notwithstanding I was scarcely five minutes older than he was, I played his mother.

Guy Burgess enters stage left. He is in his early fifties, a man who has once been handsome but is now running to seed.

Burgess Hearing that Stalin had died one cheered up no end. It wasn't just that I was glad to see the back of the old bugger, though I was, but for the first time since I'd come to Moscow in 1951 I found I'd something to do. Death always means work for somebody, and one was suddenly very busy reading the papers, monitoring news broadcasts, collating and analysing Western reactions to the Marshal's somewhat overdue departure. However, in no time at all, they had him tucked in beside Lenin on Red Square, and life returned to what I had come to regard as normal – doing *The Times* crossword, the *Statesman* competition, reading Trollope and Jane Austen. A gentleman of leisure. Of course the most accomplished exiles are, and always have been, the Russians. They're tutors in it practically. So, in a sense we had come to the right place.

What made it harder to bear was that no one in what one couldn't help thinking of as the outside world actually knew we were here. For the first few years of our sojourn we were kept very much under wraps – no letters, no phone calls, nothing. It made Greta Garbo look gregarious. I say 'we', meaning my colleague Maclean, with some diffidence. It's dispiriting to find oneself yoked permanently to someone who was never meant to be more than a travelling companion (besides

having been a fellow travelling companion, of course).
Now it was 'we', handcuffed together in the same
personal pronoun.

Quarantine or honeymoon, our period of probation
ended when we were revealed to the world's press in
Moscow in 1956. After that, though we never exactly hit
the cocktail party circuit and still had to mind our ps and
qs, there was less – shall we say – skulking. (*Burgess
exits left.*)

Coral Dissolve to my dressing-room in the Moscow Art
Theatre one night after the performance. I am sitting there,
applying the paint-stripper, when I hear a commotion next
door. Suddenly Hamlet bursts in. Someone is being sick in
his dressing room, would I assist?

Now vomiting is not childbirth. If one is having a baby
a helping hand is not unwelcome. If one is having a puke,
one is best left alone to get on with it. Remembering
always that nausea requires patience. One of the few
lessons I have learned in life is that when one is sick it is
always in threes. Judging by the state of the carpet this
was a lesson this particular gentleman had yet to learn.
When his face came out of the basin I found I knew it,
though not by name. The moment for introductions was
long since past and Redgrave did not make them. I cleaned
the man up, noting that he was English, he was upper
class, and he was drunk. It was only later that night when
a note was slipped under my door at the hotel that I found
out he was also Guy Burgess. (*Coral has put on her fur
coat and she takes a note from the pocket.*) 'Bring a tape
measure.' Bring a tape measure?

*The motif of Stalin has faded from the screen and as we
hear Burgess singing the screen rises to reveal his very
untidy flat. There is an easy chair, a sofa and a small
table, several bookshelves filled to overflowing with
(English) books and papers and at the rear of the flat a*

*kitchenette. Through an alcove is a double bed, unmade
and the sheets unwashed and stage left is a pianola.*

Burgess (*singing off*)
Oh God our help in ages past
Our hope for years to come,
Our shelter from the stormy blast
And our eternal home.

Burgess wanders in, shaving.
Before the hills in order stood
Or earth received her frame

The doorbell rings.
From everlasting Thou art God,
It's open.
Through endless years the same.

*Burgess hurriedly clears some dirty clothes from a chair
and as an afterthought flings the heaped contents of an
ashtray under the sofa, as Coral enters through the
hallway stage right.*

Burgess (*to Coral*) Hello.

Coral (*puffed*) The stairs!

Burgess I know. I'm sorry. Recover. What a splendid coat.
Let me take it. (*He buries his face in the grand fur coat
before dropping it, pretty unceremoniously, on the sofa.*)
Mmm. Have a drink.

Coral Please.

Burgess I've just been tidying up. (*He sweeps some stuff to
the floor and removes his soap and towel.*)

Coral One moment. My soap. This is my soap.

Burgess It is. It is. 'Palmolive – for that schoolgirl
complexion.'

Coral So it was you who took my cigarettes?

Burgess One wasn't well. (*He hands her a glass, which she surreptitiously cleans on her skirt. He pours her a drink.*)

Coral My Scotch?

Burgess smiles.

Burgess One should have asked.

Coral You even took my face powder.

Burgess I know. One is such a coward. Still. You came. I thought you'd chuck. (*He raises his glass in a toast.*)

Coral I nearly did. I seem to have trekked halfway across Moscow. Is there something in the Communist Manifesto against taxis? One never sees any. And that woman on the door downstairs!

Burgess I know. How did you get past her?

Coral I gave her my lipstick.

Burgess I can't think what she'll do with it. I'm always struck by her pronounced resemblance to the late Ernest Bevin. They could be sisters.

Coral Did you enjoy the play?

Burgess What play?

Coral Our play. *Hamlet.*

Burgess Loved it. Loved it. I liked the look of Laertes. He goes rather well into tights.

Coral That's what he thinks.

Burgess He looked as if he'd put a couple of King Edwards down there. That apart, of course, such a pleasure to hear the language so beautifully spoken.

Coral I was told you were asleep.

Burgess No. Though one did have a tiny zizz. After all, one has seen it before. Are there still a couple of music-hall comedians on the wireless called Nat Mills and Bobby?

Coral I don't know them.

Burgess Their catchphrase was, 'Well, why don't you get on with it?' I always feel they would have come in handy in *Hamlet*. Still. The comrades lapped it up. But they do, of course, culture. How do you like Moscow?

Coral Loathe it, darling. I cannot understand what those Three Sisters were on about. It gives the play a very sinister slant.

She walks about the flat.

Burgess It's hardly luxury's lap, I'm afraid. A pigsty, in fact. I used to live in Jermyn Street. Tragic, you might think, but not really. That was a pigsty, too. By their standards it's quite commodious. Palatial even. One is very lucky.

Coral What is that smell?

Burgess Me probably.

Coral No. Besides that. If it's our lunch, it's burning.

Burgess Oh. Now. It might be. (*He gets up unhurriedly and goes into the kitchenette.*) Yes, it is. It was stew. (*He peers into the pan.*) One could salvage some of it? (*He shows it to Coral.*)

Coral Hardly.

Burgess Perhaps not. (*He returns to the kitchen with it.*) However. All is not lost. I managed to scrounge two tomatoes this morning, and . . . quite a talking point . . . a grapefruit. Shall we perch? I generally do.

He draws Coral's chair to the table and himself sits on the arm of the easy chair.

Coral (*faintly*) Treats.

He puts a tomato on her plate and eats his like an apple.

Burgess Garlic?

Coral No, thank you.

Burgess I love it. (*He eats several cloves.*) Yum yum. Now. Tell me all the gossip. Do you see Harold Nicolson?

Coral I *have* seen him. I don't know him.

Burgess Oh, don't you? Nice man. Nice man. What about Cyril Connolly?

Coral I haven't run into him either.

Burgess Really? That must be quite difficult. He's everywhere. You know him, of course?

Coral As a matter of fact, no.

Burgess Oh. One somehow remembers everyone knowing everyone else. Everyone I knew knew everyone else. Auden – do you know him? Pope Hennessy?

Coral (*manfully*) The theatre's in a terrible state.

Burgess Is it?

Coral Three plays closed on Shaftesbury Avenue in one week.

Burgess That's tragic. Some ballet on ice is coming here. The comrades are all agog. I'm rather old-fashioned about ice. I used to direct at Cambridge, you know. That's how I know your star, Mr Redgrave. I directed him in *Captain Brassbound's Conversion*. It was an average production, but notable for a memorable performance by Arthur

Marshall as Lady Cicely Waynflete. Happy days. One thinks back and wonders, did one miss one's way. What would have happened had one gone into the theatre? Nothing, I suppose.

Coral Who knows, you might just have been Kenneth Tynan's cup of tea.

Burgess Oh, do you think so? Do you know him?

Coral Slightly.

Burgess He happened after we came away. You're not eating your tomato.

Coral I'm not hungry.

Burgess I am. (*He takes it.*) This garlic!

Coral Do you see many people here?

Burgess Oh yes. Heaps of chums. You don't know what you're missing with this tomato.

Coral There's your other half, I suppose.

Burgess What? Oh yes. He's taken up the balalaika. We play duets.

Coral Maclean?

Burgess No. Oh *no*. Not Maclean. (*He bursts out laughing.*) Taking up the balalaika! Maclean's not my friend. Oh, ducky. Oh no, not Maclean. He's so unfunny, no jokes, no jokes at all. Positively the last person one would have chosen if one had had the choice. And here we are on this terrible tandem together – Debenham and Freebody, Crosse and Blackwell, Auden and Isherwood, Burgess and Maclean. Do you know Auden?

Coral You asked me. No.

Burgess (*going over to the kitchenette*) Sweet man. Don't look. The seeds get inside my plate. (*He swills his teeth*.) People ask me if I have any regrets. The one regret I have is that before I came away I didn't get kitted out with a good set of National Health gnashers. Admirable as most things are in the Soviet Socialist Republic, the making of dentures is still in its infancy. (*Pause.*) Actually, there's no one in Moscow at all. It's like staying up in Cambridge for the Long Vac. One makes do with whoever's around.

Coral Me.

Burgess No, no. And in any case I asked you here for a reason. Did you bring a tape measure?

Coral I did. (*She produces it.*)

Burgess Good. (*Burgess puts on his jacket. His suit is well cut but shabby, the knee of the trousers darned and darned again.*) I want you to measure me for some suits. From my tailor. I only have one suit. It's the one I came away in and I've fallen down a lot since then.

Coral But I shan't know where to start. What measurements will he want?

Burgess Measure it all. He'll work it out. He's a nice man.

He gets her pencil and paper. She draws the figure of a man on the paper.

Coral Won't your people here get you a suit?

Burgess What people?

Coral The authorities.

Burgess Oh yes, but have you seen them? Clothes have never been the comrades' strong point. Besides, I don't want to look like everybody else, do I? (*He bends his arm for her to measure.*) I seem to remember doing this.

Coral Your arms can't have altered.

Burgess I never cared tuppence for clothes before . . .
Measure me round here . . . I was kitted out in the
traditional garb of my class. Black coat, striped trousers.
Pinstripe suit and tweeds for weekends. Shit order, of
course. Always in shit order. But charm, I always had
charm.

Coral (*measuring away*) You still have charm. She said
through clenched teeth.

Burgess But not here. Not for them. For charm one needs
words. I have no words. And, short of my clothes, no
class. I am 'The Englishman'. 'Would you like to go to bed
with the Englishman?' I say. Not particularly. One got so
spoiled during the war. The joys of the black-out. London
awash with rude soldiery. (*He says a Russian phrase.*)
Skolko zeem, skolko let.

Coral What does that mean?

Burgess *Skolko zeem, skolko let?* It means the same as our
'*Où sont les neiges d'antan?*' Nostalgia, you see, knows no
frontiers.

Coral Do you speak Russian?

Burgess I manage. Maclean's learned it, naturally. Swot. I
haven't. I ought to, simply for the sex. Boys are quite thin
on the ground here. I can't speak their language and they
can't speak mine, so when one does manage to get one it
soon palls. Sex needs language.

Coral is still busy measuring.

Coral At least you've found a friend.

Burgess Tolya? Yes. Except I'm not sure whether I've
found him or been allotted him. I know what I've done to
be given him. But what has he done to be given me? Am I
a reward or a punishment? He plays the balalaika. I play

the pianola. It's fun. He's an electrician with the ballet. Of course he may be a policeman. If he is a policeman he's a jolly good actor. Forster lived with a policeman, didn't he? You know him?

Coral shakes her head.

Nice man. Getting on now, I suppose.

Coral I feel I'm somewhat of a disappointment in the friends department. I gather Paul Robeson is coming here. Now I know him.

Burgess Do you? He's a big favourite with the comrades. What with being black, and red. I remember when I was posted to the Washington Embassy the Secretary of State, dear old Hector McNeill, had me in his room and gave me a lecture about what I should and shouldn't do when I got there: I mustn't be too openly left-wing, mustn't get involved in the colour question, and above all I must avoid homosexual incidents. I said, 'To sum up, Hector, what you're saying is, "Don't make a pass at Paul Robeson".'

Coral I wouldn't either.
    Nobody will believe me when I go home. 'What did you do in Moscow, darling?' 'Nothing much, I measured Guy Burgess's inside leg.'

Burgess I shouldn't think one's inside leg alters, do you? It's one of the immutables. 'The knee is such a distance from the main body, whereas the groin, as your honour knows, is upon the very curtain of the place.'

Coral Come again.

Burgess *Tristram Shandy.* Lovely book. Of course, you wouldn't do that.

Coral Do what?

Burgess Go round telling everybody. My people here wouldn't like that.

Coral (*looking up from her knees*) No?

Burgess No. A hat would be nice. I've written down the name of my hatters. And my bootmaker.

Coral It's a trousseau.

Burgess Yes. For a shotgun marriage.

Coral How do you know he won't say no, your tailor?

Burgess Why should he say no? It would be vulgar to say no.

Coral Well, I'll see what I can do.

She prepares to go. Burgess doesn't make any move.

Burgess Don't go yet. I don't want you to go yet. You mustn't go yet.

Coral Can't we go somewhere? You could show me the sights.

Burgess In due course. But we can't go yet. I have to wait for a telephone call. When the telephone call comes I'm permitted to leave.

Coral Who from?

Burgess Oh . . . you know . . . my people. It's generally around four.

Coral That's another two hours.

Burgess Yes. 'What then is to be done?' as Vladimir Ilyitch almost said. I know. I can play you my record.

He puts a record on the gramophone. It is Jack Buchanan singing 'Who stole my heart away?'. They listen to this in its entirety.

Good, isn't it? It's Jack Buchanan.

Coral Yes.

Burgess Is he still going?

Coral Yes.

Burgess Did you ever come across him?

Coral Yes. I did actually. We nearly got married.

Burgess And?

Coral He jilted me.

Burgess Oh. Small world. Still. It's a good record. (*He puts it on again.*)

Coral And so we sat there in that dreary flat all through that long afternoon waiting for the telephone to ring. From time to time he played his record and I had to listen to my ex-beau. I was puzzled as to how he had managed to get all his books there.

Burgess Someone sent them. A well-wisher. The desk belonged to Stendhal.

Coral Did you have that in London?

Burgess Yes.

Coral Couldn't the same person who sent you your books get you the suits?

Burgess No.

Coral No?

Burgess No.

Coral When I came into the flats I noticed a boy sitting on the stairs playing chess.

Burgess Police. When I first came I used to be shadowed by rather grand policemen. That was when I was a celebrity. Nowadays they just send the trainees. I wish I could lead them a dance. But I can't think of a dance to lead them.

Mind you, they're more conscientious than their English counterparts. All that last week before we left we were tailed. Maclean lived in Sussex so on the Friday evening we went to Waterloo, dutifully followed by these two men in raincoats. They saw us as far as the barrier and then went home. On the very civilized principle, I suppose, that nothing happens at the weekend. It was the only reason we got away. (*Pause.*) Waterloo the same, is it?

Coral Yes. (*Pause.*) What do you miss most?

Burgess Apart from the Reform Club, the streets of London, and occasionally the English countryside, the only thing I truly miss is gossip. The comrades, though splendid in every other respect, don't gossip in quite the same way we do or about quite the same subjects.

Coral Pardon me for saying so, dear, but the comrades seem to me a sad disappointment in every department. There's no gossip, their clothes are terrible and they can't make false teeth. What else is there?

Burgess (*gently*) The system. Only, being English, you wouldn't be interested in that. (*Pause.*) My trouble is, I lack what the English call character. By which they mean the power to refrain. Appetite. The English never like that, do they? Unconcealed appetite. For success. Women. Money. Justice. Appetite makes them uncomfortable. What do people say about me in England?

Coral They don't much any more.

She gets up and starts tidying the room. Folding clothes, washing dishes. Burgess watches.

I thought of you as a bit like Oscar Wilde.

Burgess laughs.

Burgess No, no. Though he was a performer. And I was a performer. Both vain. But I never pretended. If I wore a mask it was to be exactly what I seemed. And I made no bones about politics. My analyses of situations, the précis I had to submit at the Foreign Office, were always Marxist. Openly so. Impeccably so. Nobody minded. 'It's only Guy.' 'Dear old Guy.' Quite safe. If you don't wish to conform in one thing, you should conform in all the others. And in all the important things I did conform. 'How can he be a spy? He goes to my tailor.' The average Englishman, you see, is not interested in ideas. You can say what you like about political theory and no one will listen. You could shove a slice of the Communist Manifesto in the Queen's Speech and no one would turn a hair. Least of all, I suspect, HMQ. Am I boring you?

Coral It doesn't matter. (*She investigates the bookshelves. Takes a book out. Puts it back.*)

Burgess I'll think of a hundred and one things to ask you when you've gone. How is Cyril Connolly?

Coral You've asked me that. I don't know.

Burgess You won't have come across Anthony Blunt then?

Coral No. Isn't he quite grand?

Burgess Very grand. That's art. Art is grand. Art and opera. It's the way to get on.

Coral Is he nice?

Burgess Not particularly. Though nice is what you generally have to be, isn't it? 'Is he nice?' So little, England. Little music. Little art. Timid, tasteful, nice. But one loves it. Loves it. You see, I can say I love London. I can say I love England. But I can't say I love my country. I don't know what that means. Do you watch cricket?

Coral No. Anyway, it's changed.

Burgess Cricket?

Coral London.

Burgess Why? I don't want it to change. Why does anybody want to change it? They've no business changing it. The fools. You should stop them changing it. Band together.

Coral Listen, darling. I'm only an actress. Not a bright lady, by your standards. I've never taken much interest in politics. If this is communism I don't like it because it's dull. And the poor dears look so tired. But then Australia is dull and that's not communism. And look at Leeds. Only it occurs to me that we have sat here all afternoon pretending that spying, which is what you did, darling, was just a minor social misdemeanour, no worse – and I'm sure in certain people's minds much better – than being caught in a public lavatory the way gentlemen in my profession constantly are, and that it's just something one shouldn't mention. Out of politeness. So that we won't be embarrassed. That's very English. We will pretend it hasn't happened because we are both civilized people.

Well, I'm not English. And I'm not civilized. I'm Australian. I can't muster much morality, and outside Shakespeare the word treason to me means nothing. Only, you pissed in our soup and we drank it. Very good. Doesn't affect me, darling. And I will order your suit and your hat. And keep it under mine. Mum. Not a word. But for one reason and one reason only: because I'm sorry for you. Now in your book . . . in your *real* book . . . that probably adds my name to the list of all the other fools you've conned. But you're not conning me, darling. Pipe isn't fooling pussy. I *know*.

The telephone rings.

Burgess Pity. I was enjoying that. (*He picks up the phone.*) You spoiled the lady's big speech. *Da. Da. Spassibo.* (*He puts the phone down.*) Finished?

Coral I just want to be told why.

Burgess It seemed the right thing to do at the time. And solitude, I suppose.

Coral Solitude?

Burgess If you have a secret you're alone.

Coral But you told people. You told several people.

Burgess No point in having a secret if you make a secret of it. Actually the other thing you might get me is an Etonian tie. This one's on its last legs.

They have got up ready to go when Tolya, a young Russian, comes in.

Ah, here's Tolya.

He kisses him.

Tolya. This is Miss Browne. She is an actress. From England.

Tolya (*pronouncing it very carefully*) How do you do? How are you?

Burgess Very good. If you give him an English cigarette he'll be your friend for life.

Coral does so. Tolya takes a cigarette but is then fascinated by the packet and takes that also. He examines it carefully then hands it back.

Coral No, please. Feel free.

Coral lights his cigarette with her lighter.

Tolya Thank you.

But now her lighter has caught his eye and he takes that too, flicking it on and off, fascinated.

Tolya *Chudyessna!*

Burgess Oh dear. Sorry.

Reluctantly Tolya offers the lighter back.

Coral (*resigned*) No, please.

Burgess (*taking the lighter and handing it back to Coral*) No, you mustn't. He'll take anything. He's a real Queen Mary. But you . . . wouldn't be able to order him a suit, would you? Off the peg. He'd look so nice.

Coral (*desperately*) Anything. Anything.

Tolya (*in Russian*) *Ya hotyel bwi eegrat dlya nyeyo.*

Burgess *Da? Samnoy?*

Tolya *Konyeshna.*

Burgess Tolya wants us to play you a tune. Let him. He'd be so pleased. Just five minutes.

They embark on the duet 'Take a pair of sparkling eyes' from Gilbert and Sullivan's The Gondoliers. *Burgess shouts above the music.*

What do you think? Reward or punishment?

The music continues as the lights fade, hiding the room.

Coral When we left the flat he took me to a church not far from where he lived. I've since been told that it was kept open just to indicate that there still were such places. The singing was very good. Apparently it was where the opera singers went to warm up for the evening's performance.

As a rule I don't have much time for men's tears. It's like

blowing smoke rings, crying is a facility some men have. And it wasn't as if there was anything particularly English about the service. It wasn't like church or school, and yet when I looked at him the tears were rolling down his cheeks. He left me outside my hotel.

Coral goes stage right, leaving Burgess in the spot, stage left.

Burgess Something else you could do for me when you get back. Ring the old mum. Tell her I'm all right. Looking after myself. She's been here once. Loved it. Too frail now. I would come back to see her but apparently it's not on. Still got to stand in the corner, I suppose.

'Let him never come back to us.
There would be doubt, hesitation and pain.
Forced praise on our part, the glimmer of twilight,
Never glad confident morning again.'

Good old Browning. Goodbye. *Dosvidanya.*

The light fades on Burgess as Coral comes on, right, in a different coat and hat. A Tailor enters, left, wearing a tape measure and carrying a swatch of samples.

Coral I'd like to order some suits.

Tailor Certainly madam.

Coral You've made suits for the gentleman before, but he now lives abroad.

Tailor I see.

Coral hands him her bit of paper.

Coral I took his measurements. I'm not sure they're the right ones.

The Tailor looks at the paper.

Tailor Oh yes. These are more than adequate. Could one know the gentleman's name?

Coral Yes. Mr Burgess.

Tailor We have two Mr Burgesses. I take this to be Mr Burgess G. How is Mr Burgess? Fatter, I see. One of our more colourful customers. Too little colour in our drab lives these days. Knowing Mr Guy he'll want a pinstripe. But a durable fabric. His suits were meant to take a good deal of punishment. I hope they have stood him in good stead.

Coral Yes. They have indeed.

Tailor I'm glad to hear it. Always getting into scrapes, Mr Guy. And your name is . . .?

Coral Browne.

Tailor There is no need for discretion here, madam.

Coral Truly.

Tailor My apologies. (*He looks at her in recognition.*) Of course. And this is the address. I see. We put a little of ourselves into our suits. That is our loyalty.

Coral And mum's the word.

Tailor Oh, madam. Mum is always the word here. Moscow or Maidenhead, mum is always the word.

The Tailor exits left leaving Coral in the spot right.

Coral And so it was with all the shops I went into, scarcely an eyebrow raised. When the parcels arrived he wrote to me, the letter dated 11 April 1958, Easter Sunday, to which he adds, 'a very suitable day to be writing to you, since I also was born on it, to the later horror of the Establishment of the country concerned'.

Burgess, left, now takes over the letter.

Burgess I really find it hard to know how to thank you properly. Everything *fits*. No need for any alterations at all. Thank you. Thank you. In spite of your suggestion – invitation, to visit your friend Paul Robeson, I find myself too shy to call on him. Not so much shy as frightened. The *agonies* I remember on first meeting with people I really admire, E. M. Forster (and Picasso and Winston Churchill). H. G. Wells was quite different, but one could get drunk with him and listen to stories of his sex life. Fascinating. How frightened one would be of Charlie Chaplin.

One more thing. What I really need, the only thing more, is pyjamas. Russian ones can't be slept in, are not in fact made for the purpose. What I would like if you can find it is four pairs of white or off-white pyjamas . . .

A Shop Assistant brings on a chair, right.

Assistant If you could take a seat, madam, I'll just check.

Coral '. . . *Four* pairs. Quite plain and only those two colours. Then at last my outfit will be complete and I shall look like a real agent again.' (*She looks twice.*) 'Then I shall look like a real gent again.'

The Shop Assistant returns.

Assistant I'm afraid, madam, that the gentleman in question no longer has an account with us. His account was closed.

Coral I know. He wishes to open it again.

Assistant I'm afraid that's not possible.

Coral Why?

Assistant Well . . . we supply pyjamas to the Royal Family.

Coral So?

Assistant The gentleman is a traitor, madam.

Coral So? Must traitors sleep in the buff?

Assistant I'm sorry. We have to draw the line somewhere.

Coral So why here? Say someone commits adultery in your precious nightwear. I imagine it has occurred. What happens when he comes in to order his next pair of jim-jams. Is it sorry, no can do?

Assistant I'm very sorry.

Coral (*her Australian accent gets now more pronounced as she gets crosser*) You keep saying you're sorry, dear. You were quite happy to satisfy this client when he was one of the most notorious buggers in London and a drunkard into the bargain. Only then he was in the Foreign Office. 'Red piping on the sleeve, Mr Burgess – but of course.' 'A discreet monogram on the pocket, Mr Burgess?' Certainly. And perhaps if you'd be gracious enough to lower your trousers, Mr Burgess, we could be privileged enough to thrust our tongue between the cheeks of your arse. But not any more. Oh no. Because the gentleman in question has shown himself to have some principles, principles which aren't yours and, as a matter of interest, aren't mine. But that's it, as far as you're concerned. No more jamas for him. I tell you, it's pricks like you that make me understand why he went. Thank Christ I'm not English.

Assistant As a matter of fact, madam, our firm isn't English either.

Coral Oh? What is it?

Assistant Hungarian. (*He exits right.*)

Coral Oh, I said, and thinking of the tanks going into

Budapest a year or two before, wished I hadn't made such a fuss. So I went down the street to Simpsons and got him some pyjamas there. Guy wrote to thank me and sent a cheque for £6 to treat myself to supper at the Caprice. Which one could, of course, in those days. In those days. Anyway, that was the last I heard of him. He never did come back, of course, dying in 1963. Heart attack.

This comedy I was in at the Cambridge, *Affairs of State* – I played the wife of an elderly statesman. 'Your friends were great men in their time,' I had to say, 'only those who've managed to stay alive can now hardly manage to stay awake.' And that, of course, would have been the solution for Burgess, to live on to a great age. Had he been living now he would have been welcomed back with open arms, just as Mosley was a few years back. He could have written his memoirs, gone on all the chat shows, done *Desert Island Discs* . . . played his Jack Buchanan record again. In England, you see, age wipes the slate clean. (*She gets up.*) If you live to be ninety in England and can still eat a boiled egg they think you deserve the Nobel Prize.

Now smartly suited, wearing an overcoat and Homburg hat and carrying an umbrella Burgess stands in the spot stage left, the picture of an upper-class Englishman. Accompanied as if on the pianola he starts to sing 'For he is an Englishman' from Gilbert and Sullivan's HMS Pinafore.

Burgess
For he might have been a Roosian,
A French or Turk or Proosian,
Or perhaps I-tal-ian.
For in spite of all temptations
To belong to other nations,
He remains an Englishman,
He remains an Englishman.

As Burgess sings he is drowned out by the full chorus and orchestra in a rousing climax, but before the music stops the light has faded on Burgess and the screen drops in, bright and blank and Coral stands in front of it as though after a film screening.

Coral At supper one night, after a showing of the film of this story in 1983, I met Lord Harlech, who as David Omsby-Gore had been Minister of State at the Foreign Office at the time Burgess was wanting to come back and see his mother. The Foreign Office and the security services were in a blue funk apparently. All the threats of prosecution that were conveyed to Burgess were pure bluff. Harlech said there was nothing it would have been safe to charge him with. Egg on too many faces, I suppose.

'And what about the others?' I said. 'What others?' he said. I said I'd heard there were others. Still. But he just smiled.

A QUESTION OF ATTRIBUTION

An inquiry
in which the circumstances are imaginary
but the pictures are real

A note on the paintings

A Question of Attribution is concerned with two
paintings, Titian's *Allegory of Prudence* in the National
Gallery and the *Triple Portrait*, formerly attributed to
Titian, which is in the collection of HM The Queen. The
play owes a great deal to two articles in which these
paintings are discussed, 'Titian's *Allegory of Prudence*' by
Erwin Panofsky (in *Meaning in the Visual Arts*, Peregrine,
1974) and 'Five Portraits' by St John Gore (*Burlington
Magazine*, vol. 100, 1958).

One of the points made by Blunt in the play is that there
is a strong resemblance between the 'third man' in the
Triple Portrait and Titian's son, Orazio Vecelli as he
appears in the *Allegory of Prudence*. Should anyone be
interested enough to compare the actual paintings they
would be in some difficulty as at the moment the *Triple
Portrait* (which has recently been re-titled *Titian and
Friends*) cannot be seen. It used to hang at Hampton
Court but since the 1986 fire it has not been on public
view. Indeed, I have not seen it myself, knowing it only
from the photographs which illustrate Mr St John Gore's
article. There is a certain appropriateness about this,
though, as one of the criticisms made of Anthony Blunt as
an art historian was that he preferred to work from
photographs rather than the real thing.

AB

FIGURE I   The *Triple Portrait* before cleaning: *Titian and a Venetian Senator* (Witt Library, Courtauld Institute of Art).

FIGURE 2   The *Triple Portrait* after cleaning: *Titian and Friends* (Royal Collection Enterprises Ltd).

FIGURE 3   *Allegory of Prudence* (copyright the National
Gallery).

FIGURE 4 Details from the *Allegory of Prudence* and *Triple Portrait*.

Characters

Blunt
Chubb
Phillips
HMQ
Colin
Restorer

A Question of Attribution was first performed at the Royal National Theatre, London, on 1 December 1988 as part of a double bill entitled *Single Spies*. The cast was as follows:

Blunt, Alan Bennett
Restorer, David Terence
Chubb, Simon Callow
Phillips, Crispin Redman
Colin, Brett Fancy
HMQ, Prunella Scales

Director, Simon Callow
Designer, Bruno Santini
Lighting, Paul Pyant
Music, Dominic Muldowney

Anthony Blunt's room at the Courtauld Institute where he is the Director. The time is the late 1960s. There is a large eighteenth-century double door and a fine ormolu mounted table serving as a desk but in all other respects the room is a functioning office, the bookshelves crowded with reference books and with piles of octavo volumes on the floor. Above the desk and upstage of it is a projection screen with a slide projector on a nearby side-table.

Blunt stands left of the screen and the Restorer, a humbler figure in a dustcoat, to the right. Their positions resemble those of saints or patrons on either side of an altarpiece and some effort should be made in the production to create stage pictures which echo in this way the composition and lighting of old masters.

Blunt Next.

On the screen a slide of the Triple Portrait *before cleaning (Figure 1).*

Restorer More of the same, I'm afraid. It's an ex-Titian. Now thought to be by several hands.

Blunt Called?

The Restorer consults a catalogue or printed sheet.

Restorer *Titian and a Venetian Senator.*

Blunt And this is Titian on the left. He's not by Titian, certainly.

Restorer No. He's a copy of the Berlin self-portrait.

Blunt I don't know about the other gentleman.

Restorer He's been identified as the Chancellor of Venice, Andrea Franceschi.

Pause.

Blunt I should warn you. I don't have an eye. K. Clark was saying the other day (I don't *think* the remark was directed at me) that people who look at Old Masters fall into three groups: those who see what it is without being told; those who see it when you tell them; and those who can't see it whatever you do. I just about make the second category. It means I can't date pictures. Made a terrible hash of the early Poussins. Couldn't tell which came first. For an art historian it's rather humiliating. Like being a wine taster and having no sense of smell. (*Pause.*) People find me cold. I don't gush, I suppose.

Restorer Not much to gush about, this lot. Mind you, wait till you see Holyrood.

Blunt I'm not saying painting doesn't affect me. Ravished, sometimes. Well, what do we do? Give it a scrub?

Restorer Couldn't do any harm.

Blunt On. On.

A slide of a painting of St Lawrence being roasted over a grid comes up on the screen.

What frightful thing is happening here?

Restorer *The Martyrdom of St Lawrence.*

Blunt groans.

Blunt Art!

Blunt steps from the office set to a podium or lectern, stage left, and we should have a sense that he is in the

*middle of a lecture. The lecture is illustrated by slides
projected on the screen; these slides include Giovanni
Bellini's* Agony in the Garden, *an* Annunciation *and
other appropriate images, details and martyrdoms.*

Were we not inured to its imagery, however, it would seem
a curious world, this world of Renaissance art; a place of
incongruous punishments, where heads come on plates
and skulls sport cleavers, and an angel, tremulous as a
butterfly, waits patiently for the attention of a young girl
who is pretending to read.

Doomed to various slow and ingenious extinctions the
saints brandish the emblems of their suffering, the cross,
the gridiron and the wheel, and submit to their fate readily
and without fuss, howling agonies gone through without a
murmur, the only palliative a vision of God and the
assurance of Heaven. Remote though all this is from our
sensibility, there is a sense in which one might feel that it is
all very British. For flayed, dismembered, spitted, roasted,
these martyrs seldom lose a drop of their *sang-froid*, so
cool about their bizarre torments, the real emblems of
their martyrdom a silk dressing-gown and a long cigarette-
holder; all of them doing their far, far better thing in a
dignified silence. About suffering they were always wrong,
the Old Masters. (*Slide.*) In Bellini's *Agony in the Garden*,
for instance, the apostles, oblivious to all considerations
but those of perspective, are fast asleep on ground as
brown and bare as an end-of-the-season goalmouth, this
sleep signifying indifference.

Above them on a rocky promontory of convenient
geology, Jesus kneels in prayer, an exercise that still goes
on in some places, though with less agony and less
certainty of address, this praying of less interest to the
budding art historian or to the social historian or even to
someone who has just wandered into the gallery out of the
rain (and it is salutary to remind ourselves, here at the

Courtauld Institute, that that is what art is for most people) . . . this praying, as I say, of less interest to them than the reaper on the edge of a field in a Breughel, say, who has his hand up a woman's dress, another exercise that still goes on in most places, though with no agony but the same certainty of address. Here is threshing, which we now do mechanically. Here is sex, which we do mechanically also. And here is crucifixion, which we do not do. Or do differently. Or do indifferently. It is a world in which time means nothing, the present overlaps the future, and did the saint but turn his head he would see his own martyrdom through the window.

> *Blunt turns and on the other side of the stage, right, we see the double doors open to reveal a man in a trilby and raincoat carrying a briefcase. This is Chubb.*

Judas takes the pieces of silver in the Temple at the same moment as in the next field he hangs himself. Christ begs God in the garden to free him from a fate that is already happening higher up the hill.

> *As the lectern or podium disappears Blunt steps back into the office where Chubb is waiting. Chubb is seemingly vague, seemingly amiable. Socially he is not in the same class as Blunt, who is sophisticated and metropolitan; Chubb, while not naïve, is definitely suburban. The slides on the screen have changed to photographs of various young men, taken singly or enlarged from group photographs of colleges and teams; all date from the thirties and are in black and white. Following each denial by Blunt a new photograph comes up on the screen.*

Blunt No. No. N . . . no.

Chubb Sure?

Blunt It's the neck. The *neck* could be Piero della Francesca.

Chubb Who's he?

Blunt Well, he was many things, but he wasn't a member of the Communist Party. (*Pause.*) And in answer to your earlier question, the larger question, I would only say . . . again . . . it seemed the right thing to do at the time.

Chubb One more?

Blunt Do I have a choice?

Chubb switches off the screen.

Chubb You're probably tired.

Blunt Not particularly.

Chubb All these functions.

Blunt I don't go to what you call 'functions'.

Chubb If you're in charge of the Queen's pictures you must often have to be in attendance.

Blunt Yes. On the pictures.

Chubb I'm disappointed. Don't you see the Queen?

Blunt The Crown is a large organization. To ask me if I see the Queen is like asking a shopgirl if she sees Swan or Edgar.

Chubb My wife saw her the other day. When she was visiting Surrey.

Blunt Your wife?

Chubb The Queen. She was up at six o'clock and secured an excellent vantage point outside Bentall's. Her Majesty was heard to say 'What a splendid shopping centre'. I wonder what she's really like.

Blunt Look her up. You must have a file on her.

Chubb Yes, we probably do. I meant, to chat to. Hob-nob with. As a person. You can't, of course, say. I appreciate that.

Blunt Why can't I say?

Chubb Royal servants can't, can they? Keeping mum is part of the job. It's like the Official Secrets Act. (*Pause.*) I'm sorry. That was unkind. More snaps?

Blunt says nothing.

Some people do this for pleasure, you know. Holidays. Trips abroad. 'This is a delightful couple we ran into on the boat. He's in the Foreign Office and he's a lorry driver.' You must often get asked round to watch people's slides.

Blunt Never.

Chubb You don't live in Purley.

Blunt No.

Chubb switches on the screen with another photograph.

How many more times. There is no one else that I know.

Chubb This morning I got up, cup of tea, read the *Telegraph*, the usual routine. Nothing on the agenda for today, I thought, why not toddle up to town and wander round the British Museum, sure to come across something of interest. Just turning into Great Russell Street when I remember there is something on the agenda. Your good self! What's more, I'm due at the Courtauld Institute in five minutes. So I about turn and head for Portman Square.

Pause.

Blunt And? I was under the impression this narrative was leading somewhere.

Chubb The point is, we sometimes know things we don't know. A bit of me, you see, must have known that I was coming here. (*He switches the screen off.*) Have you ever caught Her Majesty in an unguarded moment?

Blunt I thought it was my unguarded moments you were interested in.

Chubb It's just a titbit for my wife.

Blunt My function here is not to provide your wife with fodder for the hairdresser's.

Chubb She thinks my job is so dull.

Blunt And mine?

Chubb I'm sure you have colleagues who'd be delighted to be in your shoes.

Blunt Really? Having to see you all the time?

Chubb Oh. I was under the impression you enjoyed these little get-togethers. I always do.

Blunt You nearly forgot.

Chubb I forgot it was *today*. I thought you looked forward to these little chats. I thought it helped you relax. 'All the time.' It's only once a month. I now feel I'm a burden. (*Pause.*) We could always scrap them. It's true we don't seem to be getting anywhere.

Blunt I wouldn't want that.

Chubb You've only to say the word. I don't know, I must have got hold of the wrong end of the stick. I thought this was the way you wanted it.

Blunt It is. It is.

Chubb The alternative isn't ruled out. If you feel that . . .

Blunt I don't feel that at all. I . . . I had a late night.

Chubb You *were* at the Palace!

Blunt Initially, yes.

Chubb I knew you were. My wife saw your name in the paper. Well, I'm not surprised you're tired. You must always be on tenterhooks, frightened to put a foot wrong, having to watch every word. You must find it a terrible strain.

Blunt This?

Chubb *No.* Talking to the Queen. What is she really like?

Blunt Should we look at some more photographs?

Chubb In a moment. I'm upset that you find our talks wearisome.

Blunt I don't. I don't. It was an unforgivable remark. And not the case. On the whole I find them . . . stimulating.

Chubb Do you? Now truthfully.

Blunt They keep me on my toes.

Chubb I'm glad. Are you liked, by the way?

Blunt By whom?

Chubb I don't know. It occurs to me that you work rather hard at being a cold fish.

Blunt My pupils like me. My colleagues . . . I don't know. I have a life, you see. Two lives. Some of my colleagues scarcely have one.

Chubb They don't know about your other life.

Blunt In the Household.

Chubb I see. In that case, three lives. But who's counting.

(*He laughs. Suddenly switches on the screen with a new photograph.*) You don't know this boy? Not a boy now, of course. Might have a beard.

Blunt Should I? Who is he?

Chubb Nobody.

The next photograph is of a guardsman in uniform.

Blunt No.

The same guardsman now naked.

Chubb Goodness gracious. How did that get here? Dear me. Just think if one of your students knocked at the door. Two gentlemen looking at a picture of a naked guardsman. What would they think?

Blunt They might think it was Art. Or they might think it was two gentleman looking at a picture of a naked guardsman. They would be profoundly unstartled by either.

Chubb switches off the screen.

Chubb Do you ever go to the National Gallery?

Blunt One has to from time to time. Though I avoid opening hours. The public make it so intolerable.

Chubb I went in the other day.

Blunt Really?

Chubb First time in yonks.

Blunt Good.

Chubb No, not good. Not good at all. Better off sticking to museums. Museums I know where I am. An art gallery, I always come out feeling restless and dissatisfied. Troubled.

Blunt Oh dear.

Chubb In a museum I'm informed, instructed. But with art . . . I don't know. Is it that I don't get anything out of the pictures? Or the pictures don't get anything out of me? What am I supposed to think? What am I supposed to feel?

Blunt What do you feel?

Chubb Baffled. And also knackered. I ended up on a banquette looking at the painting that happened to be opposite and I thought, well, at least I can try and take this one in. But no. Mind you, I hate shopping. I suppose for you an art gallery is home from home.

Blunt Some more than others. Home is hardly the word for the Hayward.

Chubb But you'll know, for instance, what order they all come in, the paintings?

Blunt Well . . . Yes . . . one does . . . quite early on . . . acquire a sense of the sequence, the chronology of art. Shouldn't we be getting on?

Chubb You see, I don't have that. I've no map. And yet I know there's a whole world there.

Blunt Yes.

Chubb I'm determined to crack it. I'm like that. A year ago I couldn't have changed a fuse. Started going down to the library, the odd evening class; I've just rewired the whole house. What I thought I'd do with this was start at the beginning before artists had really got the hang of it . . . perspective, for instance, a person and a house the same size (I can't understand how they couldn't just see). And then I'm planning to follow it through until the Renaissance when the penny begins to drop and they start painting what is actually – you know – *there*. How does that strike you as an approach? It's not too sophisticated.

Blunt No. One couldn't honestly say that. It incorporates one or two misconceptions, which it would not at this stage be very useful to go into. Mustn't run before we can walk.

Chubb Tell me. I don't want to get off on the wrong foot.

Blunt Shouldn't we be looking at more photographs?

Chubb In a minute. The chronological approach is a mistake?

Blunt Not in itself. But art has no goal. It evolves but it does not necessarily progress. Just as the history of politics isn't simply a progress towards parliamentary democracy, so the history of painting isn't simply a progress towards photographic realism. Different periods have different styles, different ways of seeing the world. And what about the Impressionists or Matisse or Picasso?

Chubb Oh, I think they could do it properly if they wanted to. They just got bored.

Blunt is exasperated.

That's the way art galleries are arranged. Crude beginnings, growing accomplishment, mastery of all the techniques . . . then to hell with the rules, let's kick it around a bit.

Blunt But why should a plausible illusion of nature be the standard? Do we say Giotto isn't a patch on Michelangelo because his figures are less lifelike?

Chubb Michelangelo? I don't think they are all that lifelike, frankly. The women aren't. They're just like men with tits, and the tits look as if they've been put on with an ice-cream scoop. Has nobody pointed that out?

Blunt Not in quite those terms.

Pause.

Chubb Are you sure your students like you?

Blunt Discussion is seldom at this level.

Chubb You're finding me wearisome again.

Blunt These painters – Giotto, Piero – they aren't so many failed Raphaels, Leonardos without the know-how. Try to look at them as contemporaries did, judge them on their own terms, not as prefiguring some (to them) unknown future. They didn't know Raphael was going to do it better.

Chubb To be quite honest I haven't got to Raphael. But where have I heard that argument before?

Blunt If you were planning on going to the British Museum, how was it you remembered to bring the photographs?

Chubb I know. It's exactly the same argument you were using to explain what you did in the thirties: it seemed the right thing to do at the time. Giotto didn't have a grasp on perspective and neither did you. The difference being, of course, that art has no consequences.

Blunt How did you remember the photographs?

Chubb I didn't. I nipped up to the office for them. Good try, though. (*He switches on the screen and the photographs start again.*)

Blunt No.

Photo.

No.

Titian and a Venetian Senator *now comes up on the*

screen as we saw it in the opening scene with two figures. The Restorer stands right of the screen as before.

Restorer This was before cleaning. (*He punches up a slide of the picture after cleaning, now with a third figure* [*Figure 2*].) This is after cleaning.

Blunt I thought there must be something there. With just the two of them, it didn't make sense as a composition.

Restorer Quite. Though it doesn't make a lot of sense as a composition now.

Blunt No?

Restorer Look at Titian. The scale is all wrong. He looks as if he belongs in a different picture.

Blunt He does, of course. It's a copy.

Restorer Yes.

Blunt From the Berlin self-portrait.

Restorer Yes.

Blunt But at least we know who he is. And who the Chancellor is. But who is the new man? An X-ray, do you think?

Restorer Can't do any harm.

Blunt Wish it were a better picture. Got the velvet rather well.

The Restorer disappears as a photograph of more young men comes up on the screen.

Chubb And who is the other figure?

Blunt I don't know.

Chubb You've identified him before in a different context.

Blunt So why are you asking me again?

Chubb It's the context we're interested in.

Photograph.

Who's this?

Blunt His name was Baker. He was at Oxford. Balliol, possibly.

Chubb Handsome.

Blunt Is he?

Chubb Isn't he?

Blunt Dead, anyway.

Chubb Naturally. When was that?

Blunt The death?

Chubb The photograph.

Blunt August Bank Holiday, 1935. Margate.

Chubb Vanished world. Hooligans on scooters nowadays.

Photograph.

Who are these gentlemen?

Blunt Chums of Burgess. Cameron Highlanders, I think. Kilted jobs anyway.

Chubb Two in a row. Progress.

Blunt Not really. I don't suppose they had access to any information above latrine roster level.

Chubb They probably had other qualities.

Blunt I once had a photograph of Burgess with his head under one of their kilts.

Photograph.

Chubb This one?

Pause.

Blunt Yes.

Chubb Odd, isn't it, that its the irrelevant details that you can recall. An August Bank Holiday in Margate. Not Worthing. Not the Seaforth Highlanders but the Camerons. (*Chubb drops several slides on the floor. He picks them up.*) Facts, faces, you might be expected to remember you forget.

Blunt That's the way with memory. The canvas is vague. The details stand out.

Chubb It could get tiresome.

Photograph.

Blunt No.

Photograph.

No.

A slide of Titian's Allegory of Prudence *has come up on the screen, in colour [Figure 3].*

N – Oh yes.

Chubb Sorry. Must have picked up one of yours.

Blunt No. Leave it. At least I can tell you their names. But perhaps you know it. It's in the National Gallery. How far have you got on your safari through the nation's masterpieces? Have you reached Titian?

Chubb Don't tell me. Venetian. Sixteenth century. A contemporary of Tintoretto and Veronese. In some sense the founder of modern painting.

Blunt In what sense?

Chubb Well, in the sense that he painted character.

Blunt Mmm, though it's not the slightest use knowing that unless you recognize one of his pictures when you see one.

Chubb Is this typical?

Blunt Actually, no.

Chubb Ah.

Blunt Though it is Titian at the top of his form. Done towards the end of his life . . .

Chubb Didn't he live until he was ninety-nine?

Blunt That has been disputed. What cannot be disputed is the style, shining with all the autumnal magnificence of his *ultima maniera*.

Chubb Too plush for me, Titian. All fur and fabric. Don't like the look of that dog.

Blunt That's because that dog is a wolf. (*He points to a creature on the right.*) That dog is a dog.

Chubb Still wouldn't want to be the postman. Who are they all?

Blunt The old man on the left is Titian himself.

Chubb He *looks* ninety-nine.

Blunt . . . The middle-aged man in the centre is Titian's son, and the young man on the right is probably his adopted grandson.

Chubb I don't care for it, quite honestly.

Blunt Oh.

Chubb Something of the three wise monkeys about it.

Blunt That's not an altogether foolish remark.

Chubb Good for Chubb. Why?

Blunt Because it's an emblematic painting, a puzzle picture. A visual paraphrase of the *Three Ages of Man*, obviously, but something else besides. The clue is the animals.

Chubb Was he fond of animals?

Blunt Titian? I've no idea. Shouldn't think so for a moment. People weren't.

Chubb Rembrandt was. Rembrandt liked dogs.

Blunt Rembrandt's dogs, Titian's age. I can see you've been down at the Purley Public Library again. Except that Rembrandt's dogs are different. Rembrandt's dogs tend to be just dogs. This dog is hardly a dog at all.

Chubb You mean it's a symbol of fidelity?

Blunt It can be.

Chubb Hence Fido. And the wolf is a symbol of gluttony.

Blunt One hopes the security of the nation is not being neglected in favour of your studies in iconography.

Chubb One picks it up, you know.

Blunt (*sharply*) Well, if you do 'pick it up', pick it up properly. Yes, a dog is a symbol of fidelity and a wolf of gluttony, but occurring together as they do here, in conjunction with the lion, they are disparate parts of a three-headed beast which from classical times onwards has been a symbol of prudence. Hence the title of the picture: the *Allegory of Prudence*.

Chubb And I thought I was getting the hang of it.

Blunt There isn't a 'hang of it'. There isn't a kit. A wolf can mean gluttony, a dog fidelity, and treachery a cat. But not always. Not automatically. Take the owl. It can be a bird of wisdom, but since it is a bird of the night it can represent the opposite, ignorance and wilful blindness. Hardest of all to accept, it can be just an owl. Of course, one shouldn't blame you. You're just carrying over the techniques of facile identification favoured in your profession, into mine . . . where it isn't quite like that. Appearances deceive. Art is seldom quite what it seems.

Chubb Back to the drawing-board. Perhaps we should do some more.

Blunt Art?

Chubb Facile identification.

Blunt No.

Photograph.

No.

Photograph.

No. Actually, that face does ring a bell.

Chubb Yes? (*He goes back to the last photograph.*)

Blunt I've seen it.

Chubb Who is he?

Blunt I told you. Titian's son.

Chubb I thought for one delirious moment we were about to make progress.

Blunt Where is it? Come along, come along. This is how you learn.

Chubb goes back through the photographs until he reaches the Titian again.

I have seen him. Where?

A knock at the door. Phillips, a student, stands silhouetted in the doorway.

Phillips It's Phillips, sir.

Blunt I shan't keep you a moment. I have to teach now. Since Mr Phillips is paying for his time I think he has priority. Perhaps you might wait outside, Phillips, we haven't quite finished.

Chubb We haven't even started.

Phillips exits. Chubb gathers up the photographs and puts them in his briefcase.

I'm not good at cracking the whip. I enjoy our talks.

Blunt (*consulting a reference book*) So you keep saying.

Chubb Eyebrows are beginning to be raised. The phrase 'stringing you along' has been mentioned. The feeling is, you see, that you may just be the baby thrown out of the sleigh to slow down the wolves.

Blunt And who are these wolves?

Chubb They're like this one (*in the Titian*). They look back. They're the ones with hindsight. You've told us some names. You've not told us the names behind the names.

Blunt Can I ask you something? Who else knows?

Chubb Do you mean, down the road? Somebody had to be told. You were promised immunity, not anonymity. What do you think of the Wallace Collection? Should I go there?

Blunt Their Poussin apart, it's a bit chocolate box.

Chubb They have the *Laughing Cavalier*.

Blunt Exactly. Come in, Phillips.

Chubb leaves as Phillips comes in.

327

Phillips I've seen him once or twice. He comes into the library.

Blunt Yes. He's a mature student.

Phillips I'd say he was a policeman.

Blunt Do you have a suit?

Phillips Suit?

Blunt Jacket, trousers, preferably matching. Even, by some sartorial miracle, a waistcoat.

Phillips I do, as a matter of fact.

Blunt And is it handy, or is it in Thornton Heath?

Phillips I think I can put my hands on it without too much trouble.

Blunt Well, go away and put your hands on it and your legs into it and telephone me here at two o'clock.

Phillips Why, what's happening?

Blunt Nothing. A little extra-mural work. Off you go.

Phillips goes as the lights fade. Blunt turns to gaze at the Allegory of Prudence *then switches off the projector as the scene changes.*

Blunt's room recedes, a red carpet runs the breadth of the stage, gilt console tables appear and an elaborate banquette, set against a wall covered in (not over-exciting) paintings. We are in a corridor of Buckingham Palace and prominent among the paintings hanging on the wall is the Triple Portrait *(Figure 2).*

Colin, a young footman in an apron, comes on carrying a picture. He puts the picture down as Phillips, now in a suit, follows him carrying a step-ladder and looking wonderingly at the pictures and the furniture.

Colin Jumble. Bric-à-brac.

Phillips This is a Raphael.

Colin The regal equivalent of the fish-slice or the chromium cake-stand. A downstairs attic, this corridor. (*Pause.*) And it's not Raphael. It's school of.

Phillips How would you know?

Colin Because I dust it.

Phillips keeps looking up and down the corridor.

Nobody's coming. Sir is out practising with his horse and cart, and madam is opening a swimming-bath. Though in the unlikely event anyone does come by, disappear. They are happier thinking the place runs itself.

Phillips is looking at an ornate clock.

Like that, do you?

Phillips Liking doesn't necessarily come into it.

Colin It's ormolu. I've always had a soft spot for ormolu. Childhood, I suppose. Ormolu's fairly thin on the ground in Bethnal Green.

Phillips is now looking at a painting.

Phillips Some of these are in terrible condition.

Colin I can't think why. They get a wipe over with a damp cloth quite regularly.

Phillips How did you come to work here?

Colin It was either this or the police force. I had the qualifications. Presentable. Good-looking in a standard sort of way. I might even be thought to be public school until I opened my mouth. But of course you don't open your mouth. That's one of the conditions of employment. So are you top boy?

Blunt has come on, unseen by Phillips.

Phillips What?

Colin Earned yourself a trip to the Palace, you must have something.

Blunt He does. A suit.

Fool of a policeman on the gate. Insisted on going through my briefcase. He said, 'Do you have anything explosive?' I said, 'Yes, I certainly do. An article for the *Burlington Magazine* on Sebastiano del Piombo that is going to blow the place sky-high.' Not amused. I've been walking through that gate for ten years.

How are you today, Colin?

Colin Perfectly all right, thank you.

Blunt looks at the Triple Portrait.

Blunt We're going to take these gentlemen down and put this in its place. This, (*He hands the replacement picture to Phillips.*) as you can see, is an *Annunciation*. Perhaps, Phillips, you could give us a technical description of the panel.

Phillips Well, it's constructed of two planks, joined by a horizontal brace . . .

Blunt Two planks of what?

Phillips Wood.

Blunt Oak? Ash? Chipboard?

Phillips It's probably poplar.

Blunt Why?

Phillips Because it generally is. (*He turns it over.*)

Blunt So that's the back finished, is it? What about the frame?

Phillips Gilt.

Blunt Old gilt or modern gilt?

Phillips I can't tell.

Blunt Colin, any thoughts?

Colin Modern, I'd have said. Relatively, anyway. Glazing generally well-preserved. Some worm but there seems to be very little re-touching. Number of holes have been repaired, particularly round knots in the wood. It *is* poplar, actually. Some re-touching here, see. Minute flaking along the outline of the angel's robe. A few *pentimenti* visible to the naked eye, most clearly the fingers of the Virgin's left hand. Reserve judgement on the attribution, but a preliminary impression would suggest Sienna.

Blunt Good. Phillips, the steps. Colin, would you move the banquette.

Blunt looks fixedly at the Triple Portrait *on the wall.*

Hold the steps. (*He ascends the steps.*) This painting was in the collection of Charles I where it was ascribed to Titian, and it hung with other, rather more plausible, Titians in the palace at Whitehall.

Blunt is addressing this speech to the painting while examining it closely. Meanwhile Colin spots Someone approaching off-stage right. He nudges Phillips, indicating he should go.

Colin Sir.

Blunt Shut up. It was sold off after Charles I's execution but was recovered by Charles II and hung quite happily in the royal collection, nobody having any doubts about it at all until the end of the nineteenth century. Titian's beard is so badly done it looks as if it hooks on behind the ears.

Colin and Phillips hurriedly scarper, stage left. The stage is empty for a moment or two as Blunt goes on talking to the picture.

One lesson to be learned from paintings as indifferent as this, is that there is no such thing as a royal collection. It is rather a royal accumulation.

HMQ has entered, quite slowly. She looks. She is about to pass on.

Could you hand me my glass. (*Blunt puts his hand down without looking.*) It's on the table. Come along – we haven't got all day.

HMQ thinks twice but then hands him his glass.

Thank you. I thought so. Where are my notes? (*He comes down, still with his back to HMQ.*) You're supposed to be holding the steps. I could have fallen flat on my face.

HMQ I think you already have.

Blunt Your Majesty, I'm so sorry.

HMQ Not at all. One was most instructed. You were about to make a note.

Blunt It can wait, Ma'am.

HMQ No. Carry on, do it now. Ignore me.

Blunt Very well, Ma'am.

HMQ looks at the picture while Blunt scribbles a note.

HMQ And how did we accumulate this particular picture?

Blunt It belonged to Charles I, Ma'am.

HMQ King Charles I?

Blunt Ma'am. It was thought to be by Titian.

HMQ And now it isn't?

Blunt Not altogether, Ma'am.

HMQ I suppose that is part of your function, Sir Anthony, to prove that my pictures are fakes?

Blunt Because something is not what it is said to be, Ma'am, does not mean it is a fake. It may just have been wrongly attributed.

HMQ Yes. It's a fine face, though he looks as if he could do with some fresh air. Who is he?

Blunt His name is Andrea Franceschi. He was Chancellor of Venice.

HMQ We were in Venice two years ago. Unusual place. So. Now that it's a fake, what are you planning to do with it? Put it out for the binmen?

Blunt A painting is a document, Ma'am. It has to be read in the context of art history.

HMQ Has art always had a history? It's all the thing now, isn't it, but one doesn't remember it when one was young. There was art appreciation.

Blunt Art history is a part of art appreciation, Ma'am. We know that in this painting the old man is Titian himself; it's copied from one of his self-portraits. That's the Chancellor of Venice, but this other gentleman is something of a mystery. I'm trying to identify him, and with your permission, Ma'am, I'd like to remove the painting to examine it at my leisure.

HMQ Remove it? I'm not sure I want that. It would leave us with a horrid hole.

Blunt I have something to put in its place, Ma'am. (*Indicating the* Annunciation.) It's an *Annunciation*.

HMQ Yes, I know what it is.

Blunt You're not attached to this particular picture, are you, Ma'am?

HMQ No, but it's there, you know. One's used to it.

Blunt I think it was Gertrude Stein who said that after a while even the best pictures turn into wallpaper.

HMQ Really? This wallpaper is pure silk. I was shown some silkworms once in Sri Lanka. It's their cocoons, you know.

Blunt Yes. I had understood Ma'am wasn't going to be here this afternoon.

HMQ Obviously. I had understood I wasn't going to be here, either. I was due to open a swimming pool. Completed on Friday, filled on Saturday, it cracked on Sunday and today it's as dry as a bone. So this afternoon one is, to some extent, kicking one's heels.

Blunt That must make a nice change.

HMQ Not altogether. One likes to know in advance what one is going to be doing, even if one is going to be hanging about. If I am doing nothing, I like to be doing nothing to some purpose. That is what leisure means. (*She indicates an object on a table.*) This ostrich egg was given us by the people of Samoa. It hasn't quite found its place yet. Titian.

Blunt Ma'am?

HMQ That isn't really your period, is it?

Blunt In what way?

HMQ You are an expert on Poussin, are you not?

Blunt That's right, Ma'am.

HMQ Chicken.

Blunt Ma'am?

HMQ Poussin. French for chicken. One has just had it for lunch. I suppose it's fresh in the mind. It was one of what I call my All Walks of Life luncheons. Today we had the head of the CBI, an Olympic swimmer, a primary school headmistress, a General in the Salvation Army, and Glenda Jackson. It was a bit sticky.

Blunt I've been to one, Ma'am. That was a bit sticky, too.

HMQ The trouble is, whenever I meet anybody they're always on their best behaviour. And when one is on one's best behaviour one isn't always at one's best. I don't understand it. They all have different jobs, there ought to be heaps to talk about, yet I'm always having to crank it up.

Blunt The truth is, Ma'am, one doesn't have much to say to people very different from oneself. If you'd had the General in the Salvation Army, the Archbishop of Canterbury and the President of the Methodist Conference, they could all have talked about God, and lunch would have been a howling success.

HMQ Yes. And guess who would have been staring at her plate. And think if they were all actors.

Blunt At least they would talk, Ma'am.

HMQ Correction, Sir Anthony. They wouldn't talk. They would chat. One doesn't want chat. I don't like chat.

Blunt Weren't we chatting about Poussin?

HMQ Were we? Well, we mustn't. We must do it properly. Feed me facts, Sir Anthony. I like a fact. What were his dates?

Blunt 1595 to 1665.

HMQ Seventy. A good age for those days. How many pictures did he do?

Blunt Er . . .

HMQ Don't you know?

Blunt I've never been asked that question before, Ma'am. He wasn't a prolific artist.

HMQ Have we got any?

Blunt Paintings, no, Ma'am, but what you do have is a priceless collection of drawings.

HMQ Oh dear. So many of my things are priceless. Doubly so, really. Priceless because one can't put a price on them, and then if one did one wouldn't be allowed to sell them. Do you have pictures?

Blunt One or two, Ma'am.

HMQ Are they valuable?

Blunt Yes, but they are not invaluable. Though I do have a Poussin.

HMQ You mean you have one and we don't? Something wrong there.

Blunt Do you take any pleasure in acquisition, Ma'am?

HMQ Why? I'm not asking you to make me a present of it. That was one of my grandmother's tricks, Queen Mary. Acquired no end of stuff. Accumulated it. But pleasure in buying things? No. I like buying horses, as everybody knows, but why not? I know about them. But you're right.

One more Fabergé egg isn't going to make my day. Go on with your work. Don't let me stop you.

Blunt It seems rude.

HMQ I'm used to it. My days are spent watching people work. My work is watching people work.

Blunt Very well, Ma'am. (*He goes on making notes.*)

HMQ What is it you want to know about the painting?

Blunt Many things. It's a problem picture.

HMQ Not to me. But then I don't suppose wallpaper can be a problem, can it? Where will you take it?

Blunt The laboratory.

HMQ Oh dear. I don't know. But I'm inclined to say no. It's the constant *va et vient* of one's things. A monarch has been defined as someone who doesn't have to look round before sitting down. No longer. One has to look round nowadays because the odds are the Chippendale is on exhibition. (*She picks up a bowl.*) This rose bowl was a wedding present from the people of Jersey.

Blunt Do you still have all your wedding presents, Ma'am?

HMQ Not all. For instance, it was 1947. Clothes were still rationed. Result was, one was inundated with nylons. I don't still have them. Do you like it?

Blunt Not altogether, Ma'am.

HMQ I do, quite. But then I've never set much store by taste. That, after all, is your job. In mine, taste isn't such a good idea. When one looks at my predecessors the monarchs with the best taste . . . I'm thinking of Charles I and George III and IV . . . made a terrible hash of the rest of it. I don't think taste helps. Do you paint?

Blunt I'm afraid not, Ma'am. I have no skill in that department.

HMQ Nor me. The Prince of Wales paints, and my husband. They both claim it is very soothing. As a child I found it the reverse. My colours always used to run. I like things to have a line round them.

Blunt Ma'am must have had more experience of painters than most.

HMQ In what way?

Blunt Through having your portrait painted.

HMQ Oh, that. Yes. Though one gets the impression that as artists portrait painters don't really count. Not nowadays anyway.

Blunt They're seldom standard-bearers of the avant-garde, Ma'am.

HMQ They would hardly be painting me if they were. One doesn't want two noses. Mind you, that would make one no more unrecognizable than some of their efforts. No resemblance at all. Sometimes I think it would be simpler to send round to Scotland Yard for an Identikit. Still I can understand it when they get me wrong, but some of them get the horse wrong too. That's unforgivable.

Blunt It's true none of them quite capture you.

HMQ I hope not. I don't think one wants to be captured, does one? Not entirely, anyway.

Blunt You sound like one of those primitive tribes who believe an image confers some power on the possessor.

HMQ If I believed that, Sir Anthony, I am in the pocket of anyone with a handful of change.

Blunt Portrait painters tend to regard faces as not very still lives. There was one eminent portrait painter who said he wished he could hang his sitters upside down by the leg like a dead hare.

HMQ Yes. Well, one Minister of the Arts wanted to loose Francis Bacon on me, and that's probably how I would have ended up. He did the Screaming Pope, didn't he? I suppose I would have been the Screaming Queen.

He laughs. She doesn't. She picks up something else.

This is charming, isn't it? It's antelope horn. A gift from the National Association of Girls' and Mixed Clubs. Nowadays, of course, they don't even do sketches; they take photographs, then take them home and copy them. I think that's cheating.

Blunt I'm sure Michelangelo would have used the camera, Ma'am, if it had been invented. And Leonardo would probably have invented it.

He laughs, but she doesn't.

HMQ You see, I would call doing it from a photograph, *tracing*. Art, to my mind, has to be what we used to call freehand drawing. If you paint it from a photograph one might as well have a photograph.

Blunt The portrait everybody likes best does look like a photograph.

HMQ The Annigoni. I like that one too. Portraits are supposed to be frightfully self-revealing, aren't they, good ones? Show what one's really like. The secret self. Either that, or the eyes are supposed to follow you round the room. I don't know that one has a secret self. Though it's generally assumed that one has. If it could be proved that one hadn't, some of the newspapers would have precious little to write about. Have you had your portrait painted?

339

Blunt No, Ma'am.

HMQ So we don't know whether you have a secret self.

Blunt I think the only person who doesn't have a secret self, Ma'am, must be God.

HMQ Oh? How is that?

Blunt There is no sense in which one could ask, 'What is God really like?' Never off duty – he must always be the same. It must make it very dull. There can be no gossip in Heaven.

HMQ Good. I don't like gossip. This clock shows the time not only here but also in Perth, Western Australia. In certain circumstances it could be quite handy. I suppose for me Heaven is likely to be a bit of a comedown. What about you?

Blunt I'm not sure I'll get in, Ma'am.

HMQ Why on earth not? You've done nothing wrong. Your father was a clergyman, after all. Are all owners co-operative about lending their pictures?

Blunt None as co-operative as yourself, Ma'am.

HMQ That is the kind of remark, Sir Anthony, were it in a play, to which one would reply 'Tush!'

Blunt Truly, Ma'am.

HMQ Well, I think I'm going to blot my copybook on this one and persuade you to take St Sebastian instead.

Blunt He wouldn't be much use to me, Ma'am.

HMQ Not much use to anybody. I find him faintly ludicrous. Turned into a human pincushion, and he just looks as if it were a minor inconvenience.

Blunt The saints tended to be like that, Ma'am. Though

there's more excuse for St Sebastian as he didn't actually die of his wounds.

HMQ Oh. That was lucky.

Blunt He survived and was flogged to death.

HMQ Oh dear. Out of the frying-pan into the fire. And what about this *Annunciation* you want to foist on to me? Where's it been? In the cellar?

Blunt Hampton Court.

HMQ Same thing. What should I know about the *Annunciation*? Come along. Facts.

Blunt The Virgin is traditionally discovered reading. It's quite amusing that as time went on painters tended to elevate the status of the Holy Family, so that Joseph, from being a simple carpenter, eventually comes to be depicted as a full-blown architect; and the Virgin, who to begin with is just given a book, ends up with a reading desk and a whole library, so that in some later versions Gabriel looks as if he is delivering his message to the Mistress of Girton.

   He laughs. She doesn't.

HMQ Girton, Cambridge?

Blunt Yes, Ma'am.

HMQ I opened them a new kitchen. Their gas cookers are among the most advanced in East Anglia. You see, one reason why I prefer that to this is that in a home (and this is a home, albeit only one of one's homes) one doesn't want too many pictures of what I would call a religious flavour. I mean, this isn't a church. Besides, this (*the* Triple Portrait) I think is rather unusual, whereas *Annunciations* are quite common. When we visited Florence we were taken round the art gallery there, and there – well, I won't say *Annunciations* are two a penny, but they certainly were quite thick on the ground. And not all of them very convincing. My husband remarked that one of them looked to him like the messenger arriving from Littlewoods Pools. And that the Virgin was protesting she had put a cross for no publicity. Fortunately, Signor de Gasperi's English was not good, or we should have had the Pope on our tracks. (*HMQ picks up an object.*) Do you know what this is made out of? Coal. Given us by the Welsh miners. How long would you want it for, my Titian? My fake Titian.

Blunt A few weeks.

HMQ Oh, very well. You see, what I don't like is the assumption that one doesn't notice, one doesn't care. Still, we're off to Zambia next week, so that will cushion the blow. One never stops, you know. Governments come and go. Or don't go. One never stops. Could I ask you a question, Sir Anthony? Have I many forgeries? What about these?

Blunt Paintings of this date are seldom forgeries, Ma'am. They are sometimes not what we think they are, but that's different. The question doesn't pose itself in the form, 'Is this a fake?' so much as 'Who painted this picture and why?' Is it Titian, or a pupil or pupils of Titian? Is it someone who paints like Titian because he admires him and can't help painting in the same way? The public are rather tiresomely fascinated by forgery – more so, I'm afraid, than they are by the real thing.

HMQ Yes, well, as a member in this instance (somewhat unusually for me) of the public, I also find forgery fascinating.

Blunt Paintings make no claims, Ma'am. They do not purport to be anything other than paintings. It is we, the beholders, who make claims for them, attribute a picture to this artist or that.

HMQ With respect, Sir Anthony, rubbish. What if a painting is signed and the signature is a forgery?

Blunt Forgery of that kind is much more a feature of modern or relatively modern paintings than of Old Masters, Ma'am.

HMQ Again, Sir Anthony, I find myself having to disagree with you. We were in Holland not long ago and after we had been taken to see the tulips and a soil structure laboratory, Queen Juliana showed us her Vermeers. One has a Vermeer, so one was quite interested.

Blunt I think I know what you are going to say, Ma'am.

HMQ gives him a sharp look.

. . . but please go ahead and say it.

HMQ Thank you, and (though you're obviously ahead of me) she showed us some of the forged Vermeers done by a Mr . . .

Blunt Van Meegeren.

HMQ Quite. Those were forgeries. Of Old Masters.

Blunt Ma'am is quite right.

HMQ Moreover, these Van Meegerens didn't seem to me to be the least bit like. Terrible daubs. God knows, one is no expert on Vermeer, but if I could tell they were fakes why couldn't other people see it at the time? When was it, in the forties?

Blunt It's a complicated question, Ma'am.

HMQ Oh, don't spare me. Remember I could have been opening a swimming bath.

Blunt What has exposed them as forgeries, Ma'am, is not any improvement in perception, but time. Though a forger reproduce in the most exact fashion the style and detail of his subject, as a painter he is nevertheless of his time and however slavishly he imitates, he does it in the fashion of his time, in a way that is contemporary, and with the passage of years it is this element that dates, begins to seem old-fashioned, and which eventually unmasks him.

HMQ Interesting. I suppose too the context of the painting matters. Its history and provenance (is that the word?) confer on it a certain respectability. This can't be a forgery, it's in such and such a collection, its background and pedigree are impeccable – besides, it has been vetted by the experts. Isn't that how the argument goes? So if one comes across a painting with the right background and pedigree, Sir Anthony, then it must be hard, I imagine – even inconceivable – to think that it is not what it claims to be. And even supposing someone in such circumstances did have suspicions, they would be chary about voicing them. Easier to leave things as they are in every department. Stick to the official attribution rather than let the cat out of the bag and say, 'Here we have a fake.'

Blunt I still think the word 'fake' is inappropriate, Ma'am.

HMQ If something is not what it is claimed to be, what is it?

Blunt An enigma?

HMQ That is, I think, the sophisticated answer. It's curious, Sir Anthony, but all the time we have been talking, there has been a young man skulking behind one of my Louis XV *bergères* (a gift from the de Gaulles). Do you think he is waiting to assassinate one, or does he have an interest in that particular *ébéniste*?

Blunt My assistant, Ma'am.

HMQ I think it's time he was flushed from his lair. Come in, hiddy or not, young man.

Phillips comes on left.

Blunt This is Mr Phillips, Ma'am, a student at the Courtauld Institute.

Phillips Your Majesty.

HMQ What do you plan to do with your art history?

Phillips I am hoping to go into one of the big auction houses, Ma'am.

HMQ Jolly good. That should keep you out of mischief. Did you ever consider that, Sir Anthony?

Blunt No, Ma'am.

HMQ Oh. Well, I must be on my way. Not, I think, a wasted afternoon. One has touched upon art, learned a little iconography, and something of fakes and forgery. Facts not chat. Of course, had I been opening the swimming bath I would have picked up one or two facts there: the pumping system; the filter process; the precautions against infectious diseases of the feet. All facts. One never knows when they may come in handy.

Be careful how you go up the ladder, Sir Anthony. One could have a nasty fall.

Blunt Ma'am.

HMQ Mr Phillips. (*HMQ exits left.*)

Phillips She seems quite on the ball.

Blunt Oh, yes.

Phillips The furniture, the pictures. I thought it was all horses.

Colin enters left.

Colin What the hell was madam doing here? What happened to the swimming bath?

Phillips There was a leak.

Colin I bet that made her shirty. They like their routine.

Blunt Strange about the Royal Family. They ask you a great deal but tell you very little.

Colin What were you talking about?

Blunt I was talking about art. I'm not sure that she was. Come on, let's get this bloody picture down.

Blunt watches as Colin takes down the Triple Portrait *and replaces it with the* Annunciation. *As Colin carries off the* Triple Portrait *the Palace set disappears and Blunt, pointer in hand, is once more found lecturing at the Courtauld Institute.*

And should we compare these two paintings it is plain straightaway that they do not compare – at any rate in terms of quality. One, the *Allegory of Prudence*, (*Slide of the* Allegory of Prudence [*Figure 3*]) wholly authentic, Titian at the height of his powers, the other (*Slide of the* Triple Portrait [*Figure 2*]) a hotchpotch, a studio job, Titian's hand possibly to be detected in the striking central figure but nowhere else. But let us leave quality and authenticity aside while I direct your attention to two of the personages depicted in the paintings.

A composite slide with Titian's son from the Allegory of Prudence *on the left and the third man from the* Triple Portrait *on the right (Figure 4).*

On the left, Titian's son Orazio Vecelli as he appears in the *Allegory of Prudence*. No doubt about him or his identity and rather a bruiser he looks, like one of those extravagant villains in an early Chaplin film. On the right, altogether more civilized, if not so well painted, is this gentleman.

Younger, perhaps, and with a beard which has not yet achieved its full tropical luxuriance, but with the same eyes, the same nose, surely this is the same man. Titian's son also. The identification has never been made, and I make it now only tentatively and, I hasten to say, to no larger purpose, because even if correct I cannot say it helps to solve the riddle of this picture – if indeed it is a riddle worth solving. But riddle there undoubtedly is as I shall show you. Let us look at the painting as it was when it first turns up in the collection of Charles I some three hundred and fifty years ago. Catalogued as *Titian and a Venetian Senator*, you will note that it then contained only two figures.

Slide of the Triple Portrait *before cleaning (Figure 1).*

When I was appointed Surveyor of the Queen's Pictures, I had the painting cleaned, and the presence of the mysterious gentleman on the right was revealed.

Slide of the Triple Portrait *after cleaning (Figure 2).*

So, having started with two men, we now have a third man. And that is how the picture looks at the moment. But that is only how it looks. Because in addition to being cleaned, I also had the picture X-rayed. And the X-ray revealed a fourth man.

Slide of an X-ray photograph of the Triple Portrait.*

And that was not the end of it either, for if we rotate the X-ray we find behind the original pair and the third and fourth man the rather more substantial figure of a fifth man.

* As reproduced in the *Burlington Magazine*, vol. 100, 1958.

Slide of the X-ray rotated.

The fifth man, you will doubtless be relieved to learn, is the last of the sitters lurking in this somewhat over-populated canvas. Who all these figures are and who painted them we do not know. It may be that the third man is indeed Titian's son, but even so that does not help us identify the fourth man or the fifth. And why, you're entitled to ask, does it matter? This is not an important picture, just a murky corner of sixteenth-century art history that wants clearing up but won't be. It matters, I suggest to you, as a warning.

Slide of the Triple Portrait *(Figure 2).*

This painting is a riddle, and this and similar riddles are quests one can pursue for years; their solution is one of the functions of the art historian. But it is only *one* of his functions. Art history is seldom thought of as a hazardous profession. But a life spent teasing out riddles of this kind carries its own risks . . . a barrenness of outlook, a pedantry that verges on the obsessive, and a farewell to common sense; the rule of the hobby horse. Because, though the solution might add to our appreciation of this painting, paintings, we must never forget, are not there primarily to be solved. A great painting will still elude us, as art will always elude exposition.

The transition from lecture hall to Blunt's room begins as the light grows on Chubb, in raincoat. He picks up a paper from Blunt's desk and reads it.

Chubb A long time ago when I first started, I thought . . . or thought that I thought . . . that art was in the front line. I used to review then. I was the art critic of *The Spectator* . . . and I sang the praises of realism from Rembrandt to Rivera, deplored Picasso and abstraction . . . inaccessible to the people, I suppose. What none of us, I suppose, realized then was that the people would mean the public to the extent it does today.

Blunt enters. He is in full evening dress with the ribbons and medals of his various orders and decorations. He carries a bottle of whisky and two glasses.

What's this?

Blunt My speech. The Academy Dinner.

Chubb I hadn't planned on calling. I saw your light was on.

Blunt Yes. I suppose it's what you'd call a function.

Chubb Who was there?

Blunt Oh, everybody. Including your boss. We chatted. Do you not get invited to occasions like that?

Chubb No.

Blunt You should.

Chubb I'd feel a bit lost.

Blunt Oh, I don't think so. They were all there.

Chubb Who?

Blunt The great and the good. Everybody on your list. Your little list.

Chubb Anyway, I don't have the clothes.

Blunt Clothes are the least of it. Your wife would like it. Plenty to goggle at. And in the absence of the public one can see the art. Drink?

Chubb Thank you. I came to give you a warning. There is a time coming, soon, when your anonymity will cease to be in any practical sense useful.

Blunt Yes, yes, yes.

Chubb You must understand that your situation does not improve with time. More and more questions are being asked. The wolves, if you like, are getting closer. We may have to throw you off our sledge now. The consequences will be embarrassing, and not only for you. For us too. It will be painful. You will be the object of scrutiny, explanations sought after, your history gone into. You will be named. Attributed.

Blunt And as a fake I shall, of course, excite more interest than the genuine article.

Chubb There is someone else. Someone behind you all. All the evidence points to it.

Blunt The evidence! Once upon a time, when Berenson began his pioneer work of listing and attributing the paintings of the Italian Renaissance, he would sometimes come across groups of works in which he detected a family resemblance. They pointed to the existence of artists to whom he could not give a name. And there was one, a group of drawings, that resembled – but were not – the work of Botticelli. So he called the putative author of these drawings Amico di Sandro – the friend of Botticelli. But as the work of attribution progressed, Berenson came to see that these drawings were actually the early work of the Florentine painter, Filippino Lippi. There was no Amico di Sandro. He had been invented to fit the evidence, but he did not exist.

Chubb It's funny you should mention Berenson. I've just got on to him. Fascinating chap. Only wasn't there another group of paintings he was puzzled about? Of the Mother and Child? Same situation, they resembled one another in style but he couldn't put a name to the artist. The one element they all had in common was that the Christ child wasn't portrayed as the usual torpid, overweight infant but as a real, live wriggling baby. So this process of attribution called into being a painter Berenson called the Maestro del Bambino Vispo . . . the painter of the wriggling baby. I've not got very far in my studies in art history, of course, and you'll correct me if I'm wrong, but that attribution . . . the Maestro del Bambino Vispo still stands. He did exist.

Blunt Yes. That's right. He did. But whether your man existed, or still exists, is a different matter. But very good. You might have made an art historian.

Chubb Yes? Did I miss my way?

Blunt Not really. Both our professions carry the same risks, after all . . . a barrenness of outlook, a pedantry that verges on the obsessive, a farewell to commonsense, the rule of the hobby horse. You with your hobby horse, me with mine.

Chubb punches up the X-ray of the fifth man.

Chubb Who are they all?

Blunt Oh no, not more photographs. (*He looks round at the screen.*) I'm sorry. I thought they were yours, not mine. When I was in the security service art used to be a haven, you know. A refuge. In the silly, knowing jargon of the spy story, a safe house. Not so safe now. Everybody's into art.

Chubb Including me.

Blunt Still, I think it will last my time. But who are they all? (*Blunt switches the slide off.*) I don't know that it matters. Behind them lurk other presences, other hands. A whole gallery of possibilities. The real Titian an Allegory of Prudence. The false one an Allegory of Supposition. It is never-ending.

Chubb and Blunt sit looking at one another for a long moment before the lights fade.

15. Dec. 03   Midwest   Sr. 20   70/42